YOUR WRITING WELL: COMMON-SENSE STRATEGIES & LOGIC BASED SKILLS, IN 15 ESSAYS FOR THE 21ST CENTURY

COPYRIGHT © 2014 INTERNATIONAL PUBLICATIONS MEDIA GROUP. ALL RIGHTS RESERVED.

COVER © INTERNATIONAL PUBLICATIONS MEDIA GROUP

WRITTEN BY: DR. BOB DAVIS

EDITED BY: FRANCOIS WILSON

COVER DESIGN BY: SAM ELTOSAM

PUBLISHED BY: INTERNATIONAL PUBLICATIONS MEDIA GROUP
    51 MACDOUGAL STREET
    SUITE 338
    NEW YORK, NY 10012

SUMMARY

Essay 1:

Introductory Ideas about Writing

This introductory essay for Your Writing Well highlights intellectual and psychological realities and concerns about writing that you would like a writing teacher to talk about:

How this book of essays is different from any other writing book published, and how its efficient synthesis of writing theory, with examples, offers all that you've been looking for to improve your prose.

Why thinking and writing are inseparable partners in one process, why I define writing as codified thought, and what codified thought means.

Why writing well pertains principally not to talent but to mastered skills and strategies whose principled logic most people can learn.

How to engineer each written document's information architecture for a particular audience and its demographic characteristics.

Why all public writing is educational and therefore has persuasive purposes.

Why writing cannot be purely objective, ought not be rigidly standardized in format, and logically allows for freedoms whose availability you possibly never were taught.

What the important differences are between logical rules and stylistic choices of grammar.

Why English is the global or international language of the twenty-first century, and what that means to all of us using English to communicate.

Essay 2:

Writing from the Inside Out: A Case Against Reliance on Templates, and In Defense of the Organic Way to Write

Preliminary to understanding how my book explores and discusses content and organization, this essay defines my "organic methodology" for developing and organizing written information. Advising against rigid superimpositions of template structures and organizational models, this essay explains how writers can conceive, nurture, develop, and raise to maturity the living organism that any essay is, so that it stands naturally on its own.

Essay 3:

Using a Word™ Document Before Writing Formally,

To Compile Thoughts, Brainstorming Results, & Research Material, And To Find Relationships among the Body's Structural Bones

This essay explains fourteen reasons why every writer will benefit from using a Word™ document to contain initial thoughts, brainstorming results, and research information, all before formally writing any text. These fourteen reasons will help all writers to begin developing and organizing their thoughts.

Essay 4:

Brainstorming, Learning More About What You Do and Do Not Know, And How to Use Your Brain to Think About Discovering the Purposeful Focus of the Text You'll Write.

Before formally writing out or typing up a text or essay, writers first must explore and discover the subject they're writing about, to learn more and to think more broadly and deeply about it. Brainstorming strategies help to accomplish that goal, and learning about the two hemispheres of the human brain allows writers to brainstorm more thoroughly before deciding, with certainty, what their total purpose actually is. This essay includes Initial Strategies for Restricting Your Purpose and Focus Thought as Energy; Energy and

Physics' Law of Attraction Matters of Energy in the Human Brain's Two Hemispheres Brainstorming

Journalistic Listing; Listing with Other Mental Modes; Conversation; Ways to Leave Notes for Future Transcription onto your Word document; Mapping; Freewriting; Template-Stimuli;

Essay 5:

Organizing Your Document's or Essay's Body as a Skeletal Ouline (Classifying, Paragraphing, Topic Sentences, Transitions)

Organization, if organic (and the words' roots do suggest likeness), is inseparable from content, forming itself according to how the content shapes itself within the document or essay. This essay presents methodologically an organic process of organization for the "body" of any written piece, whose product is a skeletal outline of one-word labels and labeling phrases structuring that piece's entire anatomy.

Essay 6:

Parts of Speech" Mirror All Existence

Knowing and understanding English grammar's "parts of speech" may seem like a grade school activity that lacks relevance to adult writing, but in fact that knowledge is essential in all discussions of the logic of grammar, punctuation, and sentence structure. Easy to learn, however, the parts of speech simply mirror the actual operations of our world and our lives. This essay defines English's seven important parts of speech and explains why and how in grammar's systems they represent the reality that surrounds and exists within us.

Essay 7:

Grammar: Logic vs. Style

For many adult professionals and younger students, grammar has become or is becoming a frustrating, even fearful impediment to feeling easy and natural about writing with English. Confusion prevails, so avoidance ensues. This essay introduces the distinction between grammar's "rules" based on logic, which are the only rules, and grammar's prescriptions based on stylistic preference, which are options and thus available choices, not logical necessities.

Essay 8:

Grammar Between You and Me: Mostly About Pronouns

What annoys American English teachers and some professionals and parents about incorrect grammar usage is less that people are wrong grammatically than that they just won't learn how easy it is to get their grammar right. This essay highlights some of the most common English grammatical errors resulting from illogical pronoun usage.

Essay 9:

Eliminating Wordiness, Eleven Simple Strategies

One of the most overlooked features of effective writing is conciseness or essential wording, especially when word or page limits are required. By eliminating needless wordiness, writers not only add clarity to their prose but also gain additional space within which to write more information.

Essay 10:

Sentence Combining

Also eliminating wordiness, usually repetition, sentence combining additionally trains writers to examine the parts of their ideas and to strategize how best to organize those parts in each sentence. This essay approaches sentence combining by introducing dependent and relative clauses, and participial, appositive, and absolute phrases.

Essay 11:

Easily Confused or Misused Words and Phrases

Contained in this essay is an alphabetized list helping writers to avoid commonly committed errors in diction and phrasing, errors that always have perplexed writers of English. With definitions, explanations, and examples, the list includes spelling (principle or principal?), verbs (lay down or lie down?), non-existent words (irregardless), and illogical phrasing (center around).

Essay 12:

Punctuating Points to Remember

Focusing on six principles of comma usage—or its lack—that can seriously affect a sentence's logic, and also explaining with thorough but brief discussions how to use the semicolon, colon, and em dash, this essay helps writers to understand when, where, and why punctuation may or may not be required to keep a sentence's construction accurate. Ample examples are given for every principle examined.

Essay 13: Evidence

To be persuasive, public writers must think carefully about acquiring useful evidence and using it strategically. Claims, opinions, beliefs, reminders, and proposals expressed in public writing must be defended with evidence, so this essay discusses different kinds of evidence and guidelines for using evidence advantageously.

Essay 14:

Thesis Statement, and Introduction and Conclusion Strategies

You neither can introduce nor can conclude a document or essay until you know, in total, what it is you're introducing and concluding, so writing your introduction and conclusion should come after the body's skeletal outline has been fully thought out and organized. This essay offers and investigates strategies for your writing well the final stages of your document's or essay's developmental process, which includes your necessary introductory thesis statement.

Essay 15: Diction

Diction, or the words we speak and write, preoccupies our thoughts every day and therefore deserves discussion in at least one essay. Here I focus on the variability of English-language usage between English-speaking countries and among regions in the United States, clarifying for native and international speakers how much of English is not standardized, and why; strategies for converting vague nouns, adjectives, and verbs to more specific diction; strategies for processing visual imagery, including description, metaphors, and similes; the music of English diction, its sounds and rhythms, as well as appropriate moods for each document or essay; and slang, jargon, and colloquialisms.

A Ph.D. of nineteenth-century British literature, Bob Davis has taught university English for over thirty-five years. In Manhattan now, he's a freelance editor and writer, language consultant for corporate and individual clients, and at New York University the creator and professor of a four-course writing curriculum for graduate students in the forty-five M.A. and M.S. professional studies programs. His published work includes instructor manuals for five college-level reading and writing anthologies, along with two volumes of literary criticism, style-diverse nonacademic prose, and poetry. He has been copy-chief for AOL Digital City New York, has development- and copy-edited over twenty volumes of literature for Houghton Mifflin's New Riverside Editions, edited online for The College Board and Pearson, and also edited for magazines, advertising agencies, architectural builders, and philanthropic foundations. He is in love with and loves his wife.

— Dr. Bob Davis

ESSAY 1

Introductory Ideas about Writing

Writing publicly, I expect people to explore Your Writing Well, this collection of essays, and from it to discover new skills and strategies about writing. But expect which people? For whom am I writing these essays? Why them? What are their particular concerns and needs? How do I remove or reduce those concerns and fulfill those needs? What must I do to make these real people trust me and hear what I have to say?

To answer those questions, I've had to combine personal and professional knowledge from my academic and business experience as an English-language teacher, tutor, editor, consultant, and author—have combined it to induce what I hope is a conclusive, insightful vision of my audience, the readers of this essay, you among them. I've had to give serious time to view and carefully review the diverse people commonly denominated by a need to write well and, equally important, by their desire to write well; now, here, naturally I'm hoping that I've identified my audience and that this introductory essay's responses to writing-issues still unresolved in their minds will prove that I've accurately judged their concerns and expectations.

I'll begin with a simple but always true premise about writing: Every written document or text, large or small, demandingly intricate or easy-going, is written to educate a particular audience of the importance and rightness of what we have to say. All public writers are educators; all public writing attempts to "educate," which means to lead away, away from ignorance. So why else do we write publicly, but to impart information significant to us and, we presume, possibly to someone else? The "someone else" for this book of essays is you and others like you, my audience. Because this introduction will identify those likenesses, I've had to think about and factor into my writing what I should write about and how to manage its tone and style; to do that, I've needed to understand at least some of your relationship with writing.

Defined another way, all of our writing except for personal diaries and journals—and usually even those—is a persuasive exercise with educational intentions. The very act of communication, of taking ideas and opinions, emotions and feelings, and events and experiences beyond one's private self is an attempted validation of their value, their worth for sharing. And as writers we must persuade or convince our audience of that value or worth. If you're feeling happy about a change in or contribution to your life and want in writing to tell someone about it, you assemble a case of evidence that persuasively actualizes your happiness so that your reader understands and appreciates your enthusiasm encased in words. If you write a proposal for your place of employment, you'll thoroughly investigate and research whatever background information is required to persuade your readers of the proposal's value, contrasting its improvements with the status quo's norms. If when analyzing an art or sporting event you want to convince people of its merits or demerits, you'll cite specific evidence from different evaluative categories and use logical reasoning to integrate that evidence into persuasive conclusions.

Persuasion also supervises any academic essay, whatever its focus and purpose. Persuasion's importance to writing begins with us personally, within ourselves, because as writers it is mandatory to us that what we say be as true as we can make it be. Some kind of duty, some inner contract with responsibility assumes significance when we commit to writing, to codifying our thoughts on paper, something formal and inherently ethical about doing it accurately and respectably. I doubt you ever have intended to lie or tell falsehoods when you write, or ever wanted to present a matter haphazardly, incompletely, or as a half-truth. Rather, we adopt an almost zealous commitment to expressing convincingly what we think is true, and usually we won't leave it alone until we believe that what we've written articulates that truth as we see it. Writers generally dislike criticism of their work because they themselves are literally on the line, the printed line, and to hear disagreement or to see disapproving red ink assaults the truths presented by the labors of their mind and the passions of their heart. Writers set out to be persuasive, and they don't like to be told they aren't.

Theorists sometimes distinguish persuasive writing from "objective writing" or unbiased informative writing, in which the writer makes no judgments or persuasive statements about the subject(s). More honestly, I think, even with fact-only reports[1], no purely objective or unbiased writing exists, only kinds and degrees of subjectivity. Subjectivity certainly prevails in newspaper journalism, for example, because each reporter's individual human perspective is slanted according to the uniqueness of who she or he is: everyone's point of view is multi-faceted and -focused from genetic inheritance and its predispositions in us, from systems of national and regional culture and of family training, family income and how it's used, education and sports, teachers and coaches, friends and acquaintances, and all that's personal, such as free will and choice. At the very least, this subjective slanting influences which parts of the news story each reporter deems necessary to report, how each part is sized relative to the others and prioritized within the whole report, how to integrate and thus organize the report's component parts, what to highlight in a sidebar to accompany the report, and of course what words to choose to tell it all. Except for proper nouns and spelled mathematical symbols, words themselves have no inherent objectivity but instead are defined frames with boundaries into which we step to paint our own pictures.

Numbers are objective, so long as they remain relative to other numbers[2]; language never has been and cannot be objective, not totally. Although honesty requires us to maintain impartiality when in our writing we work with facts and universal truths, as in scientific studies and lab reports or financial reports, and although honesty requires us also to remove apparent bias if it tilts evidence or skews our reasoning, yet in fact when we expose our opinions and beliefs we personally select only that evidence and craft only that reasoning which allows us to persuade our readers of our presentation's value. Objectivity lacks choice, but when we write we constantly are choosing. Not every move we make as writers will be a decisively purposeful intellectual choice, but always there will and must be conscious decisions made when architecturally we draft and then construct a creation of thought that's meticulously built according to our own blueprints, immediately functional at every turn, and rewarding to inspect and study, with all rough edges smoothed and streamlined according to our personal standards.

So as educators who need and want to educate persuasively, we first must identify the specific readers, or audience, for whom our content is intended to do that. Most written communications are likely to have a particular readership, an individual or group of individuals whom we know or of whose general demographics we are aware. And because as writers we know in most instances more about what we have to say than our audience does, it's up to us to decide in advance how much or how little need be said to educate our audience properly and thoroughly yet concisely. Knowledge of our audience informs in advance the why, what, and how we write. Most written pieces are not intended for a universal readership, so we must expect in our written documents certain kinds of persuasive predispositions and certain degrees of emotional slanting, as well as intentional omissions or emphatic inclusions used for impact. This book of essays, which I've written for you, has required at every point in my writing that I think about your needs and choose how to satisfy them, so I'm doing my best to practice what I preach.

Essentially, what a text says and how it's said must adapt to and accommodate the intellectual and emotional needs of its audience. For an interoffice memo, you'll know who in the company will receive your document, how much or how little they already know about your message's background and conceptual presuppositions, what your and their context-sensitive priorities must be with regard to your memo's subject, and where to intone seriousness or informality in your writing's voice. If you were writing to a group exclusively of teen females, or to a PTA membership mostly of moms, then you'd know that among other appropriate writing choices for those audiences there's no need to use singular masculine pronouns: "he" for a subject, "him" for an object, or "his" for possessive. Instead, for the moms you might write, "Each among you must see beyond her past beliefs and vote for what she knows is most practical for our children now, this school year." For any professional or academic text you write whose audience is uncertain to you, ask your instructor or advising manager the specific or general audience for whom you're writing; then, you'll be better able to determine the necessary amount of background information to include and whether or not to define conceptual terminology.

In a sense, writing for an audience requires also that we become political or, in campaigning politicians use different forms of a speech for different audiences, having their writers vary the speech's explanatory language, examples, slants, and humor for the demographic variables in each new group hearing the speech. Political speech-givers don't address an issue at a $1000/plate dinner in the same manner as they do at a lunch with plant workers, any more than you and I wear the same clothing to a job interview as we do to a bar; each new occasion reflects its own appropriate stylistic choices, although the speech's purpose and logic remain resolute. And because our ability to capture attention and to hold it will vary from audience to audience, as will gaining that audience's approval and support, it's essential to know the people for whom we're writing.

If at first you lack knowledge about your audience, as I did when considering this project, then spend more time thinking about which group(s) of people will read your document, and then define their demographics, if you can: gender; place of residence, U.S. or other country, U.S. state and even city; urban, suburban, rural, or other residential lifestyle; age group, and the kinds of generational experiences, values, strengths, and limitations people at that age may have; general level of education and specific field of study; specific careers, positions held, kinds of training, and professional knowledge: political affiliation, if relevant; religious affiliation, if relevant; degree of familiarity with what your text will present; degree of interest in your presentation; and any expectations, sensitivities, biases, aversions, and moral concerns held by your audience which you must referee prudently to keep readers listening without psychological and emotional disturbance. With that knowledge, a writer can prioritize explanations, strategize how much or little to say about issues, adjust the psychological force and tone presented, and anticipate rebuttals or opposing points of view.

This introductory essay's content already has begun to define who you are and will continue to do so, both explicitly and implicitly, by identifying your professional, academic, and personal expectations with regard to writing, acknowledging the kinds of psychological hardships you may have when writing, and setting an emotional tone that eases your mind intellectually and allows you comfortable access to new ideas about writing skills and strategies; certainly a broad range of people, all of you have limitations in common that this essay and the others examine and will help you to rise above.

I assume that you've chosen to read this essay because you have difficulty writing your thoughts as well and as fast as you'd like to and, possibly, as well as you need to. This book of essays' title, Your Writing Well, suggests that contained here is not only instruction to help you upgrade to "well" the quality of your writing, but also a personal reservoir, a well, or resource of knowledge to quench your thirst for improvement each time you draw from it. I intend to help you minimize your difficulty with writing and to offer logical skills and strategies for accomplishing that, and also to educate you about the importance of language, English specifically, and of respecting and writing it in the twenty-first century.

We're all aware that the new millennium has initiated and is spinning planet Earth's first interactively webbed or distributed social system: since 2000 the world as a "global village" has become increasingly networked by economy, the influence of IT electronics and social media, and, at the uniting source of it all, English language communications. Communicated knowledge in English continues to help universalize new ideas, interests and procedures, standards and values, and social and cultural trends as the global village's electronic merger of time and space reticulates the filaments of our planet's intellectual existence.

It's safe to say that English is planet Earth's international or global language. English is the most widely spoken and taught language in the world, although there are more native speakers of Chinese, Spanish, and Hindi than of English. Estimates vary, but 2010 statistics show approximately 500 million people using English as their first language and 750 million more as a secondary language, while "an estimated two billion are trying to learn it as their linguistic passport to business success and global access. China leads the pack" and last year, 2011, "bec[a]me the world's largest English-speaking nation of more than 300 million" (Francis), a highpoint destined to elevate since "there are now an estimated 30,000 organi[z]ations or companies offering private English classes in China" (Thorniley). To China's northeast, every Japanese student takes English language courses from the seventh grade through the final year of high school. Studying compulsory English beginning in the third grade, South Koreans value English so enthusiastically that medical operations to elongate one's tongue for better English pronunciation are "so common that the government has produced a film in an effort to shock parents into shunning the practice" (Marks). In January 2003, President Gloria Macapagal-Arroyo of the Philippines ordered that country's Department of Education to restore English as the medium of instruction in all schools and universities. In India, 125 million people speak English, twice the total population of England. About 90% of all European Union schoolchildren study English. Israel's public education requires English as a second language. Of Africa's 27 countries, 14 use English as their sole principal language or as one in a set of principal languages. Spoken on almost all Caribbean islands, English is the only official language of Trinidad and Tobago and the first language of 94% of Jamaica's population. And we can't forget native English speakers living in the U.S., the United Kingdom, Canada, Australia, and New Zealand, about 310 million in total.

Extraordinary in its breadth of use and depth of influence, the global diffusion of English remains one of America's most profitable commodities, an inexhaustible natural resource. British imperialism and its imposition of the English language on other cultures began globally during the Renaissance and by 1922 had suffused the English language through one quarter of the world's population, who lived on one quarter of the world's land mass; U. S. imperialism has expanded its own territorial boundaries for two centuries, either continuing to broaden or reinforcing use of the English language. An adaptive hybrid language with proven ability to meet new cultural and communicative needs, English in the twenty-first century now is the dominant, international language of world trade and business, scientific publications, world politics and diplomacy, technology and electronic communications, and sports and other entertainment. "The number of people using English for international communication is increasing on an unprecedented scale," says Burt Channing of Columbia University, "and the spread of English shows no signs of stopping."

Surviving as the unstoppable international language of business and commerce, English has been fit enough to make the earth revolve commercially. Best estimates show that more than half of all business deals in the world now are conducted in English. English is the working language of the Asian trade group ASEAN and the official language of the European Central Bank, despite that bank's Frankfurt location and despite neither Britain nor any other predominantly English-speaking country being a member of the European Monetary Union. Swiss banks use English at the senior level; Swedish boardrooms use English almost exclusively. In the French daily newspaper Le Monde, 95% of advertised jobs require a high competence in English. Commercial globalization and outsourcing, in addition to English's use for senior-level officiating, also account for the spreading mandatory use of International English this century: many of the world's most powerful transnational corporations have created a high demand for people in foreign countries who speak English, a conspicuous trend in India and China, where there is fast-growing recognition that gainful career opportunities are available when English is learned. As our world becomes more and more commercially globalized, its commercial operators will continue to need a steady but expansively adaptable global commercial language. English still supplies that demand; consequently, if people want to do business internationally or may need to operate on the international periphery, they will need English for their communications. While multinational companies may localize their products and market them in a language other than English to meet domestic needs, the trend in those companies' local staff communications is to use English for internal meetings, for documenting those meetings, and for writing the reports, plans, and e-mails that inform and govern those companies' financial performance. Over 10,000 corporations worldwide use the Test of English for International Communication, or TOEIC®, an English language proficiency test for non-native speakers of English; in

2010, more than 6 million people registered to take that test. If money talks, then increasingly it's talking in English.

Not just the international language of business and commerce, "English has been the language of science for the last 50 years and is likely to remain as such" (Haneline). No one seems to disagree that "The prevalence and dominance of English in science is a global fact" (Ammon, ix). Used in "more than half of the world's technical and scientific periodicals" (Ling), English is the principal working language at international scientific conferences. With the English language's internationally "self-reinforcing loop of language flow," in which "Abstracting services insist on English-language abstracts [and] citation indexes often include only English-language citations," it's no surprise that "English appears to dominate scientific discourse, and English-speaking universities invariably head the lists of leading scientific institutions" (Tonkin). This explains why, in the world's largest scientific database, the Science Citation Index (SCI), 90% of all cited scientific articles are in English; the remaining 10% are divided among Japanese, Russian, German, and French.

Politically, international treaty has made English the official language for maritime and aerial communications as well as an official language of international diplomacy, of the United Nations, and of many other international organizations, including the International Olympic Committee. In fact, thousands of organizations around the world use English as their official language, and, "According to the Union of International Associations' Yearbook . . . from about 12,500 international organizations in the world . . . a sample . . . showed that 85 per cent . . . made official use of English" (Crystal, 79).

Also facilitating the English language's integration into international communication is the U.S.'s lead in the computer technology industry and, as a result, the development of significant sums of software using English; this means "About 80% of the information stored in the world's computers [is] also in English" (Ling), while 85% of computer home pages are in English (myenglishforlife.com). On the Internet, English is used almost three times more than Chinese, the second most frequently used Internet language; and "three quarters of the world's mail, and its telexes and cables are in English" (Ling). Facebook has provided its 700 million users (mid-2011 statistic) the software to translate other languages into English.

In addition to online information, the entertainment industry disseminates English globally: film and television are the dominant cultural media of our time, broadcast sports are viewed around the world, and pop music with English lyrics rides sound waves across the planet. The United States dominates the motion picture industry: "80 percent of all feature films given a theatrical release are in English" (Crystal, 91). Daily, English is transmitted by five of the world's largest broadcasting companies—CBS, NBC, ABC,

BBC, CBC—to over 100 million people (Ling). Sports programming spreads English usage with sport-specific terminology from baseball, football, basketball, boxing, and horse-racing. [3]

So what, you rightfully may ask, does all this information about the global use and continuing spread of English have to do with you, personally? Possibly more than you realize. If you foresee that you may have central or even tangential involvement with transnational and cross-cultural enterprising, then consider this: because English already is integral to the world's commercial, intellectual, and entertainment interactions, writers using English for international purposes must safeguard the language's power by respecting and actualizing its potential for precise communication. Americans no longer are in a position to be carefree and careless about written English, now that our language has become the global standard for communication. America globally is losing some of its economic leadership now, but English itself continues to lead the world's economy; consequently, no longer can native speakers risk muddying the writing of English with impure, slow-moving, slack prose, and no longer can we potentially risk misleading or misinforming audiences with indistinct, dense thought. As guardians of the world's language of choice, we must assume responsibility for communicating ideas with English that is concisely informative, sequentially logical, unambiguously expressed, and mechanically precise; to do so will help to keep us afloat in the economic mainstream.

Everything that you will learn in this book of essays teaches you to accomplish those purposes and will better prepare you for communicating with English in our increasingly changing world. But you may ask, again rightfully, why this particular book of essays?

Written not for a standard publishing house or academic press, *Your Writing Well* offers itself electronically to English practitioners looking for smart responses and fast remedies to their difficulties with writing. My professional experience with American profit and non-profit business, in prep school, undergraduate, and graduate school education, and on the Internet proves to me that too many smart people don't know how to write logically, clearly and concisely, and self-confidently. When in 2005 I'd begun to write a book about writing, I titled it *Writing for Smarties* because of all the "Dummy Books" at that time. What I knew then and know now about my audience is that their deficiencies as writers are not a lack of intelligence; rather, having fallen through the cracks along their educational way, and now hobbling as writers, these diverse people—and you probably are one of them—recognize writing's importance to their own success but lack some of the know-how, the skills and strategies, to improve the quality of their prose. Each writer's success is determined somewhat by her or his talent, but it's important to realize that talent is just a small part of successful professional, academic, or personal writing, maybe 10% to 20% of what goes into a person's written creations.

Besides, talent pertains more to "creative writing" of novels, short stories, plays, and poetry. For writers of "expository prose," however, prose that in business, technology, and academics "exposes" by explaining proposals and processes, theories and positions, and issues and opinions—for writers of expository prose the remaining 80% to 90% of writing ability comes not from talent but from the skills and strategies that must be learned and naturalized, from techniques used for developing content and organization, and from logic-based requirements applied to grammar, punctuation, and sentence structure. As is true of any skill—playing a piano, for example, or dribbling a basketball—we must practice to get better at it. That's why piano teachers and basketball coaches exist: to help players refine whatever their personal talents may be but also to compensate for whatever they lack in talent, by using needed skills and strategies to become more proficient. Some of us may be more talented with a particular skill, but all of us with practice will improve.

Although skills and strategies usually must be taught or coached, personal adaptation individualizes them when ultimately we display them in public; nobody dribbles a basketball or plays Mozart exactly the same. Nobody writes the same, either, although some of what we've been taught or coached along the way becomes essential, integral, necessary to what and how we perform. Thus the basic moves on the court and the keyboard of piano or computer begin with steadfast principles of logical design that we must master, after which we infuse that mastery of systems into our unique performance of basketball, piano, or writing. And as also is true of practicing any skill, ultimately we find that it becomes instinctive or second natured to us, a "no-brainer": at the basketball game do we think about dribbling as we move down the court, nor at the piano recital do we think about forming a chord or what comes after it. Similarly, practicing the many elements of writing helps to mature writers' understanding of the best moves and correct choices to make and thus to avoid having to pause to think about those elements.

Keep in mind at all times, however, that except for descriptive grammatical principles, whose written use is either correct or incorrect, writing's "rules" and "regulations" must be flexible because of each text's unique set of variables, including audience; prudent practicality must rule and regulate how a writer manages each different text, guaranteeing that each part of the content and organization will be more correct, more logical, thus preferable as a whole. Writing well does not proceed according to hard-set "rules" and irrevocable "regulations" governing propriety or correctness. Throughout this paragraph I've quoted "rules" and "regulations," because for a written text's content and organization there are common sense guidelines but not rigid programs of acceptability. As a writer you must have freedom to explore, discover, develop, and demonstrate your unique understanding of the world, and part of this freedom is knowing that style-based rules and regulations is self-contradictory and must not obstruct your friendship with your own ideas and prose.

Your Writing Well responds to the multiple demands of smart native and nonnative writers of English who know their writing can improve, who want practical guidelines for its improvement, wish to communicate decisively in whatever work they perform, but can't be bothered by wasting time trying to find and then to learn the essential strategies and skills for writing well. Knowing that about you, *Your Writing Well* condenses a century of writing theory into a brief book of essays about "writing as a whole"; also, because writing is writing is writing, *Your Writing Well* lays out essential keys to unlock treasures for writing well any kind of text—and to write it faster, after practice has helped to broaden and deepen one's instincts. Whether you're interested in "business writing" or "technical writing," academic research or critical analyses, a thesis or dissertation, proposal or memo, personal correspondence or minutes from a meeting, you name it, Your Writing Well opens up the resources for writing successful texts.

Of course library and bookstore shelves already stack more than enough information to teach writing; however, when we examine the current titles in print, it's evident that multiple books are needed for a writer to learn how to write as a whole. The vital limitation of existing books about writing is that they focus on just one or two of the four modes of writing instruction: expressive, rhetorical, formalist, or mimetic. These books lack all-inclusive writing theory and practice; they gag writers with overstuffing while discouraging them from getting the soup-to-nuts food-for-thought they crave and can digest. In effect, many of these overly academic texts distract struggling writers—certainly have distracted me, probably have distracted you—with cumbersome singular interests that neglect writers' broader needs. Singular interest in some of these texts also misleads writers to use mechanical methods and template models that disregard the essential nature of thinking and disallow freedom of self-expression.

Consequently, my essays are for all writers at any level in any professional or personal pursuit who are too busy to separate educational wheat from chaff and who still are looking for a clearly synthesized and quick overview of all four modes of writing: the personal psychology, organic aesthetics, energy physics, and neuroscience of process-driven expressive writing theory; the intellectual, ethical, and emotional judgments and audience-politics of rhetoric, along with practical strategies for how to develop and shape knowledge and to reason when thinking critically; the linguistic logic or descriptive rules—the formalism—of usage and prose mechanics; and the best elements of mimetic style, emulative models that provoke thought. For my audience it is useful—it is necessary—to have a single book of essays delivering this synthesis efficiently and understandably. *Your Writing Well* does that with simple sophistication. There is no other text like it.

Wary of prescriptive rules and formats that narrow and restrict, *Your Writing Well* expands and clarifies writers' freedoms while emphasizing English's enduringly logical usage requirements. Whereas Strunk and White's early-twentieth-century The Elements of Style usefully advised three generations of English writers what not to do when writing and how to avoid substandard English usage, my book of essays leads twenty-first-century writers through newsworthy ideas about what they can do and ought to try, and why and how to do that. Common sense and sensible psychology help to support the explanations and directives suggested here, while, for mechanical principles, the necessities of descriptive grammar underlie the skills taught, logic-based skills of grammar, punctuation, and sentence structure whose usage is either correct or incorrect. I'm certain that my audience wants to learn once and for all the difference between logic-based and style-based grammatical standards.

But is written English really so important to individuals' interaction, their public society, and, now, the increasing internationalism of our world? Isn't it possible to remain productive with oral speech and with numbers and images, and just to ignore writing altogether? Possibly so, for some people, but not for you and me, so I want you to take a moment to consider or to reconsider why language and the writing of it are so important to us.

It's helpful to remember that language in general—grammar, grammar's labels and requirements, and sentence structure—is a mirror reflecting or representing the actual world, what it contains, how it operates, and the classified groupings, meanings, and values we assign to all of it. Language's individual words, each word's "part of speech," and language's linguistic systems using those parts of speech exist to help us reproduce our world, to stack it up with our own information architecture, to actualize structurally with words both the physical and metaphysical existence external to us, and the intellectual, psychological, and emotional existence within us. We humans are unique among animals for our creation of the magnificent symbolic system of language, whose words "represent" reality; that is, words present reality again, using letters to encode in identifiable labels whatever exists and is going on. Language thus allows us to translate and to express what and how we think and feel, and what we know and believe, so that other people can understand our perceptions of the world and of ourselves. Math, also a symbolic system, principally is about quantifying the world, but when its estimable representations end we use language to qualify meaning.

The Oxford English Dictionary (O.E.D.) contains over 600,000 defined English words, each symbolically representing at least one tangible feature or intangible quality of existence's complexity; keep in mind that many words have more than one defined meaning because they include different "parts of speech," for example "rose" as a noun ("The rose is fragrant"), "rose" as a past-tense verb ("She rose from bed"), and "rose" as an adjective ("The rose dress [what kind of dress?] is beautiful"). Furthermore, although each year some words die from disuse, thousands of others are born to accommodate humanity's ever-expanding experiences and knowledge, new words especially from institutional bureaucracy, science and technology, and medicine and pharmaceuticals, while descriptive terminology such as "bling" also enters the newly represented picture of life. The Global Language Monitor, July 23, 2011, reports that, more than the O.E.D.'s number of words, "there are currently 1,009,753 words in the English language" (http://www.languagemonitor.com/), a sum resulting from a "proprietary algorithm, the Predictive Quantities Indicator (PQI), which attempts to measure the language as currently found in print." But whatever the total of words, the English language teems with diction because human life is rich with realities that for infinite reasons must be represented symbolically with language.

 Writing out groups of words also is symbolic, an extensive series of representations. I like to think of writing as "codified thought," as thinking that's placed into codes, the symbolic codes of language: 26 alphabetic letters, single or combined use of letters into words, words into sentences, sentences into paragraphs, and so forth—in total, the formally managed and systematized exposition of whatever subjects are focused on and need to be expressed to other people. Writing is not the same as speaking in conversation, however, because with speech we formulate language spontaneously and haven't time to codify the impulsive rush of all our mental signals. We use whatever words come to us at the moment, because we haven't time to search for better ones. Perhaps we use "like" whenever a lapse occurs in appropriate word-choice—"She was like w-a-y happy that I like went to her uh-like weekend getaway"—but listeners usually don't care or even notice, because as impromptu conversationalists we don't require ourselves to speak with formal diction, and we certainly don't speak with formal paragraphs.

 Conversational thinking usually isn't premeditated, so we risk incoherence in the sequence of our spoken thoughts, if in fact there's any sequence at all when we converse; maybe the discussion is random questions and answers, back and forth, or an exploratory, random dig for information. Among many ways to aid ourselves as conversing speakers, therefore, you or I can gesticulate for emphasis and as listeners can read body language from other speakers, who read ours. We listen for tonal emphases. We see other people's eyes—"the windows of the soul"—and interpret facial characteristics as prompts for us to repeat or explain ourselves. In conversation, listeners can ask what speakers mean, and speakers can restate their ideas. Conversation has at least two lanes of interaction; writing is a one-way street.

 Conversation is vocal and composed of sound waves or energy, whereas another way to think of writing is as the conversion of energy to mass: with written language, we amass and arrange graphically on paper or screen the thoughts that exist in our brain as a result of investigating, reading, and deliberating. We make visually concrete what originally is abstract: we cannot see or literally grasp thoughts, because they are energy. We know that thoughts are energy vibrating at different frequencies because brain waves are the rapid fluctuations of energy voltage between parts of the cerebral cortex. We further know that thoughts are energy because the brain, like any machine, requires fuel for work; mental machinery fuels itself with calories, a unit of heat energy. In fact, the brain burns calories when we think. With writing, therefore, we convert mental energy into visible, encoded mass.

Writing is difficult, however, because it does require that thoughts be codified, does require that we capture, compile, and constitute in mass all those electrical impulses firing in our brain. Accomplishing this with complex new subjects does not happen easily—not for anyone—because at first we are relatively ignorant about those subjects. But once we defeat our ignorance, we then can share with readers our victory, which we do with writing because we want or need to use our formally mastered understanding to warrant a belief, or opinion, or proposal that we think has legitimacy and value and that ought to be expressed to and seen by other people, our audience. Negating ignorance, codified thought presents educative logic in an organized sequence that induces and clarifies our purposes with ideas honed to purity. So if you want to write informative, logically developed, well expressed texts—and certainly you do—then you must allow time to help yourself develop and codify your thoughts. Well written documents do not come as if by divine inspiration, although frequently we place ourselves before the keyboard at the last minute and assume that information will flow from our brain like anointed water from a sacred chalice. Not that way, our writing will be written well only if in advance we have thought out and organized the matter(s) and issue(s) at hand. You know this is true. How many times have you waited until the night before a deadline at work or in school, reviewed your materials and considered as well as possible whatever crosses your mind about them, and then composed your written text—only to realize later, after submitting it, that you forgot to say this, should have elaborated on that, definitely ought to have repositioned a few of those sentences containing important ideas, probably could have eliminated that irrelevancy, certainly might have refined how you expressed some of your ideas, and definitely should have proofread it one final time for greater mechanical precision.

Wouldacouldashoulda.

The necessity of adequate time given to writing has motivated theorists during the past generation to teach writing as a process, because thinking itself is a process; ideas require time to grow and be harvested, relished and preserved. Rather than presuming that writing is about manufacturing a finished product from a template or from an exemplary model by a famed writer, many theorists now appreciate that the overwhelming majority of writers can and will additionally benefit from approaching writing as a series of interrelated steps, what I will call an organic development of materials (see Essay #2) that is very much alive and therefore capable of growth and change. All written texts are living organisms. All texts must develop, be fed and nourished, and exercised and trained before we can deem them mature and in shape.

Because they are vital or alive as energy, ideas grow organically whenever they connect similar ideas' energy to themselves. As the ideas enlarge, they literally become more intelligent, more informed, more coherently scoped because of their increasingly composed energy. And because with written texts we gather kindred intellectual energy for the purpose of deliberate creation, the magnetic force of our subject becomes increasingly strong and better able not only to recognize, hear, and attract additional relevant meaning, but also knowingly to repel insignificance—the "bad vibes" or alien properties incompatible with our written document. Soon, every set of ideas brought together and composed becomes its own force field. As I explain further in Essay #3, in physics a force field is the space surround-ing any radiating body whose electromagnetic oscillations can exert force on any similar body not in contact with it. Therefore, as we continue to talk, read, and think about our text's subject, these increasingly forceful force fields will attract additional related energies from numerous sources in our professional, academic, or personal environment. Some ideas will be obvious connections and explicitly related, some less apparent and only implied; however, as intellectual force fields develop in power, they also develop in definition and clarity of purpose so that we know what works and doesn't work with them.

And when our conscious intellectual energy becomes vitally compounded, we find that our high-energy bonds also draw up related insights from the deep pool of our subconscious, a reservoir of mental energies. Some theorists assert that "What often passes for subconscious thought are those thoughts at the edge of your vibrational signal range. Sort of like something at the edges of your peripheral vision: it's there, but you can barely make it out" (http://kjmaclean.com/SubconsciousMind.html). But no matter how we map the territories where our thoughts reside, the fact remains that intellectual forces will attract similar forces—wherever they come from.

After you as a writer have drawn enough thoughts from inside and outside of yourself, and after separate force fields of thought have amassed their own particular boundaries, then a written text's subject begins to assume shape—because it now is informed. An essay's form, or organization, becomes inseparable from its content, because with a guiding purpose you have discovered, gathered, sorted through, dismissed parts of, and arranged the information you need, which becomes a coherent whole, the totality of your text's information. Possibly all along you have foreseen parts of the text's body—force-field sections, which are potential paragraph topics. Or possibly you have recognized and understood some of those parts of its body but only now, after time has passed, begin to understand the function and importance of interconnections you hadn't forecasted or anticipated. And maybe smaller points of information whose value you previously didn't and couldn't have foreknown now also become relevant and useful.

No matter how an essay's body becomes informed—and keep in mind that the process of discovery and information-gathering sometimes will feel random and seem speculative at first—we can say safely that no body of information ever is complete in its beginning. Each document's body's unique mass, converted from unique fields or patterns of energy, will develop most fully after compatible energy fields have gathered force and developed or amassed materially. Of course you will aid that material development by nourishing and shaping it, but you also will be able to see it develop on its own as it proliferates naturally.

Writing, in total, is how we codify our thinking for logic and coherent development of information so that, in turn, as knowledgeable educators we make our text persuasive, genuinely convincing, thus valuable and valued, even if it's just an e-mail. As writers we have expertise about something which must be shared, given attention, and of which we must take it upon ourselves to become persuasive educators. We all know that we write expository prose not principally to hear ourselves talk, or for its creatively intellectual experience, or just for the practice of it, but instead because we want or need to educate someone about something, whether it's a proposal to a company's CEO or a memo to a group, whether an essay for a class or a letter to a friend or family member.

My educational goal for my audience, you and others, whose goal is better writing, is to focus directly on what really matters when you think to write and, with efficient guidance, to help you make progress, to improve your thinking skills and writing skills, and to gain the confidence that improvement provides. But you must be a patient and perseverant reader if you want to be educated and to learn.

Like writing, reading also requires mastery of a set of applied skills; when attained, that mastery helps you not only to understand and remember lessons about writing well, but also to observe from other writers' management of prose how to strengthen or newly enable your own writing abilities. Practiced reading obviously sensitizes us more observantly to how writing can be written, so that we pick up ways and means of writing that we'd not before seen, thus not known. This kind of imitative process is well studied and proven by scholars and teachers, and confirmed by life experience. But as is true with writing, the patience and perseverance required to read takes time—time especially to read well. I understand that reading well and learning well from reading may not yet be a high-speed experience for you; possibly you're not a fast reader. That's okay: fast reading is worthless if you don't understand and can't remember what you read. Fast reading may help some students to earn a higher score in the reading comprehension section of the Verbal SAT or GRE, among many other tests, but those timed tests and the practical abilities they evaluate are based on rapid short-term memory, not on long-term memory that allows the founding and compounding of broadly based meaning. At your own best speed, therefore, which in fact will increase as you practice, reading well will help you to have a larger, more detailed and integral picture of what you're studying, a picture with more lines of reasoning, more vivid lessons, and a more broadly spread canvas of individual features.

Not everything that you read in my essays may seem interesting to you at first, but as a reader you also must train yourself to dismiss your ennui, to overcome tedium and keep your mind open to new ideas and possibilities. Sometimes, it's not that the subject you're reading about lacks interest but rather that you aren't or don't think you're interested in it; therefore, as I said before, be patient and perseverant, and attempt to understand all that you read. If you find that you've passed over a sentence or two, or more, then reread whatever you missed along the way. These oversights happen with everyone, so be mindful about rectifying them and also mindful about looking for value or interest in what you read.

Lingering in the forefront of my mind as I begin to conclude this essay is—and now we all rightfully may ask—if I've sufficiently identified the audience of *Your Writing Well*. Let me review: you and the others whom this essay explicitly profiles and writes for need greater self-assurance about your mastery of certain aspects of prose, and therefore want additional skills and strategies to understand and to improve and vary how you develop, organize, and express ideas. Second, you'd like reassurance that your particular deficiencies as a writer absolutely can be improved, since writing is a manageable skill-set that you're smart enough to learn if you give it some time. Third, because time is valuable to you, you haven't the patience to plod through coursework or to explore books' multiple, sometimes cavernous passages to find the purposeful, valued pieces of advice and explanation that you need; you want thorough, resolute, but relatively quick instruction. Fourth, you'd like my instruction to contain simple, lean logic, what's commonsensical for all writing but perhaps new, overlooked, or forgotten. Fifth, for once and for all you'd like a straightforward understanding of grammatical principles whose application is logically either right or wrong, as distinct from style, whose flexibility requires preferential choice and isn't about correctness or incorrectness. Sixth, you've always preferred writing that comes naturally and is true to you, not stamped with template structures and rigid strictures, so you want instruction that frees rather than imprisons you and your abilities. Last, you're interested in becoming or you already have become part of the twenty-first century's electronically webbed and woven networks of knowledge communicated by words, and principally English words, mastery of whose writing will be advantageous to you by keeping you current as a participant or observer in global developments.

If you know I've hit the bull's-eye or at least scored by hitting your target, then I encourage you to continue reading these essays; I want them to benefit you as a thinker and writer of thoughts, simply that, because I'm certain that your writing well profits not just you and your processing of ideas, but also the audiences with whom you communicate.

REFERENCES

[1] Fact-only exposition, such as scientific or financial reporting, is presupposed by and presented according to a writer's intentions, even when no interpretation or evaluative explanation is involved; the facts always are prioritized and stacked up according to proposed goals and desired results, which nullify pure objectivity.

[2] Numbers relative to other numbers have exactitude, so that we assuredly can conclude that 4 times 2 is 8 and only 8. However, when numbers are used as contextual representations of meaning, thus relative, they lose their objectivity. Is a 3.4% annual salary increase a good raise? Why is the difference between an 89% and 90% so psychologically important, if only one point? Is a person tall if 6"1? Will $225,000 buy a dream home?

[3] English popularizes expressions taken from many sports, expressions used especially in business and commerce and in politics. Most of these expressions are metaphors, suggesting that actions, behaviors, and attitudes in life are like specific characteristics of sports. Some expressions are common in more than one sport: "team player," "sidelined," "out of bounds," and "long shot." Possibly the largest sports source of idiomatic usage, baseball gives us "play hardball," "step up to the plate," "make a pitch," "throw a curve," "pinch hit," "hit a homerun," "hit the ball out of the park," "get to first base," "touch base," "to choke," "to strike out," "to be off base," "a bench-warmer," "come out of left field," "get a rain-check," "be in the major/minor league," "play the field," "right off the bat," "bases are loaded," "three strikes and you're out," and "a hit." Football has given us "kick things off," "take the ball and run," "score a touchdown," "second-string," "fumble," "time out," "pep talk," "put on a game face," and "hold the line." From basketball we talk about "out of bounds," "call the shots," "get caught flat-footed," "slam dunk," and "the situation is up for grabs." Boxing provides many idiomatic expressions, such as "come out swinging," "keep your guard up," "roll with the punches," "beat [an opponent] to the punch," "low blow," "sucker punch," "on the ropes," "knockdown, dragout," "take it on the chin," "get knocked for a loop," "go down for the count," "pull no punches," "saved by the bell," and "throw in the towel." Horse-racing gives us "home stretch," "jockey into position," and "Charley horse." From track, we use "jumping the gun," "up to speed," "off track," "raise the bar." And here are expressions from eight other sports: "Chips are down," "get the ball rolling," "no holds barred," "take the bull by the horns," "put the ball in [the opponent's] court," "not up to par," "behind the eight ball," and "taking the bait."

Your Writing Well seamlessly combines and reinforces the best knowledge of writing's four brands of discourse: expressive, rhetorical, formalist, and mimetic. It draws from Peter Elbow's 1981 Writing with Power, still the sovereign text of expressive theory and self-discovery through writing, which educates readers about methods for developing ideas and becoming adventuresome risk-takers. Intended principally for novice thinkers, however, Elbow's instruction relies heavily on group activity in the classroom, which affords the luxury of time for peer critiques and for ample trial-and-error; readers of Your Writing Well do not have that time and opportunity.

Another very successful writing book is Elizabeth Rankin's rhetorically focused The Work of Writing, 2001, certainly the most useful text for instructing professionals and academics how to strategize about a text's purpose, audience, genre, and voice. But because Rankin's readers already are skilled writers who want to fine-tune their texts (journal articles, books, grants, business proposals, and curriculum guides) for marketing purposes, she deemphasizes not only the foundation principles of thinking and of developing and organizing thoughts that Your Writing Well's readers require, but also guidelines for formalizing prose. At the other extreme rhetorically are the template books, notably Stanley Fish's How to Write a Sentence, 2011, and Graff and Birkenstein's They Say /I Say: The Moves that Matter in Academic Writing, 2006. I discuss these two books in Essay #2: "Writing From the Inside Out: A Case Against Reliance on Templates, In Defense of Organic Ways to Write."

Formalist writing books, which respond to back-to-basics demands, talk shop about proper usage. Along with The Chicago Manual of Style, Diana Hacker's 2011 A Writer's Reference, Seventh Ed. is the best example—and the most widely used American college handbook—of this kind. Although Hacker's book includes chapters on composing and revising, they total fewer than thirty pages, about one-twelfth of her text, whose principal focus is the micro-mechanical elements of writing. While this handbook compiles stacks of answers, the formal basics that matter most to writers get lost in the glossaried heap; for Your Writing Well''s readers, less is more.

The final instructive approach to writing, mimetic writing books, believes that learning to think well about reality is most crucial to writing well. These books offer either model essays of effective thinking accompanied by analysis, a trend begun over a generation ago in Ray Kytle's 1969-87 Clear Thinking for Composition, or theme-based anthologies of provocative essays, such as those found in Jack Selzer's 2003 Argument in America and also his 1994-2008 Conversations.

Thousands of single English words are multiple parts of speech and therefore function differently in sentences. Here are just a few: affect, bill, bow, box, date, deal, design, does, effect, felt, fit, foil, free, head, hide, hit, import, iron, last, lead, leaves, left, lie, might, mill, mine, narrow, net, oil, pants, part, paste, place, point, polish, project, prompt, protest, rest, rose, sign, smart, sow, state, tie, tip, type, want, water, well, will, wind, work.

About 80% of readers "subvocalize" or, as they read, recite to themselves most of the text's words. There is nothing wrong with this, but it does slow these readers to a rate no faster than they can talk or speed-talk. In contrast, reading visually allows greater speed because one can pass over unimportant words and learn to extract and absorb—to place in "blocks"—only what's relevant in the sentence. Visual reading of course requires a new set of skills, a set that will take time to develop if one relies on subvocalizing. Therefore, if you subvocalize, I suggest that you experiment with and practice visual reading not with professional or academic information important to your success, but with an essay from a newspaper, magazine, or online document.

Ammon, U., ed. The Dominance of English as a Language of Science. New York: Mouton de Gruyter, 2001. Channing, Burt. "What Is International English?" Columbia University Working Papers in TESOL & Applied Linguistics, 2005, Vol. 5, No. 1.

Crystal, David. English as a Global Language. Cambridge: Cambridge University Press, 2003. Francis, Diane. Financial Post, January 18, 2010.

Haneline, Douglas, Chair and Moderator. 2003 Annual conference Coverage, "English Language as a World Communication Tool: Past, Present, Prospect"
http://www.amwa.org/default/publications/journal/vol19no1/journalvol19no1.pdf

Ling, Johnny. 2001. <http://hypertextbook.com/facts/2001/JohnnyLing.shtml>

Marks, Kathy. "Seoul Tries to Shock Parents out of Linguistic Surgery," The Independent, January 3, 2004. Thorniley, Tessa. Guardian Weekly, July 13, 2010.

Tonkin, Humphrey. TheScientist.com http://www.the-scientist.com/

ESSAY 2

Writing from the Inside Out: A Case Against Reliance on Templates, In Defense of the Organic Way to Write

"Organic" has become a frustrating, possibly annoying catchword or tag, and the guy writing this essay is using it in his title. Overused application can make any word lose sense and value when its meaning, spread too wide, becomes too thin and feeble-minded; "nice" is a good example. In organic chemistry, however, because organic compounds are the basis of almost all earthly life processes, the word "organic" does make sense for bodily growth and maintenance and does positively denote whatever is natural or pure, beneficial or at least more healthful than comparable products not organic. So I wasn't surprised last year when a dry-cleaner near my home posted "Organic Dry Cleaning" above its front door; if clothing itself now can be organic, much of it made of organically raised cotton, then why can't its dry cleaning use organic products, those free of synthetic chemicals? Enter a drug store and you'll find myriad organic products for the human body, including perfume, hair color, shampoo, nail-care, deodorant, moisturizer, and toothpaste. Most grocery stores now sell organic food of all kinds including one near my home, named "Organic Avenue"; flowers and plants also can be organic. The "organic" label of federal certification assures all natural ingredients for seeding or feeding, growing or raising, producing and preserving. Colleges now offer a major in "organic agriculture."

But in aesthetic matters, always philosophical, particularly in critical theory of contemporary literature, art, and architecture, the term "organic" too often just means whatever is well constructed or unified—the resulting product but not its process. In such instances the term's use tells us nothing specific about the product's creation and development and seems a buzz-word. "Organic Way to Write" in this essay's title maybe sounds illustriously distinguished, but what does it mean to me, the writer-educator, who must persuade you that the organic way is preferable for learners of writing? Obviously I must define the term and present its operations— what it is and how it works, not only as a principle of life, but as a methodology I use when I teach writing and the thought processes writing requires.

To define vocabulary in a text's introduction is important for educating readers if a word or phrase is essential to a text's entire subject and is used repeatedly. Here, "organic" has a multifaceted conceptual meaning that controls this essay's focus, so my audience must learn immediately what the term designates. To define it, I'll borrow from early nineteenth-century philosophical and aesthetic theory, whose operative paradigm or way of perceiving the world was itself an organic model based on botany. Using that model, philosophers and aestheticians then and now have presupposed that all artistic creation and thinking, writing included, is like botanical Nature, an integrated whole whose parts take appointed places in mutual harmony consonant with the whole's total pattern and task. That last sentence, I know, requires further definition and clarification.

There are five basic similarities between the organic life of a written text and the organic life of a living plant: internality, assimilation, growth, interrelatedness, and priority of the whole. Together, these five terms mean that, from start to finish, written creation and botanical creation are about one unified purpose, even if the purpose has many parts, such as the best paper you've ever written or the wild pomegranate tree (Burchellia bubaline) in your garden.

The first similarity is that writing and botanical life evolve from a process of "internality," self-growth from the inside out, not mechanically assembled from an outside superimposition. In organic writing, internality is the writer's guiding vision, a restrictedly defined purpose with focused intellectual energy, what we call a "thesis" or directing rationale in academic exposition, or, for an analogy, what we also can call a control-center, such as the human body's central nervous system (CNS). In all humans, the CNS includes brain activity and all motor skills down to the very last twitch; therefore, we neither think nor move without our CNS, just as writing has no intelligence and no plotted progress without its generative thesis or control-center. In most botany and biology, internality begins very simply with a fertile seed from which all else grows.

Second, as growth begins, organic writing and plants use "assimilation" to convert diverse materials into one substance, the total material mass of their content. With writing, assimilation begins within the managed boundaries set by the thesis when a writer's force of purpose magnetically attracts similar but not repetitious evidence; coherence is natural as the writer's mind explores, discovers, and clusters kindred ideas into neighborhoods of thought, which, associated by ongoing classification, allows for more keenly perceived similarities and differences. Through internality and assimilation, therefore, form and content become inseparable in writing and in plants, because the inside content shapes the outward form.

Botany's and writing's third similarity is "growth," a perpetual becoming whose freedom of evolution remains formally unified because of the progressive interrelatedness of all parts. Fourth, then, is the "interrelatedness" among those parts, and between parts and the whole. All parts are related because they are generated by the same "internal" means; each part is its own effect as well as simultaneously the cause of some larger effect, therefore both means and end; in an essay, for example, a well conceived and written paragraph is an end in itself insofar as it thoroughly explores and explains one topic of the essay's subject's purpose, but that same paragraph also is the transitional means out of the preceding paragraph's topic and into that of the next, containing a set of concepts and information developed from the preceding information and upon which one's understanding or appreciation of subsequent information depends. Fifth, and last, is the "priority of the whole," without which the parts are dissociated from the cumulative integrity which the whole provides them. In total, a writer proceeds from a "first cause" inherent in all effects, whose progressive synthesis or interrelatedness ultimately becomes the whole composition.

Obviously I think that the writing of persuasive reasoning—and remember, all public writing is persuasive—as well as the sentences which that reasoning contains should not be reduced to or proceed from a predetermined mass of products; instead, written compositions should manifest an inner necessity, a generative impulse that bears itself forth materially, as a seed does its roots, stalks, stems, leaves, flowers, and fruits or cones, or as a written composition does the parts of its body—its paragraphed topics of investigation—and the introduction and conclusion to those parts. The organic process of writing is a vital process, a self-organizing formal principle or thesis, not a set of fixed products.

The way to write or the methodology that's offered in these compiled essays investigates and emphasizes how to develop any written text organically, whether it's non-academic or academic. But before proceeding to investigate my organic methodology in later essays, I want you and my other readers to think critically with me about two recent books advocating the use of templates for writing; effective persuasion—one aspect of writing well—requires that a writer consider and when possible rebut the "opposition's" general argument and particular thoughts, which I will do now.

Good sentences' structural forms have "ordained" (2) or predetermined logic, argues Stanley Fish in How to Write a Sentence (2011): this ordained logic can help untrained writers "to organize the world into manageable . . . units that can then be inhabited and manipulated" (7) by those writers' thoughts. For untrained writers to learn ordained lessons and to practice them, Fish advises that they "zero in on a form that can then be filled with any number of contents" (7), by which he means a template. Form comes first for Fish, a standard for syntax that he shares with Gerald Graff and Cathy Birkenstein's standard for strategic argumentation in They Say/I Say: The Moves that Matter in Academic Writing (2006). Both books advocate form's primacy by relying exclusively on templates, on structural models whose functional advantages come from mastering exemplary syntactic and argumentative patterns, respectively, and then deciding what to say with them.

Is Fish right to believe that "content must take a backseat to the mastery of forms, without which you can't say anything in the first place" (25)—and are Graff and Birkenstein right that the "moves that matter" in argumentation can be reduced to a set of arranged templates, because "many students will never learn on their own to make the key intellectual moves that our templates represent" (xx)? For people to write effectively and for their written texts to operate well, must they trust with certainty that content will find its proper way into syntax and argumentation if as writers they choose the proper templates? Doubtful, I do agree that "using such prefabricated formulas as learning tools need not result in writing and thinking that are themselves formulaic" (Graff xxii), but I fear that for those "many students" relying on templates the results will be counterproductive because such a process of learning is, itself, formulaic. So consider the contrary: what if, in total, content and its individual energies can and do inform sentence structure and paragraph argumentation better than the imposed form of templates can, and more thoroughly and wholly, or differently? What if we see each text first as a botanical growth in whose composition both form and content are inseparable, in which content does not take a "backseat" but instead drives forward its own necessities for syntax and argumentation?

While templates absolutely can be put to good use—for NYU graduate students I suggest templates to use as one kind of brainstorming strategy—these three authors' purpose and directives disregard writing at its best, which begins as and at all stages should be an organic activity in which sentences and arguments breatheand grow in accordance with the life of the ideas and images they represent. Not amechanical assembly-line, the writing process requires natural development, requiresenthusiastic conception, nurturance by personalized attention, logical training of ideas exercised into fitness while all along being trimmed for conciseness and developed with new, strongly related content. Although templates may be useful asspecific contextual insertions, critics Jason Arthur and Anne Case-Halferty warncorrectly that this kind of "rhetorical shorthand" with templates "seems not to allow the necessary room for development… Graff and Birkenstein inherently limit the possible insights that a writer can draw from normally multivalent academic [and non-academic] debates," thereby "encourag[ing] oversimplification and deliberate ignorance of the complexity of a given conversation" (Composition Forum 18, Summer 2008). Granted, many students possibly will not learn key intellectual moveswithout templates, but am I as a teacher and are they as writers willing to regiment and possibly restrict not just their intellectual discoveries, but also their processes ofthinking about them?

One benefit of an organic writing process, seen in the analogy with botanical growth, is that all parts of its whole product are naturally interrelated because all relationships are inspired seminally and developed by a controlling purpose (possiblywith many topics) whose content generates its own form; in effect, form and content become unified, indivisible, sui generis (when Latin does the talking). Thinking within the box of templates lends itself to boxed thinking, which may be okay if a person'spurpose to write is rigidly utilitarian and impersonal; formulas used to express ideas and to maneuver arguments are helpful to know when the mind requires standardization, but, like individual bones in a body, established forms aren't just ends in themselves but instead integral parts of and links within a larger skeletal structure supporting and expressing that body as a whole.

Regarding sentences, Fish denounces writing textbooks whose vocabulary includes names for parts of speech and for different clauses and phrases, arguing that when those books tell writers that "a sentence contains a subject and a predicate" or that "sentences consist of one or more clauses," then it follows that such declarations, "far from being transparent and incisive . . . come wrapped in a fog . . . [and] seem to skate on their own surface and simply don't go deep enough" (15). Fish thus asks his reader, "what can we offer that will go deeper?" and answers that his "bottom line can be summarized in two statements: (1) a sentence is an organization of items in the world; and (2) a sentence is a structure of logical relationships" (16). However, Fish's refutation of fog-bearing writing instruction such as that of Strunk and White and other, more contemporary writing theorists argues misleadingly, because in short time there is no actual difference between saying "a sentence contains a subject and a predicate" and Fish's own bottom line that "a sentence is a structure of logical relationships." Once a person learns that a subject is a noun- or pronoun-doer of an action, and that a predicate is the verb's action done, then a basic knowledge of three parts of speech lifts the fog and clearly reveals a logical relationship. Moreover, Fish overstates his belief that writers "confuse a taxonomy of the parts of speech with an analysis of a sentence's logical structure" (20); in truth, although taxonomy and analysis are not the same, they are two parts of one process that writers use so that they can examine a sentence's logical structure.

Fish further emphasizes that a writer's analytical appreciation of other writers' syntactic structures will improve any writer's prose, "because taking it [a sentence] apart will give you an enhanced understanding of just what kind of goodness it performs" (11). But how does Fish expect us to "take apart" or analyze a template, and share our analysis with ourselves and others, without a working vocabulary for identifying how and what the template performs? Isn't that really the guiding purpose of parts of speech anyway, one-word labels for the logical relationships that Fish tells us we should understand? If I tell you that every preposition must have its own noun or pronoun object (an object is a non-doer person, place, or thing—for example, "in Manhattan" "at midnight," "with a fork," "for them"), then we have established another logical relationship and can label it a prepositional phrase, which in English expresses either where ("in Manhattan") and when ("at midnight"), or how ("with a fork") and why ("for them"). If additionally I tell you that every prepositional phrase functions either as an adjective (adjectives usually tell us a characteristic about a noun or pronoun—"The man with expectations") or as an adverb (a characteristic usually about a verb—"The man with expectations works for results"), then our analysis of that part of a sentence is precise and our knowledge of that logical relationship is thorough. And by the way, in the preceding example we already have learned five of the seven important parts of speech; only the verb and the conjunction remain. Mastering the parts of speech and their functional logic may take a while, but, if a fourth-grader can master them, why such fussiness from Fish?

One wonders as well about the number of people actually able to analyze and "inhabit and manipulate" for themselves the complexity of sentences, as Fish requires. Musically bereft students always will have a difficult time experiencing and thus explaining the "delight and awe [Fish] feel[s] when reading and contemplating" (8) the templates he uses to illustrate the structures he encourages writers to emulate. A Milton scholar of superior sensitivity to language's rhythms and tones, Fish hopes to reduce to common sense and practicality his private series of appreciations, which, in fact, are extraordinary and rarified.

Certainly Fish also must be aware that using templates to frame what writers want to draw out, depict, or portray removes them, the writers, from their own expressiveness: with templates' preconceived, superimposed patterns, too much of any writer's voice—if not all of it—is stifled or inhibited. Infused in prose, a writer's voice can and usually does communicate heightened connection with the logic of whatever is being told; in a poetic sense, the voice achieves Alexander Pope's principle that "The sound must seem an echo of the sense" ("Sound and Sense"). Without one's voice, loss of pronouncement therefore occurs because vocal reinforcement of thought is minimized. Indeed there may be a voice already cadenced and intoned by a template, but that is not one's own voice and does not necessarily amplify the singular personal convictions that belong to each writer.

In total, for Fish, template "sentences promise . . . nothing less than lessons and practice in organization of the world," while for Graff and Birkenstein template rhetorical strategies teach students to "inhabit the worldview of those whose conversation you are joining" (29). Those promises are immense, and they can be true, to a point, but getting to each truth must proceed not by replicating stock models, but instead by personalized formulation and expression that invite conventional models only if and when they're appropriate.

Therefore, I want my audience not to think that writing well is attainable by following template instructions and replicating template models. Of course templates have sequential strategies for presentation that may be useful to business and technical writers. Nevertheless, with the intellectual communication of writing, template forms often ignore or do not anticipate individualized functions for content in projects with unique variables; such functions of content must inform organization on their own terms. My advocacy of an organic methodology for writing isn't about composing from the outside in, as we do with templates, but instead from the inside out, botanically, as natural imperatives of our intellect, psychology, and style direct.

REFERENCES

Arthur, Jason and Anne Case-Halferty. Review of Gerald Graff and Cathy Birkenstein. They Say / I Say: The Moves that Matter in Academic Writing (2006). (Composition Forum 18, Summer 2008)

Fish, Stanley. How to Write a Sentence: and How to Read One. Harper, 2011

Graff, Gerald and Cathy Birkenstein. They Say / I Say: The Moves that Matter in Academic Writing. W.W. Norton, 2006.

ESSAY 3

Using a Word™ Document To Compile Thoughts, Brainstorming Results, and Research Materials, And to Find Relationships, for Synthesizing and Classifying, Thus Organizing the Essay's Body's Structure Before You Write Formally

I first taught university "word processing" in 1981, using a computer to develop, edit, and revise academic writing; thirty years ago microprocessors didn't have chips to reduce the number of transistors used, so the Hewlett Packard I worked at was a metal dinosaur by today's standards, its pea-brained memory minimal, its hefty tail- end printer about thirty feet away. Yet to teachers and students back then, that computer was no brontosaurus, not cumbersome, not slow, but instead an agile corpus of coordinated abilities winged to fly us beyond this world's material boundaries. No longer a sci-fi supposition, "computer" denoted an electronic mode of new intellectual realities and transcendent possibilities, alluringly brilliant in power and potential. Although electricity-dependent and crash-prone, that early computer nonetheless was instructive and visually efficient, tooled for writing without scissors, Scotch tape, and inked arrows, without ink erasers or White-Out. Its remarkable word-processing abilities allowed those of us at the keyboard to edit and revise, to cut and paste at electric speed, to document, compartmentalize, and save whatever we hadn't completed, and to see clearly what we had.

By 1989—birth of the World Wide Web—empowering us all was a newly engineered supervision of information, with systems providing mind-boggling expansion and concentrated focuses. Electronic immediacy allowed sites to be spun and to spin into other newly spun sites, all interconnecting and expanding exponentially on an endless "information highway." Seemingly overnight the world sped up: by merging macroculture with micro-computing, humans allowed themselves to search for and locate new knowledge about everything. If at your birth a computer already was in your house, then you always have known its amazing potential but have less appreciation of the intellectual revolution or paradigm shift that the late-'50s to late-'80s computer industry created for writing and increasingly for imaging and sound—and for the thinking that all three media require. The final scene of the 1982 movie Koyaanisqatsi: Life Out of Balance aerially overviews Midtown Manhattan's roof grids, brushed metallic to look like microprocessors, as the fluid cinematography shows how at the beginning of that decade a cultural macrocosm—NYC, capital of the world—and cultural microcosm in a chip are analogous forms of human culture, macrocosmic and microcosmic metaphors of human self-operating.

For people in my Boomer generation, the computer literally changed the world, changed how we all were able to learn and think, and invited us to become a professional and social part of the Web's many links. Whereas people today under thirty-five necessarily have taken the computer for granted, I and others like me retain an innocent joy inspired by the innovative power and potential that the computer brought to us in the middle of our lives—and still brings. During the past decade, however, I've realized that many professional people and college students whom I've taught at all levels have forgotten or never have learned the simple value of Word™ as a useful modality for brainstorming, thinking, and thought-processing before they formally write, edit, and revise. That is why I recommend—actually, in an ideal world I'd insist—that all writers create a Word™ document for any important subject about which they must write, regardless of its length.

I'm advocating that on an appropriately titled Word™ document you immediately record your initial ideas and impressions, each on a separate line, regarding whatever subject you must write about, thus establishing their potential value. Often, just a word or phrase will trigger your recall later on, so type out your ideas using however many words it takes to remember those ideas' importance. Made more actual by your Word™ document and its preliminary content, the essay's subject will be lodged in the forefront of your mind. As new ideas cross your mind, note them, and enter them soon. If possible, read about and discuss your subject, and make notes about your reading and discussions. Enter those notes, too, and record page numbers in texts from which you later will want to paraphrase or quote. Periodically review your recorded ideas, not just to refresh your memory, but to see whether any item prompts you to think associatively and thereby to gain additional, related ideas. Note those. Also, you will begin to see patterns repeating or possibly a theme or line of reasoning emerging, none of which can happen if you aren't able to see your thoughts on the screen.

One significant result from the list on your Word™ document will be your ability to interconnect or synthesize ideas, which in turn yields new insights; in such instances the value and meaning of X combined with Y may become significantly more than just X + Y. Coupling two thoughts that you've recorded on Word™ can create an even larger magnetic force of its own, like the marriage of two compatible energies whose deep-structured union becomes magnetically greater than the sum of its parts. This relationship's greater force is better able to adopt or to procreate additional related information: we see how strongly coupled ideas can give birth to new thoughts. Furthermore, interconnecting and synthesizing while compiling new information on your Word™ list begins your important process of organization.

The preceding paragraph says "synthesize" because that word broadly denotes "putting together" or joining meanings; in that sense, a synthesis connects information from several different sources to formulate a new pattern or idea. Occurring in all aspects of thought, synthesis helps us combine ideas to improve our understanding of the matters that matter and the knowledge to know. And as a thinker and writer, remember that the philosophical operation of induction is itself a process of synthesis, of integrating and combining related and, sometimes at first, seemingly unrelated parts into new wholes, in effect a compilation of particulars adding up to a new generalized truth.

Integral to the process of synthesis is the "Law of Attraction," a fundamental concept of quantum physics that helps explain the physical universe. This law asserts that all existence—physical, metaphysical, and non-physical—is made of energy. Energy according to its own laws attracts that which is vibrating at the same speed; therefore, this physical principle also has valid implications for thinking, because all thought is energy. I mentioned in my introductory essay that thought is energy because brain waves are the rapid fluctuations of voltage between parts of the cerebral cortex; different brain waves have different frequencies. We further know that thought is energy because the brain, like any machine, requires fuel; mental machinery fuels itself with calories, a unit of heat energy, and in fact the brain burns calories when we think.

This law of physics suggests that if you are attuned to and focused intellectually on "X," then you will attract more "X" to your mind; if "Y," you'll draw more "Y." All of us have experienced this idea subliminally when we feel "good vibes" from another person or in group situations that we'd like to join—or even in certain geographical locations. In fact, the natural force inherent in the idea of the "Law of Attraction" has empowered itself as a theoretical tool in recent general psychology and, more specifically, in self-motivation practice. Take for example the still popular 2006 book and later television documentary The Secret, which I mention not for endorsement but to reinforce my point: "The message in The Secret goes far beyond the catch phrase 'you are what you think about,' and this is where quantum physics comes into the picture. Through your intention, and then your focus of attention, you will draw new thoughts and ideas that are in alignment with your focused attention. When you act on these 'inspired' thoughts, you create an energetic chain reaction". One therapeutic group refers to its use of the Law of Attraction as "Organic Psychology" (http://www.ecopsych.com/). Again, while it's not my purpose to legitimize such therapies, I find it revealing that we can use their subsuming principlehere, for an organic approach to writing.

Thus our thoughts and our ideas containing thoughts are patterns of energy; each pattern has its own unique force and, according to the "Law of Attraction," therefore draws to itself thoughts of similar frequencies. Sometimes, when we first are attracted to a thought, we do not fully understand its intellectual kinship with our existing community of ideas; still, we feel, intuit, or get the impression that it may have connective value, and common sense compels us to hold on to it, just in case. Inexplicably, at first, it too has good vibes. But because most of us may not see immediately that an individual thought is attracted—or how it is attracted—to another individual thought, it helps to see both of them literally beside one another in Word™.

Because they are vital or alive, ideas grow organically whenever they connect similar ideas' energy to themselves. As the ideas enlarge, they also become smarter, more informed, more observant, because of their increased rational energy. And because with written compositions we gather kindred intellectual energy for the purpose of deliberate creation, the magnetic force of our subject becomes increasingly strong and better able not only to attract additional relevant meaning, but also knowingly to repel insignificance—the "bad vibes" incompatible with our written document. With incompatibilities recognized and understood, our conscious intellectual energy becomes even more vitally focused, also drawing up related insights from the deep pool of our subconscious, a reservoir of mental energies. As mentioned in my introductory essay, some theorists assert that "What often passes for subconscious thought are those thoughts at the edge of your vibrational signal range. Sort of like something at the edges of your peripheral vision: it's there, but you can barely make it out" (http://kjmaclean.com/SubconsciousMind.html). But no matter how we map the territories where our thoughts reside, the fact remains that intellectual forces will attract similar forces—wherever they come from.

Soon, every set of ideas brought together by attraction becomes its own force field; in physics, a force field is the space surround-ing any radiating body whose electromagnetic oscillations can exert force on any similar body not in contact with it. Therefore, as we continue to talk, read, listen, and think about our text's subject, these increasingly forceful force fields will attract additional related energies from numerous sources in our personal and professional or academic environment. Some ideas will be obvious connections and explicitly related, some less apparent and only implied; however, as intellectual force fields develop in power, they also develop in clarity of purpose.

After we've drawn enough thoughts from inside and outside of us, and after separate force fields have amassed their own knowledge and have begun to form their particular boundaries, our document's subject comes to life and begins to assume shape because it now is informed. Possibly we begin to see parts of the essay's body—those force-field sections, or potential paragraph topics. Or possibly we have seen those parts of its body all along, but only now, after time has passed, begin to understand the function and importance of interconnections we hadn't forecasted or anticipated. Additionally, because increased thinking about our subject yields greater sophistication, small bits of information whose value we previously couldn't have foreknown also become relevant and useful now.

No matter how an essay's body becomes informed—and keep in mind that the process of information-gathering initially will be random—we can say safely that no body ever is complete in its beginning. Each document's body's unique mass, converted from unique patterns of energy called thought, will develop most fully after we apply to our thinking the Law of Attraction—after compatible fields have gathered force and developed materially. Of course you will aid that material development by nourishing and shaping it, but you also will be able to see it develop on its own as it grows naturally.

Granted, discovering potentially fusible or synthetic relationships among thoughts may require sophisticated conceptual insight acquired only through time; however, we are much less likely to find any potential relationships, let alone sophisticated ones, if we have no visibly itemized thoughts to interrelate in the first place.

Creating a Word™ document to collect and to see your thoughts for a writing project offers at least fourteen benefits, especially with an assignment or project whose destiny you don't yet see totally, clearly, and pointedly; Word™ can instruct and lead, exercise and develop, and help to organize your intelligence:

1. At all stages of research and development of ideas you will see objectified what you've thought and are thinking about, because whatever you've written is coded enough for your own recognition and understanding. This simple process locates and structures in your mind the essay's evolving boundaries, which become a vibrational field of intellectual energy initially too broad to have definable integrity, but which begin to reveal how, where, and especially why to develop, build, and place thoughts.

2. Even partial and random ideas emit frequencies and can attract to kindred vibes when symbolized in print; they become force fields of energy that can grow. Maybe you have just a seed of a thought: plant it; don't throw it away. Maybe branches of thought disconnected from their solid trunks of meaning cross your mind: lay out in lines those limbs, whatever they may signify, even if you haven't fully realized how they will or won't attach to your larger purposes.

3. Each Word™ document allows for a discovery process. Whatever theories, reasoning, observations, data, quotations, and points of interest you discover, put them in their designated Word document. Coded there, individual points quickly will begin to interconnect with conceptually related information and thus gain nascent coherence. Sometimes, when we first are attracted to a thought, we do not fully understand its intellectual relationship or importance with the community of ideas to which it belongs; that may take a while, but it never will become a community member if you don't record it on Word. While initially discovering, do not censor or discard.

4. Your initial compilation of ideas on Word™ will prompt you to think associatively about each point and, perhaps, to gain additional, related ideas and sections of a large thought. From that, you may begin to see patterns repeating, or a theme or line of reasoning emerging. That is less likely to happen if there's no compiled list of ideas on Word™.

5. Because some of your Word™ document's information will be broad and general, while some of it will be very particular, it's inevitable that you will rely on both deductive and inductive reasoning.

When you deduce, you move from general principles to particular conclusions or inferences. General: Bill eats daily at MacDonald's. Possible deductive inferences: 1) Bill has unhealthful eating habits, 2) Bill's ingestion of fats and useless calories may be negatively affecting his vascular health, 3) Knowingly or unknowingly, Bill is "super-sizing" himself into obesity, 4) Bill likes fast food. Another form of deduction is the syllogism, which juxtaposes two generalizations, proves them, and then arrives at a specific conclusion. Possibly the most notable use of deductive syllogistic reasoning is Thomas Jefferson's The Declaration of Independence. Structurally, his argument is quite simple: he must prove his major premise (If A, Then B) and minor premise (A) to arrive at a valid specific conclusion (Therefore B). In the Declaration's own words, Jefferson argues that "If a government is despotic, then it is the people's right to overthrow it," that "The government of King George III of England has been despotic," and that therefore it is Colonial America's "right to overthrow it" by declaring its independence.

When you induce, you add up and synthesize particular points of information to reach a general conclusion. Particulars: a) In early 2010, Chile had an 8.8 earthquake and Haiti experienced a 7.7 earthquake along with a devastating hurricane, b) In early March 2011, Japan was struck by an 8.9 earthquake followed by a tsunami, c) Higher global temperatures are negatively affecting global crop yields, d) Increased numbers of species are endangered globally, e) Polar icecaps are melting, f) "The situation with drinking water is already a problem in many parts of the world, and there are more than 1 billion people worldwide that do not have sufficient access to clean drinking water" (http://ecological-problems.blogspot.com/search/ label/water). From these individual points of information we can induce or synthesize possible conclusions: 1) Planet Earth is experiencing ecological imbalances, 2) The 1982 film Koyaanisqatsi, or Life out of Balance, foresaw three decades ago what is happening to the world today, 3) Human beings have lost control of natural priorities, 4) Preservationist attitudes, purposes, and management must be a new human priority.

Notice the different directions in which we logically may take our inductive and deductive conclusions. The five inductive particulars, for example, allow us to conclude general truths about ecology, or a film, or human nature, or global imperatives, and thus we can add up or synthesize ideas for different kinds of observations or total effect; similarly, we can break down ideas into particular possibilities.

The significance of gathering and listing both general and particular ideas should be apparent: these ideas are the starting points from which additional information and insights result. Without these ideas on your Word™ document, you potentially are depriving your mind—and thus your writing—of recognizing important deductive and inductive points of conclusive interest.

6. From the broad purpose and focus you initially gave to your subject, see what emerges as your information grows on its own and is guided by you. Soon, inevitably, you will need and want to begin to decide how to handle the content of this information and its forms: clay in your hands, these expanding, often malleable clumps of information can become interestingly different forms of material depending on what you include and exclude and how you arrange what remains. Remember: you can't go in every direction with an essay; therefore, using your Word™ document, begin to decide which topical directions—which parts of your subject—you need to choose as an educator, want to choose professionally, and incline towards personally. Ask yourself if, and, if so, how each of these directionally plotted ideas that you've chosen interconnects with the essay's entire map or picture; logically prove to yourself that these interconnections are strong and meaningful, so that your total content continues to remain intellectually coherent.

7. Because everything you put in your Word document will have been thought about by you, at least in a preliminary manner, you'll have a better focus on what each item's singular or multiple function is as an interrelated part of the essay's total picture. If one theory, observation, datum, quotation, or point of interest potentially belongs in more than one topic or paragraph in the essay's body, then place it everywhere until you attain greater clarity of your total purpose. Be assured that certain significant concepts and ideas may need to exist in more than one place because they assume different purposes and meanings in different contexts.

8. Systematically in 1) through 7) you are organizing the essay's content from the inside out by uniting potential relationships among its parts and, soon, classifying those parts with a unifying label whose total identification warrants a paragraph of investigation, or more; conceptual, this label names one important topical part of the essay. If one topic seems too broad, subdivide and label it with two separate but interrelated subtopics.

9. As your Word document's list of information and your understanding of it grow, and as you classify all of that information into labeled topics or paragraphs, you will begin to learn approximately how much space each topic or paragraph will require in your essay's body. Spatial allotments may be less important to you if your writing has no length requirement; however, if it does, then your document's success will heighten if you establish reasonable spatial limits for each topic that you're writing about. By approximating which of your topics will require more space, which less, you won't overextend one topic at the expense of the others; instead, a carefully weighted allowance of space among parts must exist—and will, if you see in advance the essay's proportional needs. Consequently, estimating the relative size of each of your topics will give you advanced insight into how and what extent you will use your information. Good editors often must use foresight to decide what to include and what to exclude, decisions made by estimating the merits and value-per- line of each idea; such value judgments will be easier for you when your foresight isstructured visually in front of you.

10. With this evolving list of information, itself grouped into topical paragraphs, you quickly will discover what is and isn't workable for your essay. What at first may have appeared to be an excellent idea is possibly now extraneous and won't work well with what has developed as being central to your purpose. If so, then again you've made a discovery, this time about what to discard. If you discover—and of course you have to see something to discover it—that something lacks usefulness, you won't be bothered by having to throw away a few lines of information.

11. A visual survey of your developing essay's content will help you to make increasingly informed research decisions. As is customary with any organic development, you will add and nourish here, subtract and throw away there, being more secure with the coordinated strength of what

remains. Conversely, if something is vital to your essay but presently is insufficiently developed, you will see what is absent and know better what to pursue in your additional research and conversation; also, this specific focus will save you time.

12. Using Word will allow you to bring to finality your evolving outline of information and its organizational superstructure, all before you have written a formal first draft for the essay. At this point, and on your own terms, you have guaranteed that your essay contains the force of content and stability of organization that you want, because every step of your Word document results from some kind of crafted, codified thinking: describing, defining, comparing and contrasting, classifying, labeling, arguing, and persuading.

13. You also will be able to place properly any afterthoughts that cross your mind after you've begun to write. Because our preoccupations with broad, complex subjects don't just end automatically, it's probable that new ideas and inspirations will continue to pop up and assume associative value as you write. If that happens, you then either can locate where in your skeletal outline these new bones of information belong, or you can determine immediately if they're irrelevant to the body of your essay.

14. Keeping everything in its proper place on your Word document will allow you to see and then consider if any information unrelated centrally to your subject may have tangential importance and possibly be worthy of a footnote or endnote. Professional academic and business writers often fill their documents with supplemental ideas included not in the main body of the essay but in notes, where they explicate those ideas as fully as they want to without having them interrupt the concise flow of thought in the document's body. Similarly, information of tangential importance excluded from the text's body also may serve as a premise for your conclusion.

Compiling information on a Word™ document also helps you to systematize or organize all parts your text's body. Notice the word "body," a term all of us in all nations have used to indicate the main part of any document; however, indicating not just that, "body" also tells us that writing is organic, a living organism. I point this out because we should think of a written document's body, like a human body, as having bones to structure it skeletally, and ligaments or joints to connect those bones.

There can be no stand-up body of knowledge without interconnected bones to support it purposefully. All organized parts of a document's body—all of its topics— must connect with or relate to the whole subject's purpose. For the developmental sequencing of those topical parts, each part or paragraph must connect with what precedes and follows it. Within each topical part or paragraph, all of its parts—that is, all sentences—must relate to the whole and must connect with what precedes and follows them. Within each sentence within each topic within the whole subject, the syntactic parts—the arrangement of clause(s) and phrase(s)—also must be structured so that the sentence stands logically on its own yet grows from what precedes it and anticipates what follows it (see Essay #10, "Sentence Combining"). All of this sequencing begins with and is filled by substance drawn from the "Law of Attraction." All of this interconnectedness indicates the organic nature of writing.

The content of a document's body is meaningful only if it is interconnected or organized successfully—only if its linked bones add up to and operate with unified intelligence and development. Too frequently in academic, business, technical, and legal writing, ineffective organization diminishes excellent content's quality; a written text may have probing, insightful, useful, memorable information to impart, but its disorganization or incoherence or lack of "flow" detracts from and subverts the quality of what it has to say. Whenever a reader becomes lost or momentarily confused, the writer has devalued the content's worth, regardless of its informing intelligence.

Therefore, using Word allows writers to organize interrelated bones of the document's body so that ultimately an entire skeletal structure—an outline—is created. The most common and useful linear form of organization, outlining allows you to create a graphic sequence of ideas that your essay will contain. If the central part of your essay is the "body," then an outline is that body's skeleton; each topic is a bone-group, such as the bones in our hands, or arms, or torso or legs, while every idea is a bone within its appropriate group. Notated with single words or brief phrases that serve as identifying labels, an outline's component parts usually are reducible to a single page; therefore, the writer will be able to see assembled at once what the essay's content includes and will be able easily to relocate—reorganize— parts of the outline as well as to recognize where additional last-minute information is required.

The common sense lesson overlooked by too many educators is that outlines are purposeful only after you have given yourself some time—how much? as much as you can—first to brainstorm thoughts, then to list them, and consistently to classify them or put them into groups. The problem, obviously, is that writers cannot outline content that doesn't yet exist—or, if it exists even partially, content that hasn't been fully thought out. Outlines created in advance will take on an architectural structure and graphic aesthetic of their own, but their building blocks will be either meaningless, inconsequential, or, at best, rudimentary. When outlining, too many people spend time thinking about how their information is outlined, not about what they're outlining, and that leaves them with a form lacking meaningfully structured content.

ESSAY 4

Brainstorming, Learning More About What You Do and Do Not Know, And How to Use Your Brain to Think About Discovering the Purposeful Focus of the Text You'll Write

1. INTRODUCTION

What you need to accomplish in a writing project sometimes isn't immediately clear to you, at least not as a total composition of different parts; that's because your assignment's purpose and focus possibly begin with broad, general intentions.For such situations it takes time to narrow your purpose to a defined and manageably controlled focus, a focus which when properly restricted and clarified will frame your governing set of intentions or, in academics, what we call your "thesis statement." Because a thesis statement is the central nervous systemguiding any written communication's body—because it activates, gives intelligenceto, and functionally interconnects all parts of the communication—you want to guarantee for your own satisfaction that you understand and define it as clearly as possible. So if your supervisor or teacher has not assigned a specific set of requirements for your writing, and if thus you are on your own to determine some or most of your subject's thesis, then you should devote time to examining and thinkingbroadly within the borders of your subject's territories before you begin to restrict and refine what you think your thesis is.

I've seen too many smart people decide hastily, sometimes rashly and recklessly, what they think their thesis is or should be, often because they dislike indecision and want the security of immediate guidance along a definite path; there's nothing wrong with wanting a sure, secure direction, but taking an initially obvious, dependably safe, guaranteed standard path—taking a road more traveled—mayshort-sell and lessen the latent intellectual complexity and the potential informational rewards attainable by allowing yourself time—again, time—to pursue paths as yet undiscovered but ultimately conducive to your text's purpose and focus. Hasty judgment puts blinders to our eyes, restricting our vision of all adjacent matters, and requiring us to see only what we've already planned or instinctively learned to lie straightforward ahead. While blinders work well for horses pulling carriages and prohibit distractions along known routes, they're not usually effective for humans who carry the mental responsibility of assembling complex investigations for use in arguments, critical analyses, proposals, and all other forms of exposition. Often, we write because we're still ignorant about something and need to teach ourselves what our research's results and our thoughts about them add upto and mean; then, knowing that and, further, having codified our thoughts, we can actualize it all by writing to educate others. However, without opening our eyes to broad-ranging investigation and learning, without the inevitable dot-connecting architecture that new personalized information and understandings require and effect, without our mind's eye open to alternative views in the first place—without that, we're likely to write a communication conceptually feeble or fatigued and deficient of new, comprehensive materials.

So before you begin to research further along predetermined roads with their narrow boundaries, routes, and trails, keep in mind that you want to explore and advance your subject towards what its thesis ought to be at its best—at its most cleverly synthesized, cumulatively wise, innovative, and persuasively thorough andcoherent to other people, and most rewarding to you. Formal business and educational exposition presumes that you presume you have something new to sayin public, a specialized written response to any kind of transaction or interaction, a new way or ways of thinking, and new thoughts to share.

But during your search and research, also realize that your subject's purpose and focus are likely to adjust and modify as you continue to inspect that subject and to clarify what your own intentions actually should be. Ultimately you must create one integral organism (your text or essay), but like a paramecium under a microscope it can constantly change its contours and reshape itself according to what you learn and prioritize as important. Like anything organic, a written communication's purpose will self-generate until you impose finality on its formative, processed life.

Given adequate time, your defined purpose will become apparent; I'll talk more about that in later essays, which continue to explore the process required to plot your texts. But until then, and before mapping your specific directions, be certain that you explore the subject's general territory. Begin your exploration by brainstorming, and know that the most effective brainstorming requires using both sides of your brain.

2. RIGHT- AND LEFT-BRAIN THINKING

Jacquelyn Wonder and Priscilla Donovan's Whole-Brain Thinking, a book written to improve job performance, helps us to understand why successful process-to-product writing requires both right-brain and left-brain abilities. In their chapter "Communications," the authors assert that "Nowhere in this book's workworld applications of the split-brain theory is the difference between left and right brain thinking clearer. Nowhere else is it more important to integrate the two. Written business communication [and certainly all other written communication, especially academic] would not be so difficult to compose or to understand if its writers used a whole-brain approach" (167). Integrated use of both sides of our brain makes it easier for us to write meaningfully and coherently, the authors argue.

As is true of most theory still on the frontier of inquiry, the validity of the right and left brain duality remains partly open to doubt: neuro-scientifically, not all brain activities are polar or exclusive to one side of the brain, or hemisphere. Generally, however, and regardless of "sides," both sets of opposite tendencies remain essential to whole-brain operations and holistic thinking—and thus to all writing; besides, it does seem logical that written thinking, as a whole, should require the whole brain. Therefore, because the brain houses separate sets of abilities and tendencies that in fact complement and reinforce each other, for convenience we will adopt the model of a two-sided brain. Using that, we can take the phrase "wrap my head around an idea" and expand its implications: if our brain is a sphere, with two 180° halves or hemispheres, then it will wrap itself around complex ideas only when its applied abilities come closer to 360°.

Another way of thinking about the brain's two sides' functions—this is not necessary to appreciate the point of this discussion, but it's worth noting—is to realize that "the right/left brain talk maps fairly well to yin/yang talk"(http://www.4dsolutions.net/ocn/overview.html). When we refer to yin and yang, we speak of two universal energies: "All things carry the Yin and the Yang," including mental energy, "deriving their vital harmony from the proper blending of the two forces" (Tao Te Ching, Verse 42). In effect, therefore, "This Dance of the Opposites [yin and yang] weaves its way through every facet of our lives" (http://www.aquarianzone.net/yinyang.html), so that "As applied to neuroscience and cognitive psychology, the yin would refer to the right brain and the yang would refer to the left brain". It's fair to conclude that the brain's two sides' operations, when integrated, produce a vital harmony; further, "This balance of Yin and Yang speaks to the organic nature of writing" (15), says Ralph Wahlstrom in The Tao of Writing. A look at the list of abilities generally accepted for each side of the brain, as seen two pages ahead, makes it apparent that the best communication or writing requires participation from both sides, just as the wisest and most complete balances in life are a scaled fusion of yin and yang energies. It is important to all of us and to the linguistic culture of our global village in the twenty-first century that neither side of our brain should be allowed to atrophy; we must develop both hemispheres of our brain's potential and our culture's health.

Those people who have equally refined talents and abilities in both sides of the brain are labeled "mixed dominants," but most people are genetically inclined or wired to use one side of their brain more than the other, just as few of us are ambidextrous and rely instead on either right- or left-handedness. Natural bodily balance is rare, as anyone practicing yoga rapidly learns. Reading the following lists, therefore, you'll recognize which of the brain's two sides or hemispheres your mind resides more comfortably in, and which side is more challenged. Note my repeated word "more": we all use both sides of the brain, but most of us do so disproportionately, our mind trained to follow our own diverse predispositions and influences, which favor one side over a perfect 50/50 balance of both sides. Appliedand responsive to all variables in existence, however, these imbalanced hemisphericqualities and abilities are as diverse as our active and reactive experiences are withpeople and the world. Keep in mind that the two lists itemize polar opposites, without any middle ground; consequently, if right-brain/yin is white and left-brain/yang is black, then nearly all intellectual and behavioral applications of our energy are some shade of gray. For example, when I teach a class, my instructionalmanner is maybe 65% left/yang and 35% right/yin: I'm likely to shape my purpose using left-brained intentions, using planned structures presented in a sequence which incorporates logical absolutes and facts within compartmentalized distinctions, and from which I can form strategies or draw conclusions, while alwaysallowing for the right-brain possibilities. Conversely, if I attend a jazz performance, I may be 20% left/yang and 80% right/yin, expecting a left-brain program that's structured and directed, but wanting fluidity of music, the risk-taking liberalism allowed by improv solos, the feelings expressed by the musicians and felt by me, andthe emotional theatricality that musical interconnectedness provides.

LEFT BRAIN (YANG ENERGY) - Stereotypically Masculine Perception and Knowledge	RIGHT BRAIN (YIN ENERGY) - Stereotypically Feminine Perception and Knowledge
Empirical/Objective	Intuitive/Subjective
Emphasize Fact	Emphasize Belief/Imagination
Concrete	Abstract
Objective	Emotional, Feeling
Rational, Logical	Heart, Inspiration
Head, Formal Training	
Knows Object's Name	Knows Object's Function
Sequential	Random
As Is, Present, Explicit	Symbolic, Represent, Implicit

How We Use/Apply Intelligence

YANG

1. Deduction
2. Detailed, See Parts First
3. Distinctions Important
4. Math, Science (scientia, L. = knowledge)
5. Algebra, Calculus
6. As Readers: Plot and Character
7. Preference for Being Taught,
8. Legal, Liturgical
9. Humor: Literal, Drawn to Wordplay

YIN
1. Induction
2. Holistic, See Patterns First
3. Connectedness Important
4. Science, Philosophy and Religion
5. Geometry, Trigonometry
6. As Readers: Themes and Character
7. Told Advocacy of Self-Questioning, Introspection
8. Ethical, Theatrical
9. Humor: More Alert to Nuance and Subtlety

How We Create

YANG

1. Planned, Structured
2. Mechanical
3. Directed, Within Limits
4. In the Box
5. Right Angles

YIN

1. Practical Fluid, Spontaneous, Impetuous
2. Organic
3. Free, Risk-taking
4. Out of the Box
5. Circular Undular

Formal Philosophical Orientation

YANG

1. Realism
2. Aristotle / John Locke
3. Phenomena
4. Forms Strategies
5. Self-reliance, Practicality
6. Neoclassicism
7. 18th C. ("Age of Reason"); 1950s

YIN

1. Idealism
2. Plato / Immanuel Kant
3. Noumena (Kantian Term)
4. Presents Possibilities
5. Worship, Prayer, Mysticism
6. Romanticism
7. Early 19th Century; Late 1960s

Political Orientation

YANG

1. Conservative
2. Republican, U.S.
3. Status Quo
4. Individualism

YIN
1. Liberal
2. Democrat, U.S.
3. Change
4. Communalism

View of External Nature

YANG

1. Subordinate to Humans
2. Utilitarian

YIN

1. Coordinate with Humans
2. Ecological

Human Development

YANG

1. Nature, Person's Genetics

YIN

1. Nurture, Person's Environment

By knowing your dominant, primary side, you then can recognize your subordinate, secondary side, whose set of communication skills you'll need todevelop more completely and durably. Because the entire process-to-product writingof any document relies on both sides of the brain, all of us will benefit from remembering which side of our brain is less naturally inclined and less skillfully trained to think effectively and thus to write effectively developed thoughts. We may conclude that the integrating and harmonious blending of the brain's two sides' operations is a preliminary goal for all writers, a principal principle for stimulating anew and maybe beyond how we presently evaluate everything in the world that affects and involves us.

Using both sides of the brain is becoming a renewed goal in American business as well, according to "Let Computers Compute. It's the Age of the Right Brain," an April 6, 2008 New York Times article. Its author discusses how "That alternate way of thinking [right-brain thinking] has been marginalized in corporate America....What it comes down to is that modern society discriminates against the right hemisphere," or at least it did until recently. Now, however, "business executives areturning to…right-brain thinking," especially because "now that computers can emulate many of the sequential skills of the brain's left hemisphere, it's time for our imaginative right brain."

Wonder and Donovan suggest that before we formally write any text, we should use basic brainstorming techniques; two techniques that the authors discuss use theleft-brain, followed by two that use the right. We will investigate techniques beyond the four suggested by Wonder and Donovan, but theirs are useful as initial examples. According to those authors, list-making and then defining a communication's purpose are left-side brainstorming; both approaches attempt to objectify the communication's purpose, see details, and begin to structure or plan the communication (review the preceding list). Next are two right-brain functions: first, a writer visualizes the audience, an exercise in connectedness that often is abstractand intuitive, followed by free-writing, a process during which "the words will seem to flow from your fingertips." Given free-writing's intentional omission of left-brain operations, the authors advise that you "do not analyze what you are doing, why or how—just let it happen" (168). These two right-brain strategies—audience visualization, and free-writing—help writers to explore their subject without the interruption of structure and sequential thinking, and without the restraints of rules. When integrated with the left-brain techniques, however, these right-brain contributions further develop the scope and refine the meaning of our text's content, providing a more total, 360° perspective on the subject being communicated.

Always remember that our personal talents' and skills' inclination towards right- brain or left-brain thinking has nothing to do with our being correct or incorrect, and nothing to do with the quality of our thinking or with our writing being good or bad; rather, by recognizing our major strengths and relative limitations, we learn to reinforce the latter and to use the former in balance with it, for total performance of our mind.

2. BRAINSTORMING: TAKING A LOOK AT HOW YOU THINK INTRODUCTION TO BRAINSTORMING

An industry all its own, brainstorming theory now offers software programs and numerous Web sites whose useful, common sense methods help thinkers togenerate and, later, to evaluate ideas for writing. Because brainstorming "is a part of problem solving which involves the creation of new ideas by suspending judgment" (http://www.brainstorming.co.uk/tutorials/definitions.html), we may use it freely,liberally, and beneficially. Brainstorming helps us not only to discover and developnew facts and information, but additionally to build new ideas, concepts, andtheories, modify old ones, and find new solutions. Brainstorming thus allows us tobreak our own established patterns or systems of thinking, to breathe new vitalityinto dull, listless ideas, and to add fresh perspective to stale ways of looking at ideasor issues. In effect, brainstorming liberates us from our own boxed-in modes of mental processing, allowing us to think out of the box. Very possibly, it leads to breakthrough ideas about which we otherwise never would have thought.

Brainstorming can help to generate any kind of idea about any kind of subject. If before writing you're lucky enough to know all of the parts into which your subject of communication already is compartmentalized, then it will be useful to take those parts and brainstorm about them, one at a time. However, more often, we don't know at first what all of our subject's parts are, or, even if we do, cannot yet know which ones are most important to use and will require expansion and evidence. As often as not, therefore, brainstorming is about discovering what needs to be investigated and discussed, and then how much space should be allotted to each part. Also, because your Word™ document will contain some broad, general ideas requiring further inspection, you may want to brainstorm about some of those ideas which you have recorded there.

3. BRAINSTORMING STRATEGIES

1. QUESTIONING

One way to "open doors" to the roomy potential of your subject is calling out the six journalistic questions below (the "Five Ws" and an "H") to discover answers you need to develop and, importantly, enjoy developing as you filter, collect, and arrange these brainstormed facts through the point of view you'll want to enlarge. I stress "facts" because this set of questions attempts as a whole to "objectify" the scene and our potential to understand it with facts, definable data not yet subjected to personal choices—not yet pondered over, explained, and interpreted.

1) Who? 2) What? 3) Where? 4) When? 5) Why? 6) How?

If nothing else, answering journalistic questions relevant to your essay's purpose will help you to establish important background information about your subject and to think associatively about other, possibly related ideas. As a thought process itself, asking each of these questions separately will help you to understand, first, its unique contributory nature to your subject and, second, when and why and how it interrelates with the other questions' answers. Interesting syntheses come from unexpected fusions of fact.

2. FURTHER QUESTIONING

Probing deeper into the potential breadth and depth of the journalistic questions are an additional Twenty Questions for the Writer,[1] which I've adapted from Jacqueline Berke's study of relevant questioning to develop a text's purpose; because each question itemizes a different mode of thinking, not all modes may apply to your essay's purpose, but some of them certainly will be useful:

1. What does X mean? (Definition)
2. What are the various features of X? (Description)
3. What are the essential major points or features of X? (Summary)
4. What are the facts about X? (Reporting) (= Answers to 1. Questioning)
5. What are the component parts of X? (Simple Analysis)
6. What is the significance of X? (Interpretation)
7. What is the value of X? (Evaluation)
8. What is my personal response to X? (Critical Reflection)
9. What are the types of X? (Classification)
10. What is the present status of or situation for X? (Comparison)

11. How is X made or done? (Process Analysis)
12. How should X be made or done? (Directional Analysis)
13. What is the essential function of X? (Functional Analysis)
14. What are the causes and/or effects of X? (Causal Analysis)
15. How is X like or unlike Y? (Comparison/Contrast)
16. What kind of person is X? (Characterization/Profile)
17. What case can be made for or against X? (Persuasion)

In 3), which follows, I elaborate on modes of thinking generated by someof Berke's questions, above.

18. AS AN EXTENTION of 2.: USING COMMON MODES OF THINKING

Review each point of information that you already have compiled on your Word™ document, and see which of the following modes of thinking apply to it: description, definition, summary, analysis, and comparison/contrast analysis. Not all of them will apply, but the ones that do can reveal important ideas you otherwise might not have thought about. Expect some of these modes to work together as mutually adaptiveforces and sometimes to overlap; for example, while describing, you may need to analyze and define as well. Again, placing these new brainstormed ideas on a Word™ document will help you to discover how and where each mode's informationbelongs within the essay's entire purpose.

Description: Assume you must describe a person's, place's, or thing's characteristics and qualities—facts and impressions that make each what it is; thisdescription may be only a small part of your text, but you want it to catch the reader's eye and then be memorable. For convenience while brainstorming, subdividethose noted characteristics and qualities into either X, important objective facts, or Y, subjective impressions. When you write your description, appropriately combine Xand Y, the objective and subjective.

Objective facts can be validated by weights and measures and by verifiable sensory observation, such as the sight of how a scene is structurally formed andcolored, or a smell whose rot or foulness qualifies as a stench; further, objective factscan come from certified compilations of information, as with The Guinness Book ofWorld Records, World Almanac, The National Data Book, Office for National Statistics, and statistical records from different sources.

Subjective impressions—impressions of beauty or love, for example—are slanted from each person's particular point of view and reveal personalized emotional metrics, values developed from past experiences, accumulated knowledge, presuppositions and beliefs, and tastes and inclinations. It's obvious that abstract description, as of a person's attitude or your own love of a sport, is likely to be mostly subjective and based on personal impressions and emotions.

As you collect objective data and subjective impressions, look for relationships among your listed items: it helps to categorize them into groups—to classify—and then to label those classified groups. This set of groups will let you and your reader know what are the major parts or dominant components of whatever you describe,such as beauty, or an attitude, or your sport-love. For example, after you examine your list, the attitude you want to describe might be understood if you label its components as "self-importance," "arrogance," and "condescension." Next, combinecoherently all objective and subjective details that belong to each of those three dominant components; often, the objective information provides specific examples ofyour subjective impressions.

Let your details accumulate throughout the description, so that its dominant characteristics—in this case the attitude of "self-importance," "arrogance," and "condescension"—add up in significance as objective and subjective materials blendtogether. Choose evocative words to highlight those details, so that your dominantcharacteristics further compile in force. Avoid vagueness; attain specificity or precision.

The compilation of specifics will help you to reveal your descriptive vision, to portray a person, place, or thing. Ultimately, that vision fuses objective material with your own personal responses. Your descriptive result, like a woven tapestry, tells a picture-story threaded throughout with suggestive fact and with textures and colors intoning identifiable qualities, all of them diffusing into one another and adding up to imagery that can affect your readers indelibly.

Definition: Definition explains what a word means, its essential nature. Many words have multiple meanings, thus multiple definitions. Additionally, words have adenotation ("to denote") or primary, literal meaning, and also a connotation ("to connote") or alternative, figurative meaning: denotatively, "pig" is a barnyard mammal, a swine with bristly hair, cloven hooves, snout for digging, and an identifiable oink-oink sound, whereas connotatively "pig" may be a sloppy eater, agreedy person, and a late-1960s policeman. As is true of describing, defining a word's meaning can be achieved with objective, concrete facts; with subjective, abstract impressions; or with a combination of both, which usually happens. We candefine a word's meanings by negation, or by clarifying what it isn't; by similarity, with likeness expressed through analogy, metaphor, or simile; by enumeration, listing its characteristics: and by etymology, providing the word's origin and development, whose entire history you can find in the O.E.D. (The Oxford English Dictionary).

It's very likely that your definition of a word or term also will require other modes of thought, especially description, classification, and process analysis. Also—and thisis true of anything we write—you want to be certain that your definition offers well chosen examples.

Summary: An overview or generalized reduction of content, a summary mentions a work's key points: guiding purposes and premises; issues and arguments; topicsand those topics' important supporting ideas; and themes or lessons to be remembered. A summary may provide specific points of information, but it does notelaborate on them. Summaries collect and assemble the work's most important information, pasting together whatever connections in logic unite the summarized work.

Regardless of their specific content, all summaries serve the same general purpose: condensing information. In business, however, an "executive summary"—part of a business proposal or plan—additionally serves as the first impression the proposal makes; therefore, it should capture and hold readers' attention, authoritatively and enthusiastically, enticing them to read the text's elaboration, which comes later in the document.

Analysis: When we analyze, we take a broad or general idea, premise, or operation and break it down into its component parts. Because analysis requires explanation, each component part or element contributes to a greater understanding of the whole idea. When we add up all the explained parts, the whole or general idea can be fully understood—or at least its most important parts can be understood.

Analysis usually will begin with objective fact, but it also can contain subjective interpretation. If we were to analyze why a soup tastes good, first we would examine and explain the individual foods in the soup and their tastes, as well as the ingredients of the soup's broth. We would explain how certain combinations of tastes further contribute to the soup's delicious flavor. Possibly the analysis "breaks down" the taste also into the spices or seasonings used. Possibly this soup's combinations of tastes and seasonings make it unique or at least significantly different from other soups, so we explain subjectively why the soup's unusual composition contributes to its tasting good. Also subjectively, we might explain that what makes this soup taste good is its harmony with a particular wine or bread or cheese.

If we were to analyze the ideological differences between America's Democratic and Republican political parties, we would investigate those differences according to prevailing national issues—taxes, employment, welfare, military, diplomacy, etc.— and the positions each party takes regarding them. Perhaps we would include historical differences.

Looking at a few of the different kinds of analysis provides added insight into what analytic investigations can accomplish: process analysis; comparative analysis;feasibility analysis and risk analysis; cost analysis and economic analysis; statisticalanalysis, regression analysis, and data analysis; systems analysis, requirementsanalysis, and necessity analysis; performance analysis and gap analysis; interpretive analysis and qualitative analysis; and game analysis.

Comparison/Contrast: A type of analysis, comparison/contrast usually examines and explains two things, looks for the similarities (comparisons) and differences (contrasts) between them, and often concludes which of the two is preferable. For a comparison/contrast analysis to be worthwhile, it should study two or more things within the same categorical group, for example two or more kinds ofcar, brands of soft drink, political ideologies, NBA stars playing the same position, or vacationing in France vs. vacationing in Italy. Usually there is no point or intellectual advantage in comparing/contrasting an apple with an orange, an elephant with a flea, or the Empire State Building with the NYC Public Library; writers must begin with a fair or just reason for comparatively analyzing, so that a purposeful conclusion can occur.

How a person organizes a comparison/contrast analysis will vary according to the content being investigated, but remember that you do not want to divide and keep separate whatever you analyze, first X, then Y, and next possibly Z, as if your essay actually were two or more essays. Although in some instances it may take time to explain X before you can turn to Y, and vice versa, be certain to juxtapose and thus highlight directly all significant contrasts between X and Y. Direct contrasts occur easily when sentences begin with any of these words or phrases: although, but, contrasted with, conversely, despite, even though, however, in contrast, nevertheless, on the contrary, on the one hand/on the other hand, regardless, unlike, whereas, while, yet.

Here's an example using "whereas": ("Whereas X features public settings for a fast-paced, socially youthful crowd under forty-five years, with ample dispensable money and a desire to use it, Y represents a more sedate demographic, certainly social but provided greater privacy, with settings for dinner parties, wine and book clubs, or get-togethers initiated by events of theater, music, dance, film, and sports").

Use any of the following to indicate direct comparisons: again, also, compared to, in the same way/manner, like, likewise, similarly, similar to.

Classification: I discuss classification separately, because it is an essential stage of thought in a writer's process of organizing materials.

Deduction/Inferences OR Induction/Synthesis: I also discuss deduction and induction separately, in Essay #3, because they are the two broad ways all thinkers must approach their thought processing: either 1) drawing inferences or new conclusions from established conclusions (deduction), or 2) adding up particulars or parts to make whole conclusions (induction). Both modes are essential in a writer's process of organizing materials.

19. NOTEBOOKS, CASSETTES, & BRAINSTORMING SOFTWARE

Because most of us live a hurried life and are preoccupied by many people, places, and things (nouns or pronouns), carried away by many actions (verbs), and diverted by many modifying characteristics (adjectives, adverbs, and prepositional phrases), it's not always easy to find time to think uninterruptedly about our writing assignments, let alone to apply this essay's brainstorming strategies. Therefore, I encourage you to carry a notebook or a recorder of some kind, or to consider using some kind of available brainstorming software; with that, you'll be able to record and to remember any ideas, images, clusters of thought, and words rich with implication that cross your mind. Like butterflies flittering through or around your head as you pass through the day, ideas must be netted. And because meaningful ideas usually are composed of many constituent parts and pieces of thought, you want to be certain that you don't forget any of those parts and pieces when they call attention to themselves. If something inspirational or provocative crosses your mind in the first place, usually that's because it has force pertinent enough to demand your attention. However, if you don't attend to it, you may forget it, so be sure to record whatever crosses your mind; it's very possible that it will attract other forceful ideas, too.

With no recording resources available other than your cell phone, leave yourself a voice-mail message and record it later, at home, on your Word document.

20. CONVERSATION

Often overlooked as an excellent source of brainstorming, conversation with other employees or students and with friends or family can help you to explore your subject, develop important ideas about it, and clarify where revision may be useful. Even if your conversation partners are relatively ignorant of your subject, their lack of knowledge and their questions may be enlightening to you: an intelligent but ignorant conversation partner will motivate you to recognize whatever theories or intellectual complexities require the greatest emphasis and clarification, to evaluate whatever approaches are best for explaining your subject's issues, to prioritize the importance of your essay's information, to defend your opinions and arguments more thoroughly, and to add required background information and explanations. In your conversation, gather as many ideas, suggestions, examples, sentences, and telling words as you can; write down everything valuable that your conversation partners say and that comes to your mind as a result of their responses.

Ask your conversation partners which parts of your text are most important to them. Why? Do you as writer thoroughly and clearly delineate that importance? Do omissions exist?

21. RESEARCHING

Extend your knowledge of a subject by drawing on the experience and expertise of professional thinkers in and beyond your text's concerns or field of study. Read well-chosen articles and books, and read more. Many smart people have thoughtsmartly about whatever subject your essay must discuss, so learn from them—andthen exceed these writers' personal focus by integrating into your own focus what you learn from others. Synthesize.

A normal part of all writing, research isn't the function only of a "research paper." Part of writing well is persuading or proving to your reader that you are knowledgeable of your subject, whether library researched or not; writing well grows from original ideas or intriguing questions that you want to explore in depth. Whether your knowledge-gathering takes place mostly at the library, on the Internet, or in life, it's important to prepare ahead. Preparation by research provokes you to think further and thus to write better and more meaningfully about your subject.

If you are at a university, then be certain to use your library and the knowledge of librarians at the reference desk to expedite your research and to save you time. Public libraries also employ reference librarians, who are trained to locate the materials you desire and to help you learn to access information on your own. Also, remember that many important articles are published by specific journals and therefore, because copyrighted, may not exist on the Internet.

When you use the Internet, always be certain to consider the source of your source—the URL itself. While the Internet in general is an invaluable information supplier, not everything on the Net has value or is informed and helpful, reputable and credible, and worthy of reproduction. If you cannot prove to yourself that a Web site, article, or author is legitimate and worthy of reproduction, then it's likely that your reader(s) also will not consider it a sufficiently reliable source. Furthermore, never rely exclusively on the Net for your research: learn to rely on books and especially journal articles to advance your knowledge and to reinforce your beliefs or opinions.

22. FREEWRITING

As you'd expect, freewriting means to write freely, without restrictions. Its main purpose is to allow you to discover and to develop further any subject's content. The most right-brain brainstorming strategy discussed here, freewriting requires you to emancipate yourself from the mind-forged manacles of all of writing's requirements, rules, and regulations that restrain and preoccupy most people when they write: precise grammar, punctuation, word choice, and spelling; logical sentence structure; and logical organization of sentences within paragraphs. Novice writers acquiring new knowledge of writing's rules often require precision of everything mechanical when they write and, as a result, prevent the flow of their thoughts: they turn away to the dictionary, use a thesaurus to find a better word, try to recall or search for what the teacher said about the semicolon or the non-restrictive comma, wonder if this part of the sentence is a proper modification, etc. If this is wholly or even partly true of you when you write, then you are like most other people and, also like them, are doing yourself a disservice; therefore, you may find freewriting useful for generating ideas.

When freewriting, you write without interruption whatever comes to your mind about the subject you're exploring. Without interruption. Overcome self- consciousness, forget rules, and completely disregard diction, spelling, grammar, punctuation, coherence, paragraphing—even if what you write seems nonsensicaland is replete with errors. No one but you will see what you write, and proper editing will come later. This is not the time or place for right and wrong.

Begin with a five-minute uninterrupted freewriting exercise. Let your thoughts focus on the subject-at-hand: this is a discovery process, so don't be concerned if nothing of seeming importance comes to you at first. Instead, keep writing, and when a potentially worthwhile thought does appear, pursue it, without interruption. If you can't pursue it, turn elsewhere, but keep going. If you have no idea about where or how to begin your freewriting, consider one of the questions in Brainstorming #1 or #2. Never reject any thought before writing it down: freewriting is not about criticizing your ideas or about editing. Later, upon reexamination, that thought may prove more valuable to you than initially you realized; if not, you have lost only a few seconds of time.

After your first five-minute freewriting exercise, read what you have written. (Be kind to yourself.) As you read, circle all sentences or parts of sentences or words that you think contain potential for expansion and that may contain value to your essay's subject (sometimes, you may want to circle a series of interrelated sentences). Each circle contains a "kernel idea." Next, choose the kernel idea that you feel most strongly about, and devote another five-minute freewriting exercise to it; now, you will investigate and discover even more about that particular idea, without interruption. Then do the same for the other kernel ideas.... and so on, as much as you can tolerate. Within little more than a half-hour, you will have produced pages of information about your subject—some of it useless, some of it very useful or potentially useful. Continue to circle kernels in all your freewriting, and then develop them in additional exercises. In effect, you are finding seeds of thought, planting them, and quickly nurturing their growth. Transfer to your Word document whatever information you have. And if you find freewriting advantageous, then you may want to consult some of Peter Elbow's writing.[2]

23. MAPPING

Concept Mapping and Mind Mapping® may be useful for those of you who prefer to see your subject's information graphically, in interconnected networks of circled or boxed concepts. A Concept Map usually charts several concepts, whereas a Mind Map explores just one concept. Regardless of that specific difference, mapping in general helps you to visualize information that you already know about your subject, often yielding insightful connections or relationships among its parts. Furthermore, your vision of the map's graphed information may inspire you to think more creatively and to generate additional ideas that you hadn't "seen" before: seeing these literal boxes also may help you to think "out of the box." Observe the map below, whose center states the document's subject: Causes of the French Revolution.

(http://www.studygs.net/mapping/mapping1.htm).

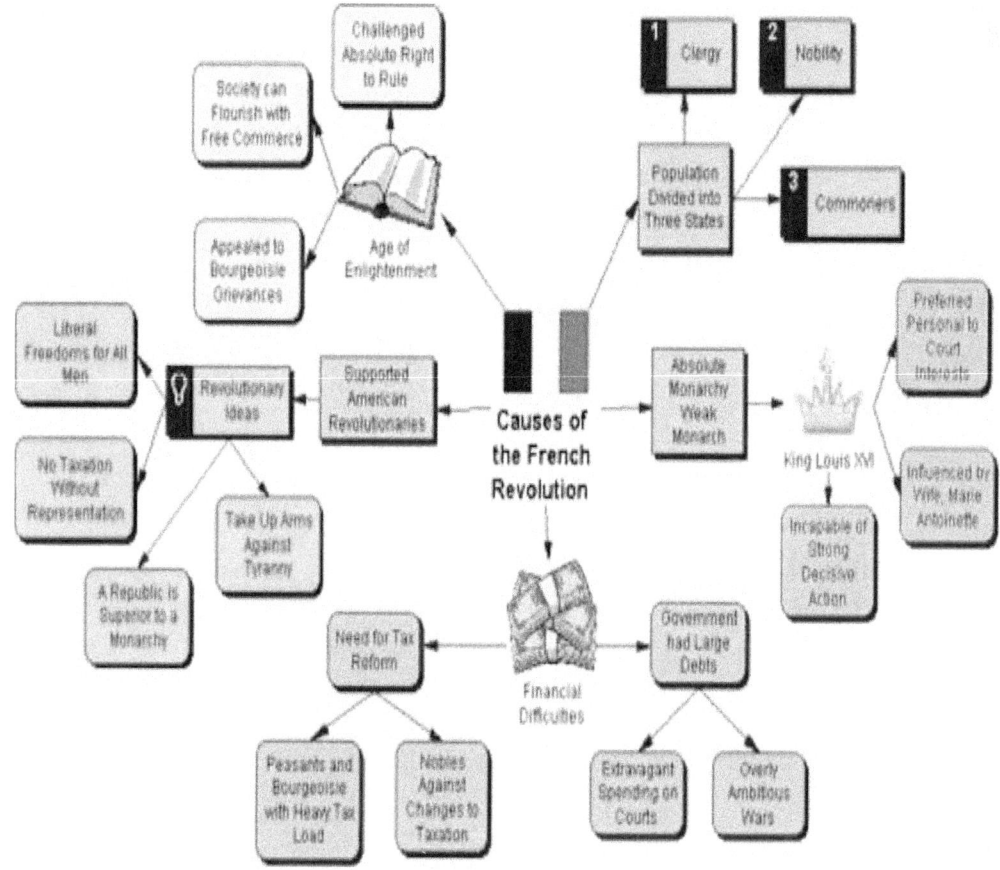

From that subject, arrows point to five conceptual topics, each labeled for easy identification. We see that the Causes of the French Revolution are analyzed topically, clockwise, into 1) Population Divided into Three States, 2) Absolute Monarchy, with a Weak Monarch, 3) Financial Difficulties, 4) Supported American Revolutionaries, and 5) Age of Enlightenment. From each of those five conceptual topics, more arrows point to color-coded subsets of ideas and information pertaining to the topics. What this map doesn't show, but what also is possible with mapping, is to draw arrows that interrelate ideas among different color-coded subsets of information; as such, these additional arrows are graphic reminders of close relationships between separate points in the essay's topics of investigation and thusmay serve as excellent transitions from one paragraph to another.

While mapping may be a valuable way for some of you to see your information's interconnections, it is only a beginning brainstorming procedure: ultimately, you still will need to outline that information in a linear sequence—because all written documents are themselves linear sequences of information. So, be inventive andplayful with mapping if you find it advantageous, but remember to list all of its information on your Word™ document.

24. TEMPLATES

Templates adapted from Gerald Graff's and Cathy Birkenstein's They Say / I Say: The Moves that Matter in Academic Writing (W.W. Norton, 2006) may help you to better identify, think about, and structure individual parts of your discussion, but certainly not all of your discussion. That book's templates are models that will give you an intellectual "feel" for how you can manage your thoughts within the expository contexts identified by the authors. Use the templates not as ends in themselves, but as launches into your own additional thinking and your own positioning about the issues your writing must explore and express.

25. "DOWN" TIME

With the above brainstorming strategies understood and, when possible, applied, don't forget that you should stop thinking when there's a need to remove yourself from the text or essay. If your ideas are seeds, then time is required for them to take root in your mind; when that happens, the intellectual growth process will bloom. If sizeable spans of time do not exist for you, then for a short duration separate yourself and divorce your mind from your written work. By consciously avoiding your mental preoccupation with the text or essay—by running, working out, practicing yoga, socializing with friends, seeing something new that will change your focus, such as a movie or a sports game—you will be better able to see again the reality of your essay—to "revise" it.

26. REVIEW OF RIGHT- AND LEFT-BRAIN BRAINSTORMING

Now that we know the general abilities associated with each side of the brain, we can identify the side to which each kind of brainstorming belongs:

RIGHT BRAIN (YIN ENERGY)   LEFT BRAIN (YANG ENERGY)

Defining Communication's Purpose

YIN	YANG
Inductive Shaping of Topics	Planned, Structured
Intuitive, Abstract	Empirical, Concrete
	List Making
Audience Visualization	Audience Demographics

	DESCRIPTION
Subjective Impressions	Objective Facts

YIN ONLY	YANG ONLY
Fluid, Spontaneous, Random Modes of Thinking/Writing	As Is, Explicit, Present, Free-writing
Find Similarities, Analogies	Conversation
Research	
Mapping	
Applying The Law of Attraction	
Find Similarities	Bring Parts Together
Sees Patterns	Finds Differences
Connectedness	Breaks Down in Parts
	Synthesis Journalist and Other Questioning
	Emphasizes Fact
	Distinctions Important

YIN AND YANG
Notebooks, Cassettes, PDAs, Tablets, Smartphones

If possible, try all of the above brainstorming techniques, discovering what each of them yields for you and which ones are most advantageous. Also, be certain that you have allowed both sides of your brain to storm.

When brainstorming's storm of ideas slows down and blows fewer winds to inspire your mind, probably it's time to further assemble what you've accumulated. A final consideration of your audience is mandatory, and then classification of your ideas ensues.

27. ESTABLISHING YOUR PURPOSE AND FOCUS FOR ACADEMIC ESSAYS

If you are writing an academic essay, here are a few suggestions to help you move closer towards discovering your purpose, which in turn leads you closer to your essay's thesis. Consider what most interests you about the general subject:

1. One particular issue, topic, or controversy worthy of investigation
2. Two or more issues, topics, or controversies which, when combined, offer a new understanding of or approach to the subject
3. Something about the subject you would like to learn more about
4. A subject whose information's importance your teacher is likely to emphasize on a mid-term or final examination
5. A new process you can formulate to attain a standard result, or, conversely an existing process you can apply to create new results
6. Something about the subject that interconnects with knowledge from another discipline or from another aspect of your coursework

If nothing comes readily to mind, then approach your purpose in any of the following ways:

Review your textbook or assigned readings and see if they contain any leads worth pursuing. For example, if you receive a writing assignment during week five of the semester, then your intellectual sophistication and understanding will have grown since you began underlining some of your reading during the first and second weeks; therefore, go back and rediscover whatever had importance or interest to you, and see if it promotes any possibilities for an essay.

Do a Google, Yahoo, or other engine search on the Internet, using an important keyword or variously combined keywords to discover additional possibilities. Think about using parts of speech to arrange a search: noun(s) first (recession; recession United States). If for your subject an adjective's quality is inseparable from the noun itself, use quotation marks: "economic recession" United States; "Darwinian evolution"; "green hoteliers." Usually, a verb with tense isn't used, but participles are: "economic recession" forecasted; "Darwinian evolution" debated; "green hoteliers" increasing.

If nothing develops from your search and research, your mind thus remaining unfocused, consult and discuss possibilities with your teacher.

ESSAY 5

Organizing Your Essay's Body as a Skeletal Ouline (Classifying, Paragraphing, Topic Sentences, Transitions)

We may think of a written document's or essay's body as a human body:

- individual bones = points of information and ideas, quotations, statistics

- purposefully classified and thus specialized bone-groups, such as those of ahand or foot = paragraphs, to structure the body skeletally

- the body's musculature supported by those bones = evidence, explanations, interpretations, the "meat of the matter"

- ligaments and joints = transitions, to connect those bones and bone-groups

- separate organs functioning behind the bones = conceptual topics of investigation, thematic purposes

- central nervous system, both the brain activating the body's intelligence and the motor-impulses guiding all of its activity and forward development = document's or essay's thesis.

In all cultures' languages, the main, central part of a document or essay is called "the body," an anatomical metaphor, so as indicated above I extend that metaphor when discussing an essay's parts and how we organize them.

There can be no stand-up body of knowledge without interconnected bones to support and stabilize it firmly. All organized major parts of a document's body—its paragraphed topics of investigation—must be a part of and relate to the whole subject's purpose. For the developmental sequencing of those topical parts, eachpart or paragraph must connect with what precedes and follows it. Within each topical part or paragraph, all of its parts—that is, all sentences—must relate to the whole and must connect with what precedes and follows them. Within each sentence within each topic within the whole subject, the syntactic parts—the arrangement of clause(s) and phrase(s)—also must be structured so that the sentence stands logically on its own yet grows from what precedes it and anticipates what follows it. All of this sequencing begins with and is infused by appropriate substance drawn from the "Law of Attraction" (see Essay #4). All of this interconnectedness indicates the organic nature of writing (see Essay #2); I assume we have inherited the word "body" because composed writing through all time and across all space has been considered organic.

Critical to any written document's success is its content's organization, which contributes to how well you will educate your audience. Assessed pragmatically, a document's content is meaningful only to the extent that it is organized well. Too often in business, technical, and academic writing, ineffective organization of information diminishes excellent content's quality; in effect, writers may have probing, insightful, useful, memorable information to impart, but their documents' disorganization and, sometimes, incoherence or lack of "flow" detracts from and subverts the quality of what they have to say. Whenever readers become lost or momentarily confused, whenever they must second-guess new information's contextual purpose or must conjecture how a passage relates to what they're already read, writers have devalued the worth of the document's or essay's content, regardless of its informing intelligence.

Any document, as a whole, should be greater than the sum of its parts; only then does the cumulative authority and influence of a writer's presentation attain the persuasive power and successful educational result hoped for. Effective organization allows that powerful result to occur, so it's very important to your writing well that you think carefully about relationships among information, for the purposes of classification, paragraphing, and sequencing.

As members of Western culture, we rely consciously and intuitively—

with our left brain and our right brain, respectively—on classification as an intellectual method for perceiving, thinking about, understanding, and expressing verbally the complexities of our world. Classification is our way of sorting out, then imposing sense on, and thus structuring the world: all that exists, and all that we know about what exists, gets placed into classes, groups, categories, or kinds. Based implicitly on physics'Law of Attraction, and inspired by all human minds' inescapable need for order andconsistency, classification's purpose is to synthetically organize large sets of data or information so as to promote universal understanding and effective communication. We see this truth brilliantly exemplified in our libraries' complex organization of books and other printed material, originally systematized by the Dewey Decimal System of classification, now by the Library of Congress Classification. Otherclassification systems may be so simple as to escape our notice, such as the fruit ata local supermarket, or the three-class color system at a traffic signal.

Classification is integral to the working infrastructures of education, government, business and industry, medicine, science, and the arts. You name it—just about everybranch and leaf of life's social organization, cultural productivity, technical networks, professional bureaucracies, mental pursuits, and moral orders is classified, producinga density of intellectual arrangements and standards that subsume nearly everything we know.[1] Whatever it may be that is classified, classification's fundamental purpose is—and I reiterate—to organize our perception, structure our thinking, add focus to our understanding, and guide our linguistic expression of the multifaceted worlds outside and inside us. If nothing else, classification helps us to recognize bothbroad and narrow objectifications of those worlds by giving language-labels to all of their parts. Without classification, we are less technical as observers of life's millionsof colorful threads, whose identities we then cannot weave into recognizable meaning for functional synthetic value. Not surprisingly, the father of Western biological classification was Aristotle, whose pursuit of skientia, Greek for knowledge (science), seems endlessly robust and diverse, always offering original findings andthoughts. To better understand classification's purposes and methods, we can lookto contemporary biology, whose hierarchical structure classifies all living organismsaccording to the extent of their similar characteristics; wherever that extent of similarity ends, a new classification begins on the next-lower level of the hierarchy. As the classification continues to descend through the hierarchy, or as differencescontinue to set apart one kind of animal from another, the organisms become more particularized. Biological classification, its methods no different from those applied to library books or to toilet paper (2-ply? 3-ply?), therefore is a process of analysis: it breaks down and investigates information from top-level generalizations to bottom-level specificities, providing labeled identification for every part in any whole system.

Also called taxonomy, biology's classification system began embryonically with Aristotle but was delivered as scientific theory by Carolus Linnaeus, an eighteenth -century Swedish botanist and medical doctor (1707-1778). As more living organismshave been discovered during the past 250 years since Linnaeus, and as thedistinctions among them have been empirically, conclusively established, biology'staxonomic categories or classes have expanded. Now, we can classify any animal—and the same is true for any plant—and can position it properly in the detailed taxonomic system of hierarchical groups.

Keeping in mind that all classification systems exist with word-labels, which help us to perceive, think about, understand, and express similarities and differences inthe world, let's take a moment to consider how human beings are classified in the taxonomic hierarchy. At the top of the taxonomic hierarchy is kingdom; there are five kingdoms, one of them for animals, to which human beings belong, along with about one million other individual species. Below kingdom comes phylum; humans'phylum is chordata, meaning animals that have a notochord or dorsal stiffening, but not specifically vertebrae. Just for animals there are ten phyla, a fact that indicates significant differentiation even at the hierarchy's top. As biological differences increase, classified organisms descend through the hierarchy, moving next to subphylum (vertebrata); then class (mammalia); subclass (theria, meaning animals that give birth to their young without using a shelled egg); order (primates); suborder (anthropoidea, animals that can hang by their arms, use stereoscopic binocular sight more than smell to identify the world, and have nails instead of claws); family (hominidae, or humans and apes of all kinds); subfamily (homininae, humans, alongwith gorillas and chimpanzees); tribe (hominini), just humans and chimpanzees, because gorillas are different in ways that humans and chimps remain similar); genus (homo); and, last, species (sapiens). Each species is a single, particular organism unique to itself, as are we humans, homo sapiens.

The myriad connections and resulting density of classified information in biological taxonomy is astounding—as astounding as the number of living species that exist on Earth, about 1,800,000. All other subjects of study, systems of operation, and practices of the human head and heart also classify the components of their information; consequently, classification is part of how we as a species have trained ourselves to think. So it follows that, for writing, which is codified or formalized thinking, classification is an essential element for writers to achieve smartly labeled and organized information, which itself yields greater insight into and comprehensibility of a subject's materials. Just as classification helps us as dwellers on Earth to intellectually navigate the complex world of animals, plants, institutional structures, and so forth, so it helps us as writers to map in our mind—and thus to map for our readers—what our subject's fields of investigation are, and, given classification's inherent analytical power, how best to plot, explore, and travel through our writing's intellectual territory.

As a writer you will find it highly useful, indeed imperative, to classify or to group your ideas in a written document so that each idea is placed with ideas similar to it and is conveniently distinguished from those that aren't so similar. Before long, you will find that some of your Word™ document's randomly brainstormed ideas begin to join into separate but neighboring communities of thought: separate, because you have been thinking of conceptual differences among your collected information; neighboring, because your writing's subject makes the grouped communities conceptually akin in the first place. Rather than allowing your brainstormed information and ideas to lie randomly scattered, either you have given them united identities, or on their own they have begun to merge by the Law of Attraction. Organization like this helps you literally to see (see Essay #3) the information with which you are and are not working.

Keep in mind that these communities or classes of thought exist for your particular purposes as a writer-educator, not for any inherent intellectual reason of their own; that is, information can be—and has been—used in countless ways, depending on thinkers' and writers' purposes. "Systems of classification are not hatracks, objectively presented to us by nature. They are dynamic theories developed to express particular views,"[2] Stephen Jay Gould reminds us. Note Gould's words "dynamic" and "particular views," which are important for their assertion that classified groups are fluid and malleable, not static and rigid—not permanent or fixed. It follows logically that the criteria used to classify sets of information may be highly subjective in purpose; may use formats based on ideology or on the methodological imperatives of a particular field of study, or theory, or social condition, or business practice, or behavior; and may reflect the changing state of science and knowledge. Classification systems within the same "kingdom" of existence change all the time, including our already-mentioned library classification, or corporate structures (Vice-Presidents subdivided into Senior V-Ps and Junior VPs), or many universities' decision to merge their sociology and anthropology departments. People impose purpose and necessity onto their classifications, for example again with the simple traffic light: by 1920, with commercial electricity and automobiles popularized, the first traffic light as we know it was invented, of necessity. Inventors could have colored it purple, turquoise, and pink, or they might have decided that there should be two levels of caution, a color for "initial caution" and a different color for "final caution." But they didn't; they classified it as we know it. It follows further that in any classification system, as in any written document, some information will be proclaimed, other information silenced. From this obvious truth we may conclude, again, as in Essay #1, that purely objective writing does not exist: your essay's classification of information will and should result from your own purposes.

Finding relationships—the compatible and cooperative assembly of information— must begin your classification process and must always underlie how you thinkabout organization. Relationship is a simple principle, and working with it from the inside out (see Essay #2) will help to guarantee connectedness of information or thecoherence that all writers aspire to achieve. The Law of Attraction fosters relationship, while larger, more forceful relationships produce stronger force fields, whose repellence of incompatible information helps us to determine differences when we are classifying. To illustrate classification for writing and the organizational processes associated with and developing from it, I'm going to use an essay subject that I gave to a group of adult continuing education students about eight years ago: "Living in New YorkCity."

Although an uncomplicated, straightforward, not noticeably theoretical subject, this essay offers many possible ideas and approaches; therefore, its informationneeds to be controlled and effectively organized. In class, first, the students compiledaloud a substantial list of brainstormed information, which I wrote on the blackboard, equivalent to compiling information on a Word™ document. Some of thestudents' responses triggered associative responses from other students; associativethinking occurs in one's individual mind, too. Although the class might have brainstormed for weeks to come, I imposed a one-session time-limit on their thinking, just as all writers must work within limits. After class I wrote down everything the class had said, in its original, random order, then took it home and typed it up for our next session. Here's the list:

expensive housing . . . Empire State building . . . many art

galleries
. . . costly support services . . . subways . . . diversity of people . . . Trump towers . . . New Yorkers sometimes are thought to be inconsiderate . . . Times Square . . . international corporations . . . New Yorkers' impressive behavior during summer '03 blackout . . . Carnegie Hall . . . publishing houses . . . weekend behavior . . . higher pay . . . Ellis Island . . . the impact of 9/11 . . . Greenwich Village . . . nightlife in the "city that never sleeps" . . . glass buildings everywhere . . . museums . . . Wall Street . . . city districts featuring all aspects of national cultures . . . rush hour . . . music . .. fashion . . . Penn Station . . . bustling walkers on streets . . . jobs in finance . . . car and taxi horns . . . skyscrapers . . . arts . . . Colonial architecture . . . Beaux Arts architecture . . . international population . . . advertising . . . perceived as a difficult place to live. . . New Yorkers as tough-minded . . . theater in general, Broadway in particular . . . diverse cuisine, countless restaurants . . . buses... high city taxes . . . Grand Central . . . Art Deco architecture. . . taxis everywhere, fleets of yellow . . . Central Park . . . positive statistics for crime . . . Harlem . . . pedicabs . . . Lincoln Center . . . medicine . . . Gramercy Park . . . waitering

When in the following session I gave this list of fifty-three items to the class, telling them that these were the bones that would serve as their essay's skeletal structure (or outline), at first they were overwhelmed: fifty-three jumbled thoughts! But that's where the organizational process of classification is so important: all of that listed information needed to be classified into bone groups or topical groups.

If you personally ever have fifty-three (probably fewer) bones requiring bodily composition, it's likely that you already will have thought about relationships among some of them; that's one of the purposes of having a Word™ document. For my class' purpose of organization, however, I suggested that students begin by using the first item, "expensive housing," as a magnet to carry through the list, to see what other items it could attract into a possible classified grouping. As the students went through the list, they realized that "housing" itself never would become the topical basis for a paragraph—there wasn't anything else about housing—but that "expensive" could; in addition to the outrageous cost of housing in New York City, their list of fifty-three bones also included expensive "city taxation" and expensive "support services," with required services such as grocery-store food, and optional ones such as dry cleaning and haircuts. Then the class took the second item, "Empire State Building," and used that as a magnetizing principle. Collecting potentially relatable items (or bones), they quickly realized that some of their brainstormed bones belonged not strictly to the category of architecture but instead to a category that they decided to call "landmarks"; the Empire State Building was such a landmark, whereas items such as "Colonial," "Beaux Arts," "Art Deco," and "glass skyscrapers" represented periods and kinds of architecture and, for intellectual clarity, needed to be a different although closely related class of information. Critical to their perception of each topical class of information—each bone-group—was the simple but differentiating label that I required them to give to it, such as "expense," "architecture," and "landmarks." Naming or labeling gives substance and unity to abstractions and to conceptual groupings. Any idea in our mind is intangible until we make it tangible, either by visual images, which are open to endless subjective interpretation, or by language, which is more self-defining. In effect, because words are material symbols that represent whatever exists and goes on in the world, naming or labeling makes ideas real.

I had my students keep in mind that the classification and labeled identification of ideas is never strictly right or wrong; rather, although certain classifications may be better or worse than others, more efficient or less so, the creation of topical groups for a document or essay always should be determined by writers' priorities and purposes as educators, their thinking, and their conceptual view of existing similarities and differences. Quite a few of the fifty-three items listed above overlap categorically and easily could belong to more than one topic; therefore, as my students did, writers in general always should impose categorical logic on their own information, differentiating, classifying, and labeling it according to their own intellectual preferences, purposes, and point(s) of view, and according to the specific life of the body they are creating.

Up to that point, seventeen or nearly one-third of the list's fifty-three items already had been classified and labeled, making the remaining two-thirds easier to group. Ultimately, my students discovered nine separate classes of information using the "magnet search" principle, nine topical groups that would form the basis for paragraphing their essay:

EXPENSE: housing...city taxes...support services

ARCHITECTURE: glass skyscrapers...Trum...Colonial...Beaux Arts...Art Deco

LANDMARKS: Central Park...Wall Street...Greenwich Village...Gramercy ark...Ellis Island...Empire State building...Lincoln Center...Carnegie Hall...Times Square

CULTURE: Nightlife...food...museums...galleries...music...theater...city districts featuring all aspects of national cultures

TRANSPORTATION: subway...bus...taxi...pedicabs

PEOPLE: diverse...international...tough...sometimes inconsiderate...impressive during summer '03 blackout...weekend behavior

JOB OPPORTUNITIES: international...corporations...finance...publishing...arts...advertising...medicine...fashion...waitering...support services...higher pay

DANGER: 9/11...perception of difficulty...statistical actualities

FAST-PACED: rush hour...Grand Central...Penn Station...walking on street...car and taxi horns

After you have classified—as my students did—all of your document's or essay's ideas, or bones, you will see that there are X-# of bone-groups containing the essay's content; if any bones remain lonely and unclassifiable, then the good news is that they don't belong in the essay. Naturally, the groups that can be classified are interrelated theoretically, at times even somewhat overlapping, because they all belong to and are bound by the same subject: again, think of the human body, whose bone-groups remain separate (there's no operative connection between myleg-bones and hand-bones) and yet have a distinctive purpose for that particular part of the body and for the total integrity of the body as a whole. Analytically you have had to assemble information into distinct groups, each united by its own content'sstrong similarities and separated from other groups' content by major and minor topical differences. Notice that the compounded information in each class or topic becomes its own force field, a separate vital set of ideas whose energy may andoften does attract additional information and examples. Part of the beauty of classification is that anything new which comes to your mind will have a designatedplace to be located; if it can't be located in its proper place, then it doesn't belong in your essay unless it's forceful enough to become its own topic of investigation.

Necessarily, any well-organized document's or essay's whole investigation—its subject—always is divided into topical parts resulting from the classification process. Some essay subjects are small and thus have a small number of topics; others,larger in scope, contain many topics. Generally, each topic is one paragraph, or oneseparable section of the whole investigation. We create each paragraph to help the reader see, graphically, that a new topic is being investigated; achieving this visually is either indentation of a new paragraph's first line, or double spacing between paragraphs. When conceived and written successfully, paragraphing also helpsreaders to outline their retention of your subject's topics of investigation, providing a developmental general summary of what's going on in the document's or essay'sbody.

Because each paragraph is informed with the content of its own particular topic of investigation, it is inevitable that every paragraph will have its own length. Therefore, because paragraph lengths naturally vary, there are no length requirements for paragraphs: paragraphs' lengths are what they are because their content is what it is. Some paragraphs inevitably will be large; others, small. Furthermore, in professional and graduate writing, paragraphs sometimes are just one or two sentences, serving as "transitional paragraphs" to help writers create a bridge between significant areas of an essay's discussion.

Sometimes, when a topic is e-x-t-r-e-m-e-l-y large and contains naturally divisible sets of sub-topical information, you may want to divide it into parts, thus giving more than one paragraph to that topic's content. In such instances, the "flow" or continuity of your discussion remains exactly the same, the only difference being that the information now moves through two paragraphs rather than uninterruptedly through just one.

With nine topics of investigation for their "Living in New York City" essay, my students next had to organize the topics themselves, had to place them in a developmental order that best told the story of living in NYC that they wanted to tell. Some organizational processes are better than others, but there are no definitive, absolute ways of structuring your content. Just remember that as an educator you want to create a progression of thought which fulfills your goals and highlights your priorities, and also which your reader will be able to follow and remember easily. Again, think of your developmental order as being the story you want to tell. Different topical organizations will tell a different story, with different emphases, different priorities, so I asked the students what kind of "attitude" they wanted to bring to the overall presentation of their ideas about living in NYC. "Positive" was their consensus, so they kept positivity in mind as their salient organizational point of view (later in this essay, you'll see an acceptably and logically organized but less positive story about "Living in New York City"). To organize their essay's nine topics, my students again had to look for relationship: I asked them to go through the list of nine and to look for any two items that seemed particularly inseparable, especially auxiliary, like a right-hand / left-hand complementation. Doing that, they realized that some of the pairings were self-evident, obvious, inevitably connected: "people" and "culture" belonged together, or, in the essay, back-to-back, because—duh, they said—you can't have culture without people; yes, that's obvious, but often the strongest logic is the most obvious logic. Earlier the students had realized that "architecture" and "landmarks" were inseparable topics, so they paired those two. Thinking in financial terms, they concluded after some dialogue (our individual mind also dialogues when thinking) that "job opportunities" and "expense" could work well together. That left three topics: transportation, fast-paced, and danger, all three of which had possible logical interconnections.

With three pairs plus three interconnected remaining topics, the students then had to refine their essay's developmental order, being certain to impose a logical "flow" onto all of it, one step at a time. The first sequence they created, one that upheld their "positive attitude," was this: ¶s 1 (expense); 7 (job opportunities); 6 (people); 4 (culture); 3 (landmarks); 2 (architecture); 5 (transportation); 9 (fast paced); 8 (danger). I asked them to think about the logic that allowed for the "flow" between every topic in this developmental order, for example what allowed "landmarks" to flow out of "culture" and into "architecture," because writers always need to consider that kind of logic—relationship—for the transitions they write to interconnect paragraphs.

Having designed their macrostructure or large organizational layout, my students now had to learn, think about, and write a topic sentence for each paragraph, with a transition built into it. A topic sentence is to a paragraph what a thesis statement is to an entire essay: it provides a general summary overview of what is about to come in the reader's journey, like a roadmap delineating the next stage of travel. Also, I have found that the easiest way to establish transitional links between preceding and new paragraphs is to build those transitions into the topic sentences, so that each new paragraph's first sentence looks back to and connects with the preceding paragraph's topic while announcing the new topic. This way, writers create two levels in their "information architecture" by "cementing" together two paragraphs.

Any document's body's first paragraph will develop easily from the introduction, which generally ends with the essay's thesis or purpose statement, of which the body's first paragraph is one topical part. For "Living in New York City," the first topic, expense, had the following topic sentence, which upheld the students' positiveattitude: "Every category of expense for living in New York City is costly and comparatively high-priced, although most residents find those expenses a small priceto pay for the paybacks they receive by living there."

Then, using the nine topics' progression—¶s 1, 7, 6, 4, 3, 2, 5, 9, 8—the students wrote the eight remaining topic sentences, each with a built-in transition that logically interconnects the new paragraph with the preceding one. Reading all eight of them gives not only a complete summary of what the essay discusses, but alsothe logical plot of the writers' story:

Transition from:

¶ 1 → ¶ 7

Despite the city's higher cost of living, its jobs opportunities are diverseand its pay proportionally higher.

¶ 7 → ¶ 6

Certainly it is the ample opportunities for work in New York City that draw such diverse national, ethnic, and racial populations to it.

¶ 6 → ¶ 4

Its international population makes New York one of the most culturally interesting cities in the world, "the city that never sleeps."

¶ 4 → ¶ 3

One notable result of New York City's culture has been and continues to be its outstanding architecture—outstanding in every way.

¶ 3 → ¶ 2

Because New York City is historically important, a person will find among the city'sarchitecture many noteworthy landmarks.

¶ 2 → ¶ 5

Access to New York's landmarks and parks is made easy not only by the city's fleetof taxis, the largest in the U.S., but by the Metropolitan Transportation Authority (MTA), whose complex system of subways and buses provides excellenttransportation throughout the five boroughs.

¶ 5 → ¶ 9

New York's busy streets, honking horns, and noisy subways contribute to the city'sfast pace.

¶ 9 → ¶ 8

Associated with New York's fast pace, if not a result of it, are people's feelings that the city is a dangerous place to work and live—although statistics prove otherwise.

To prove to my students that they could create a different organization using exactly the same material—the same fifty-three bones in the same nine bone-groups—I required them to organize the essay with a logical but different format and attitude, an attitude less "positive" than that of the other essay because of its new organizational structure. Read the following topic sentences with built-in transitions, and notice how the information "adds up" differently here. I want you to appreciate that organization is subjective and variable, and, again, that writing's messages and the persuasion of those messages, whatever they are, result from how you organize or build your information architecture—and are not purely objective sets of information:

Transition from:

¶ 1 to ¶8

Adding to people's apprehensions about New York City's expensive cost of living isthe supposed danger associated with its urban life, even though statistics indicate that for all categories of violent crime and property crime New York is a significantly safer place to live than are Los Angeles, Chicago, Miami, Dallas, Atlanta, Philadelphia, Boston, St. Louis, Detroit, and Washington, D. C.

¶8 to ¶ 9

Despite New York's relative safety, heightening the city's sense of danger may be itsfast pace, often seemingly random and unrestrained.

¶9 to ¶6

No doubt the city's fast pace creates negative stereotypical beliefs about New York'sstyle of urban life; however, because New York is a residential city, its pace more appropriately suggests that its residents, like most urbanites, are professionally busyand personally in a hurry to return home to their respective communities.

¶6 to ¶4

It is because of New York City's diverse population, who live in the city, that its culture remains so vital, so richly varied, and so accommodating to all kinds of lifestyles.

¶4 to ¶7

Another aspect of New York City's culture is its immense opportunity for jobs, whosediversity and proportionally higher pay can offset the expense of living here.

¶7 to ¶5

Getting to work is a cost-affordable, relatively convenient proposition in New York City, owing to the city's complex and efficient transportation system of subways, buses, and, at an added expense, taxis.

¶5 to ¶ 2

Traveling to work along New York's avenues and streets allows a person to view the city's historical and contemporary buildings, which provide one of the world's greatest assortments of urban architecture.

¶ 2 to ¶ 3

Included in New York City's remarkable architecture are its landmarks, both metropolitan and natural.

Not yet accomplished for "Living in New York City" was the internal organization for each paragraph. My students had organized the essay macrostructurally, stacking up each paragraph in what they believed was the best developmental order, but they still hadn't organized each paragraph's information. Again, the principle of looking for relationships was their first organizational step. For example, the topical classification and paragraph for the bone-group "job opportunities" has the following bones: international corporations…finance… publishing…arts…advertising…medicine…fashion …waitering…support services…higher pay. Students agreed that "higher pay" is true for every other bone—even waiters make more money in New York City—so they thought it could be placed either as an introductory thought or as a concluding summary thought; however, because they wanted to reinforce their existing transition with the preceding paragraph, "expense," they decided to place "higher pay" at the new paragraph's beginning. Then, using the magnet principle yet again, they took "international corporations" and decided which other items are principally international: finance certainly is, and advertising and fashion frequently are. Of the remaining items or bones, students saw two more classifiable groups: national, and local, the former including medicine and publishing (mostly national publishing houses in NYC), the latter including arts, waitering, and support services. Classification again allowed these writers to see that the "job opportunities" topic could be organized and coherently developed in a logical progression beginning with "higher pay for all," then internationally based jobs, nationally based jobs, and locally based jobs. The paragraph would flow according toan obvious, easy logic, which, as I stated before, frequently is the most useful logic.

When reviewing the bone-group paragraph of "landmarks," my students after much discussion decided that the easiest—again, easy for all—and undoubtedly educational way to organize that paragraph would be to move south to north through Manhattan, taking readers on a geographical journey that announced the ascending street numbers or general locations: Ellis Island, Wall Street (before numbers existed), Greenwich Village (1-13), Gramercy Park (18-23), Empire State Building (33-34), Times Square (42), Carnegie Hall (57), Central Park (59-110), and Lincoln Center (62-65). That logic created a graceful flow, although the students alsohad considered organizing the paragraph differently—but also educationally—with a chronological, thus historical focus: Wall Street (1640s), Greenwich Village (1712), Gramercy Park (1833ff.), Central Park (1857, planning commission; 1873, completed), Carnegie Hall (1891), Ellis Island (1892), Times Square (1904), Empire State Building (1930), and Lincoln Center (1962). Writers always have options, and it's up to them what best to opt for; my students decided that they preferred to treat "landmarks" as a tour rather than as a history lesson.

Regardless of what you choose to plot your paragraph's story, each paragraph's organization should be an organic form of the information living within that paragraph; as the word in-form (my hyphen) suggests, the form or ultimate organization evolves from the inside out, because, as with a plant, the outer shape isformed by the inner content, thus creating a composite of information. As we saw above, classification in one paragraph written by my students produced the natural model of "higher pay for international, national, and local job opportunities," whereas in another it produced the geographical model of "landmarks" moving fromsouth to north on Manhattan. Look for informing theoretical principles that can shape your paragraph's storytelling naturally and make it easy to follow; usually, those principles become apparent as soon as we look for relationships among the parts.

If, however, you're uncertain about how to organize a paragraph's information, or if that information doesn't reveal potential organizational patterns, then develop it by using one of these patterns as a starting point:

a. from the paragraph's most general idea to particular points analyzed or deduced from the generalization

b. from a general claim to particular reasons supporting it

c. from cause(s) to effect(s) or, depending on your analysis, from effect(s) to cause(s)

d. if your essay investigates a problem for which you offer a proposed solution, then introduce one topical aspect of the problem in a paragraph and offer a solution(s) for it, analyzing why each aspect of the problem is deficient and why your solution(s) is(are) superior

e. according to chronology (first, second, third, etc.)

f. according to sequence or process (this, then that, next this, then that)

g. if you see one idea or sentence in your paragraph's information that transitions really well into the next paragraph, place that at the paragraph's end and work backwards

At this point, everything in my students' essay's body was organized or placed in its proper position. Except for the paragraphs' topic sentences with transitions—and my students wrote them only to complete my instruction—nothing in the essay's body had yet been formally written. What my methodology encourages writers to create—what my students created for "Living in New New York City"—is a skeletal outline for any document's or essay's body. Notated with brief phrases and sometimes single words that serve as identifying labels for each bone ("city taxes") and bone-group ("expense"), a skeletal outline's component parts usually are reducible to a single page; therefore, a writer will be able to see assembled at once what the body's content includes and will be able easily to relocate—reorganize—parts of the outline as well as to recognize where additional last-minute information is required. The common sense lesson here is that outlines are purposeful only after you have given yourself time to brainstorm, compile information, classify, and begin to see the best development of your thoughts. Preliminary outlining is a waste of time: you can't outline content that doesn't yet exist—or, even if it exists partially, content that hasn't been thoroughly brainstormed, investigated for relationships, classified, and thought out. Preliminary outlining takes on an architectural structure and graphic aesthetic of its own, but its building blocks are either meaningless, inconsequential, or, at best, rudimentary. Writers who outline before a total thought process about their document or essay devote time to thinking about how their insubstantial, nascent information is outlined, not about what should be outlined. Such a process is form without content, and it can deceive writers into believing that their thinking is broad and deep enough when it isn't.

With the skeletal outline complete, with all bones and bone-groups positioned properly in the body, a writer now can draft the essay in formal prose. Writing will seem significantly easier to accomplish when the mind needn't focus on content and organization and instead can attend exclusively to sentence structure, the mechanics of grammar and punctuation, the expression of ideas, and word-choice. With the skeletal outline visually in front of them, writers know where they're coming from and what they're heading toward, every step of the way, allowing greater concentration on how to express what they already know, have thought about, and positioned structurally. Also now, and only now, is a writer prepared to write the thesis statement—the introductory summary statement—of the essay's purpose. Vitally important to writing any document or essay well, and also to a reader's full understanding of any document's purpose, the thesis is part of any document's introduction, so in my next essay we'll look at that, along with conclusions—the body's before and after appendages.

REFERENCES

[1] Historically and presently, Western society's classifications include—and this is a small list attempting only to establish the range of classification—age; angels; architecture; art history periods and art movements; asteroids; astrological signs; automobiles; behavior; biological existence; blood types; bodies of water; building codes; bureaucratic regulations; bureaucratic systems; causes of death; climate; clothing function, size, and style; clouds; colors; computers (ACM [Association for Computing Machinery Classification System]); continents; cooking; crimes; dances; detainee classification system (INS's DCS); disability sports; diseases (ICD [International Classification of Diseases]); doctors; drivers' licenses; Ecological Classification System (ECS); economies; endometriosis; ethnicities; fabrics; Federal Classification and Job Grading Systems; fonts; food groups; fractal art; genetic disorders; government types; grammatical parts of speech; hardware; historical periods; human body types; industrial products (NAICS [North American Industry Classification System]); intelligence; International Classification of External Causes of Injuries (ICECI) and International Classification of Functioning, Disability, and Health (ICFDH), both of them parts of the World Health Organization; jobs or employment; Lake Classification System; law (Schiller Classification System); letter grading in academics; linguistic families; literary genres; Mathematics Subject Classification (MSC); metabolism; movie ratings; music types; musical instruments; nursing; patents (USPC [United States Patent Classification] and IPC [International Patent Classification]); patients; patients' rehabilitation classification system; pencil leads; personality types; pharmaceuticals; philosophical schools of thought; prisoners; prisons; psychological traits; races; religions; résumé layouts; rocks; set theory; soil; sports of every kind, including leagues, positions, types of performance, weight groups; subway lines; suntan lotion; time; unethical practices in the legal system (15 classes); United Nations Classification System; watersheds; wines; WIPO classifications (World Intellectual Property Organization); wires; yoga; and on and on, seemingly without end.

[2] http://csmres.jmu.edu/geollab/Fichter/SedRx/Classtheory.html

ESSAY 6

Parts of Speech Mirror Life and the World

"Part of speech" refers to how a word functions, the part it plays in a sentence. In all languages each part or "lexical category" of speech has its own logical functions, but these functions may be unique to the systems of a particular language and shouldn't be applied to any other languages. English has eight parts of speech, seven of which require some thought. The eighth part, the exclamation, is self-evident because it's followed by an exclamation point: "Wow!" "Yikes!" "Duh!" "OMG!" The other seven mirror actual existence and are the principal building blocks for constructing all that we can say or write in English.

Each word in English is at least one part of speech; some words function in more than one way, having more than one part they can play, such as "design," "fit," "narrow," "palm," "prompt," "coordinate," and thousands more. When used in sentences, the worded parts of speech work together as logical constructions to define everything of matter and of envisioned imagery that matters in the world, outside and inside of us. So without your first having a defined knowledge of and ability to identify the seven major parts of speech, it's difficult for me to explore and explain ideas about how to write with mechanical precision, and difficult for you to understand those ideas.

Without these structural foundations for our ideas and understandings, written language would be quicksand swallowing all sense and sensibility and belching out thickly bubbled nonsense instead. "Guide with surely must way logic our here I" has nine easily identifiable words, each with meaning, but their structure is nonsensical and their meaning silly because the layout of words, or syntax, ignores the logical placements systematized by grammar to represent existence as it actually exists or may exist. Grammar's systems, all assembled using parts of speech, have built-in logical guides for representing whatever we want to express.

Grammar was not created to bother us with difficulties; instead, as I mentioned in Essay #1, think of grammar's labels and requirements—each word's part of speech and how the English language's systems use it—as a simple mirror reflecting or representing the actual world, what goes on in it, and what we make of it all. Even with about one million English words, it's interesting that all of them belong grammatically to one or more of just eight categories. Apples have more categories than that. In other essays of mine you can learn the descriptive logic of grammatical machinery and systems, but I've found that it's much easier to begin learning the simple logic of grammar, punctuation, and sentence structure if first you know the parts of speech, what they are and what they do by themselves, and how they can or can't interact with the other parts. You're reading these essays to learn ways to think about and use the mechanics of English, so I invite you to familiarize yourself with or to review the language's conceptual basics, the parts of speech. Thinking of each part as a concept with defined functions, and observing and experimenting with those functions' possibilities, you'll discover that what you learn here can have personal rewards and, if you give it a chance, definitely will add professional and academic profit to your writing.

Here's a sentence containing all seven important parts of speech: "Izzy and I excitedly sent red roses to Mary on her birthday."

Actual enough because possible or imaginable, those twelve words represent a simple scenario: viewed in general terms, two (or plural) people perform an action that itself is characterized by one specific quality; the action's energy delivers something to someone on a specific occasion. The example sentence's syntax or arrangement of the seven important parts of speech makes sense; its sequence of parts of speech "adds up" logically and allows me to tell the birthday story (or, if I prefer, to tell another story: "She or Mary carefully will plan reception activities for guests at Mark's wedding."). Using specific grammatical vocabulary, here's what happens in the original sentence: a proper or capitalized noun person (1st part of speech), "Izzy," and a pronoun (2nd part) substituting for a person, "I," are the sentence's compound subject or doers of an action; the subject is coordinated—made compound or plural—by a conjunction (3rd), "and," which conjoins or brings both subjects together. The verb (4th), "sent," is the action in the past that the compound subject performs, a verb whose characterizing adverb (5th), "excitedly," expresses a quality of how the two people sent it. The plural noun object of the sending ("roses") has its own characteristic, expressed by an adjective (6th), "red." Two prepositions (7th), "to" and "on," combine with their objects, respectively "Mary" and "birthday," to create two prepositional phrases that reveal more information—where and when—while "her" is another adjective, a possessive adjective expressing the characteristic of ownership.

These days mostly grammarians parse and diagram sentences, as I just did, but there's no need for you to do that; what I expect is that after completing this essay you will have a defined understanding of each part of speech and its functions, so that later you'll have working vocabulary to identify and to use the language's logic; being conversant with the parts of speech will allow you to know what I mean and what is meant by others about principles of grammar, punctuation, and sentence structure. To be conversant with the English language requires that we understand, from the bottom up, what the language is and how the language works, at least fundamentally. Nothing built intellectually, no system, can stand without a foundation or fundamental grounding, so it's important that you not dismiss the parts of speech—whatever you presently think of and feel about them.

Although the parts of speech can be complex functionally, and sometimes tricky, their basic purposes are easy to learn. What follows is theory with explanations and examples that will help you to identify, understand, and use the seven important parts of speech. Read patiently and perseveringly, as I suggested in my Introductory essay, but feel free to bypass whatever you're certain you already know—unless you want to review it.

THEORY

1), 2), NOUNS AND PRONOUNS

I asked you at this essay's beginning and also in Essay #1 to "think of grammar's labels and requirements as a simple philosophical mirror reflecting or representing the actual world." Let's pursue that truth. Most immediately noticeable in reality are physical matter and abstract matters. Our world is reducible to three categories of materialized and abstract existence: persons, places, and things. In grammar, all persons, places, and things are classified as nouns. "Things" also include all animals, all sensory phenomena, and anything conceptually abstract that exists, thus is intangible and non-empirical, such as mind, intelligence, theory, neurosis, sin, allegiance, deceit, bravery, fear, or kindness. You cannot see or touch any of the ten nouns just itemized, but for all humans they exist as discernible existences or behaviors.

Proper nouns are capitalized specific names of persons (Bob Davis), places (New York University), and things (Diet Coke). Common nouns are uncapitalized, general kinds of persons (educator or teacher or man), places (school or institution or university), and things (soft-drink or liquid or refreshment). You always can identify a common noun by seeing if you can place an article—"a," "an," or "the"—in front of it. If that works, as it does in the preceding paragraph's list of ten nouns, the word is a common noun; if it doesn't work, it's not. Thus we can say "an educator" or "the school" or "a soft-drink," knowing in all three instances that the article must identify a definite ("the") or indefinite ("a," "an") common noun. An article belongs only to a common noun. To say "The Bob Davis" makes no sense, because "Bob Davis" is a proper noun. To say "the danced" makes no sense, because "danced" is a past-tense verb. To say "Andi is a smart" or "Myles is the cute" makes no sense, because "smart" and "cute" are adjectives which, when alone, do not belong to an article; adjectives belong to nouns, so we can say "Joan is a smart person" and "Myles is the cute boy."

Someones, somewheres, and somethings fill the actual world and all our thoughts and emotions. In the actual world, and therefore also in grammar, sometimes a noun does something by performing an action, and sometimes it performs no action at all. If a noun is performing or enacting something, then grammatically we call that noun a "subject," a doer of an action—the main subject of what the sentence is about; if it isn't doing something, then we call that noun an object, a receiver of an action or what is acted on, a person, place, or thing external to the subject or doer of action. In the sentence "Jim loves food," Jim is the subject or doer of love, and the food—external to him—is the object of his love. In the sentence "Mary writes sentences," Mary is the subject or doer of the writing, and the sentences—external to her—are the object of her writing.

In sentences, as in life, all nouns can be either a subject or an object, depending on what's going on in the reality that your sentence is representing. In "Spiders spin webs," the plural common noun "Spiders"—more than one spider—is the subject performing the verb's action, "spin," while the plural common noun "webs" is the direct object of the spinning. In "Webs catch flies," the noun "Webs" now becomes the subject of the verb's action, "catch," while "flies" is the direct object of the catching. In "Flies sense movement," the noun "Flies" now becomes the subject performing the verb's action, "sense," while the noun "movement" (a thing) is the direct object of the sensing. Again, any proper or common noun can be either a subject or an object. If your name is Zoe, then you can be a subject ("Zoe enjoys movies") or an object "The teacher praised Zoe"). If you write about a rose, then the rose can be a subject ("A rose exudes fragrance") or an object ("Bill smells the rose").

Remember: if a noun does not perform a specific action or does not indicate a state of being ("to be" or "to exist"), then it is not a subject and therefore must be an object, because objects do not perform actions.

Verbs, which soon you'll read about fully, express a specific action or a state of being (again, by "state of being" I mean a form of the verb "to exist" or, more commonly, "to be" = am, are, is [happening in the present]; was, were [in the past]; will be [future]).

When we pair a noun or pronoun with a verb located in time—the past, present, or future tense—we create a clause. A clause is one of English's two broad categories of sentence structure; the other category is phrase. Both categories have different subsets or kinds. For now, just know that all that's needed to create a complete sentence is a clause that logically can stand on its own, an "independent clause: "Instructors teach." "Students learn." "Minds forget." "Interest regenerates."

"Grammar is." Conversely, any group of words that does not have a subject and verb with tense is not a clause and therefore must be some kind of a phrase.

In the preceding paragraph's two-word sentences, each of the nouns—"Instructors," "Students," "Minds," "Interest," and "Grammar"—is the subject of its sentence. The subject performs or is connected with the verb's action, or, when the verb is "to be," the subject just exists ("Grammar is."). In English, every subject must have a verb with tense—withtime, the present, past, or future—and, conversely, every verb therefore must have a subject, because all sentences—and all reality— must minimally have a subject-doer and a verb with tense to make total sense. If we write "Dolphins" by itself, we await an action to complete the subject's logic: "Dolphins swim." Those two words are a complete sentence. If we write "suffered" by itself, we await the subject of that past action: "Victims suffered." A doer ("The salamander") cannot exist without an action done, and an action done ("crawls") cannot exist without a doer. Grammar thus mirrors the philosophical truth of reality, because language's purpose is to represent reality.

Words that substitute for nouns are called pronouns. Like the nouns they substitute for, pronouns also function as either subjects or objects. Become familiar with the chart below, because the differences between the subjective and objective use of pronouns are basic to your understanding various rules of grammar:

	SUBJECT	OBJECT
First Person Singular	I	Me
Second Person Singular	You	You
Third Person Singular	He/She/It	Him/Her/It
First Person Plural	We	Us
Second Person Plural	You	You
Third Person Plural	They	Them
	Who(ever)	Whom(ever)

The easiest way to remember the subject pronouns is to conjugate a verb, as you did in grade school with your native language and probably also did when learning a new language: I eat, you eat, he/she/it eats, we eat, you eat, they eat. As subjects, those pronouns must and do have verbs.

There are three kinds of objects: 1) direct object, 2) indirect object, and 3) object of a preposition. Nouns and pronouns can function in any of these three ways.

A direct object is the person, place, or thing directly acted upon or directly receiving the action of the verb performed by the subject. In the sentence "She enjoyed the dancer," "dancer" is the direct object (person) of her enjoyment. (Don't forget that "dancer" can be a subject also: "The dancer provides pleasure.") In the sentence "His mother visited the museum," "museum" is the direct object (place) of his mother's visiting. In "I eat cake," "cake" is the direct object (thing) of my eating.

The second kind of object, indirect object, needn't concern you much, not only because you always will use it correctly, but also because it actually is an object of the preposition "to." With indirect objects, English sentence structure allows us to delete the "to" without disturbing the sentence's logic: in the sentence "Bill sent Mike the invitation," "Bill" is the proper noun subject, "sent" is the past tense verb, "the invitation" is the direct object of Bill's sending, and "Mike" is the indirect object—or actually the object of the preposition ("sent to Mike the invitation"). In effect, the indirect object is considered "indirect" because, both in philosophical reality and in real-world time, a direct object of an action must exist before there can be any person, place, or thing to receive it. For example, in "Ricardo gave New York City his blessings," "Ricardo" is the subject (proper noun person), "gave" is the past tense verb, "his blessings" is the direct object of his giving (common noun thing), and "New York City" is the indirect-object receiver of those blessings (proper noun place); as always, the indirect object, in this instance "New York City," is really the prepositional phrase "to New York City."

Nouns and pronouns can function also as objects of the preposition. Because a preposition is yet another part of speech, let's study that part of speech.

3)   **PREPOSITIONS**

Most prepositions grammatically express the physics of existence—as indicators of space and time, of where and when. Where, spatially? In the store. Near Jim's house. Around the corner. Under a tree. On the plate. Within the box. By the car. Between New

York and Philadelphia. Over the rainbow. When, temporally? At 4:00p.m. By noon. After Tuesday. Before Thursday. Around midnight. Near noon. About 2a.m. In one hour. During the snowfall. Until hell freezes over.

Notice that all prepositions must have an object—a noun or pronoun, thus a person, place, or thing—belonging to them. If I say "beside" to you, you immediately need to know "beside what?" The "what" will be a noun or pronoun functioning as an object, in this case the object of a preposition: "beside Bob" (proper noun), "beside me" (pronoun), "beside Brooklyn Diner" (proper noun), "beside the restaurant" (common noun), "beside the Kleenex" (proper noun), "beside the tissues" (common noun). Grammar's mirroring of reality completes the logical necessity that every preposition must have a noun-object.

Our descriptive observations and analyses of most persons, places, and things in the world involve spatial and temporal facts, which is why so many English prepositions indicate space and time: location, location, location, and our rides in time's winged chariot. But in addition to answering the where and when questions, prepositions answer or illustrate to a lesser extent the how ("with a fork"; "by reviewing" ["reviewing is a gerund-noun]); or why ("from eating too much"; "for a thousand reasons"); how much ("in the millions"; "over my limit"; "beyond acceptable"); and what ("In trouble"; "of the committee") For review, think again of which question(s) a prepositional phrase can answer: where (spatial location, direction, or source?) when (time)?; how or why (manner or way)?; how much (degree); or what? Notice that sometimes the same preposition can express different ideas when it is used in different contexts: "Will he arrive by midnight?" (when); "His exit ramp is by the concession stand" (where); "He will arrive by taxi" (how). { } "Bill is in his house" (where); "Bill will arrive in three hours" (when); "Bill is in trouble" (what); "In no way can Bill get out of trouble" (how).

The preposition and its noun or pronoun object become a phrase that functions either as an adjective or, more commonly, as an adverb, and sometimes as a noun; soon we also will explore adjectives and adverbs. For now, appreciate that the prepositions listed below are the most commonly used in English. To understand other grammatical and syntactic principles, you must recognize these words as prepositions; therefore, read this list a few times.

↓↓↓↓↓↓

about, above, across, after, against, along, along with, amid, among, around, as well as, at, before, behind, below, beneath, beside, between, beyond, by, concerning, despite, down, during, except, except for, excepting, excluding, following, for, from, in, in addition to, including, inside, into, like, minus, near, of, off, on, onto, opposite, outside, over, past, per, plus, regarding, through, throughout, to, toward, under, underneath, unlike, until, up, upon, versus, via, with, within, without

↑ ↑ ↑ ↑ ↑ ↑ ↑

Remember: all prepositions must have objects. Choose any of the words above, and add to it anything that makes sense, for example "among a crowd," "within an arena," "below the dome." In those three examples, we see that the objects, respectively, are a common noun person (group of persons), place, and thing. The same applies to proper nouns: "about President Obama," "inside the Empire State Building," and "with my Nikon."

4) VERBS

There are five preliminary principles about verbs that you must know:

First, actions outside and inside us are represented by verbs. Through writing's symbolism, verbs represent motions and emotions so that we can see them enacted. Also, all inactive states of being are verbs: "to be" and "to exist."

Second, to qualify as a sentence, a set of words must include a verb with tense (time) along with that verb's subject. A verb's essential form, an infinitive, has no tense; we indicate this by placing "to" in front of the verb, such as "to study," "to party," "to be," etc. (This kind of "to" is not the same as the preposition "to," which denotes direction and requires an object.) Because infinitives do not have time, they are infinite: "to study" is timeless, because we do not know when it happens. Conjugating an infinitive gives it tense, which makes it finite, with time. Minimally, therefore, a sentence must have a subject and a verb with tense, for example "She eats" (present tense), "They kissed" (past tense), or "America will prosper" (future tense).

Third, verbs either are transitive or intransitive (transitive = transition to an object, whereas intransitive is not transitional). When a sentence's verb has a direct object, then that verb exerts a transition of energy onto the object person, place, or thing, thus being transitive ("Jane eats grapes"; "Roy manages a bank"; "Billy cuts paper"). Conversely, when a sentence has no direct object to receive or to be touched by a verb's energy, grammarians name this an intransitive verb: "Roy sleeps," "Jane laughed," and "Billy will look" cannot have an object—a person, place, or thing— following the verb.

It makes no sense to write "Roy sleeps bed," "Jane laughed story [She could laugh buckets, but only metaphorically]," and "Billy will look magazine." Additional verbs that always are intransitive include "to ache," "to arrive," "to blush," "to die," "to go," "to lie," "to linger," "to sit," "to thrive," "to tremble,"

Fourth, verbs with tense can have more than one word when they have a helping verb and a participle. With verbs containing two or more words, helping verbs (or auxiliaries) "help" because they give tense to the verb. The most common helping verb in English is "to be" (am, are, is // was, were // will be"). In the sentence "I am writing," the verb for the subject "I" is two words, "am thinking"; there, "am" is a present-tense helping verb and lets us know that the ongoing or progressive action of "thinking" (the participle) occurs in the present. However, if the thinking occurred yesterday, then I help the sentence by changing the helping verb's tense to "I was thinking." The ongoing action of thinking can occur in the future, too: "I will be thinking tomorrow." The second most common helping verb in English is "to have" (have, has // had // will have). In the sentence "They have opened the store," the verb for the subject "They" is two words, "have opened"; there, "have" is a present-tense helping verb and lets us know that the completed action of "opened" (the participle) occurs in the present. Other helping verbs that you should recognize are called modals, which express the mode in which they operate:

For emphasis: do, did = "I do believe" or "I did go"

For necessity: must, should = "I must believe" or "I should believe"

For possibility and probability: can, could, may, might, would = "Mary can prove her point"; "The little engine could climb the hill"; "I may travel to China next year"; "I might have traveled to China last year, but circumstances prohibited that"; "I would like to meet you."

Fifth, although forms of "to be" frequently are used as helping verbs ("Peter was working" or "In their eighties, his parents still are driving"), sometimes forms of the verb "to be" stand on their own; in such instances, they simply announce the subject's existence or being. For example, "I am" is a complete sentence telling the reader that I exist. Usually, though, any form of "to be" standing on its own in a sentence is used as a linking verb or as a bridge that interconnects the sentence's subject with added identification about that subject. In "Bob is my teacher," the verb "is" links or equates "Bob" with "my teacher"; therefore, X = Y and, if we prefer, Y = X, so that with equal logic we can write, "My teacher is Bob." What you need to remember here is that the form of "to be" equalizes both sides of the equation; in effect, both "Bob" and "teacher" are subjects, although Y complements or adds to the subject X and, as such, is called a subjective complement. When Toni Morrison writes in her novel Paradise that "It was she who discovered the bush with stinging- hot peppers," the pronoun "It" is the sentence's subject and the pronoun "she" (not "her," which is an object) is its subjective complement linked by "was," a past-tense form of "to be." Again, if we prefer, we can reverse X = Y and write, "She was it." In addition to equating subjects and subjective complements, linking verbs can equate a subject with qualities of that subject, such as "She is beautiful" or "They were industrious"; we call the qualities of "beautiful" and "industrious" adjectives.

VERBALS: Gerunds, Participles, Infinitives

The three kinds of verbals retain a verb's action even though they no longer function grammatically as verbs.

Gerunds

An unusual kind of noun that always is a thing is called the gerund. All gerunds end in "-ing." Also, all gerunds retain what appears to be a verb's action, which is why gerunds are called "verbals"; however, not a verb, a gerund's part of speech is a noun. For example, the word "swimming" can be used to mean an activity, something that we perform: "Swimming is good for you" (here, swimming is a subject); "I enjoy swimming" (here, "swimming is an object). As you begin to discover that many English words can be used as different parts of speech, you will find that "swimming," besides being a gerund, also can be a progressive participial adjective ("The swimming fish are in a school" [what kind of fish?]) or part of a verb ("I was swimming yesterday"). Just remember that most verbs in the English language—e.g., to dance, to think, to believe, to collect, to grade—can have a gerund form and thus be a noun: "Dancing tires us out"; "Thinking can be a painful process"; "Seeing is believing"; "Her hobby is scrapbooking"; "The student resented the teacher's standards for grading."

Participles

The most commonly used verbals are participles, which by themselves always function as adjectives. A participle originally can be the part of a verb that follows an "auxiliary" or "helping verb. In "He is managing," the two-word verb contains a helping verb, "is," which gives the verb its present-tense time, and also a progressive participle, "managing," which signifies ongoing action. All progressive participles end in "-ing" and suggest ongoing or progressive action. Therefore, that sentence says that the subject, "He," manages now and hasn't yet stopped managing. In "Eloisa was singing" and "Eloisa will be singing," we find the progressive participle, "singing," preceded respectively by a past-tense helping verb and a future-tense helper. Also adjectives when by themselves, completed-action participles come from verbs whose action already has been finished or achieved, whether in the present ("is finished now"), past ("was finished yesterday"), or future ("will be finished next month"), as opposed to the progressive participle's ongoing action in any of those tenses.

The four most common completed-action participle endings are "-ed" ("Our nation was divided," "Joan's bowl is placed on the table," "The manual will be studied"); "-en" and "-n" ("Cinderella's gown was sewn by birds," "My left index finger is broken," "Tonight's movie will be shown at 9:30"); and "-t" ("Yesterday morning my toast was burnt," "Too much money is spent on useless things," "The diamonds are kept in a bank").

When we remove the ongoing-action participle or the completed-action participle from its helping verb, it no longer is a verb. Again, it automatically becomes an adjective. Let's take some of the participles illustrated in the preceding two paragraphs—"managing," "singing," "divided," "broken," "spent"—and see how we naturally use them as adjectives: "The managing agent helped me." What kind of agent? Managing—an adjective. "The singing birds heralded spring." What kind of birds? Singing. "Disunited, the United States was a divided nation during its Civil War." What kind of nation? Disunited and divided. "Joe's broken arm is in a cast." "My spent money is a cause of sadness." In each instance, the completed-action participial adjective is modifying a noun, giving that noun a descriptive quality. Still, although the participle now is an adjective, it retains its sense of action; thus we call it a verbal.

Thousands of English's single-word adjectives are ongoing-action participles or completed-action participles. What makes these kinds of adjectives particularly useful is that they retain the verb's action. Here are just a few:

"broadcast news," "breaking story," "stolen property," "hidden vault," "buried money" "sparkling jewels," "kept secret," "lost fortune," "no promising suspects," "stymied investigation," "bewildered owners," "diminishing hopes" "frustrated police," "surfacing possibility," "renewed optimism," "startling error," "mistaken identity," "sworn affidavit," "proven innocence," "hurt feelings," "unrecovered goods," "done deal," "sinking ship," "burst bubble"

"prepared dinner," "exciting menu," "braised lamb shanks," "roasted chicken," "smoked salmon," "mixed greens," "sun-dried tomatoes," "sautéed vegetables," "rising dough," "steamed rice," "baked potatoes," "creamed onions," "stuffed zucchini," "split peas," "iced tea," "sparkling water," "aged wine," "spiced apples," "cut cake," "frozen yogurt," "spooned ice cream," "forbidden fats"

"murmuring pines and hemlocks," "babbling brooks," "shining sun," "invigorating air," "changing weather," "varied temperatures," "blowing winds," "freezing rain," "fallen snow," "iced roads," "spinning tornado," "damaging hurricane" "forsaken residents"

"bathed, washed body," "shampooed, dried, and brushed hair," "applied make-up," "powdered face," "dangling earrings," "complementing bracelet," "designed outfit," "matching shoes"

Some English verbs have irregular completed-action participles. Remember: participles do not have tense, so each completed-action participle listed below must be preceded by a helping verb if it is going to function as a verb. However, without the helping verb, it is an adjective. Here are the most common:

to abide → abode, abided; to fly → flown; to sing → sung to arise → arisen; to forget → forgotten; to sink → sunk

to awaken → awoken; to freeze → frozen; to speak → spoken to begin → begun; to get → gotten; to speed → sped

to bite → bitten; to hold → held; to spin → spun

to bleed → bled; to keep → kept; to stand → stood

to break → broken; to lay → laid; to swear → sworn to buy → bought; to lead → led; to sweep → swept to catch → caught; to leave → left; to swim → swum

to choose → chosen; to lie (recline) → lain; to swing → swung

to creep → crept; to lie (be untruthful → lied; to think → thought to drink → drunk; to ride → ridden; to weep → wept

to eat → eaten; to ring → rung; to win → won

to fight → fought; to say → said; to wind →   wound

to find → found; to seek → sought; to write → written to flee → fled; to sell → sold

Infinitives

Infinitives, the last kind of verbal, are the root forms of verbs and are always preceded by "to": "to be," "to come," "to see," "to conquer," etc. Infinitives have no tense, therefore cannot be located in time, and, as such, are infinite, hence their name. Used in sentences, infinitives can function as nouns, adjectives, or adverbs: "To eat healthful foods is important" (noun functioning as sentence's subject); "Some people like to vacation" (noun functioning as direct object); "The teacher's request to turn in homework alarmed the students" (adjective modifying the noun- subject, "request" [note: "teacher's" is not the subject because it is possessive and therefore an adjective]); and "I ran fast to win the race. " (adverb modifying the adverb "fast," which modifies the sentence's verb, "ran").

REVIEW OF PARTS 1-4: NOUN, PRONOUN, PREPOSITION, VERB

The sentence "Donations gave him hope" contains the four parts of speech discussed so far. "Donations," a plural noun, a thing, is the sentence's subject, the cause or doer of the action of giving in the past tense, "gave," the verb. "Donations gave" has meaning and can stand as a sentence, but here there's also a direct object of the donations' giving: "hope" is what the donations gave; "him" ("to him") is the indirect object, in this case a pronoun, two steps removed from "Donations": "hope" came after "Donations" were given and as such is chronologically and spatially later, a step removed; "him" receives the "hope" and therefore is two steps removed. One of life's time sequences is established with the syntax or logical word-order of these four parts of speech.

5) ADJECTIVES

In life, all persons, places, and things—again, remember that "things" includes animals, mental states, and sensory phenomena—have definable qualities, characteristics, attributes. When we ask, "What kind of man?" or "What kind of park?" or "What kind of belief?" the answer can come with an adjective: "tall man" or "honest man"; "beautiful park" or "convenient park"; "institutional belief" or "core belief." Adjectives offer us words to depict nouns' qualities, characteristics, attributes, and kinds or types. Generally, we say that an adjective "modifies" a noun, by which is meant that it transforms a noun or pronoun's matter, mental process, or sensory perception by adding values, features, traits, and meanings. Adjectives can be single words: "burgundy blouse," "stalled car," "installed cabinets," "foul odor," "thirty chapters," "unusual event," "deciduous tree," "swimming salmon." Adjectives can be compound: "deliberate and unethical behavior," "soft, gentle cat," "new yellow raincoat," "weakening and devalued economy." Adjectives can be an entire phrase: "Singing in the rain [ongoing-action participial phrase], Gene Kelly became wet"; "The arrow, broken in two [completed-action participial phrase], symbolized war"; "The CEO of BlackRock [prepositional phrase] is my wife's first-cousin"; "The tunnel to New Jersey [prepositional phrase] is crowded"; "Everyone agreed with George's idea to vacation [infinitive phrase]."

Beyond adding specific descriptive information to a person, place, or thing, an adjective can modify another adjective, announcing a qualify of a quality. For example, the noun "child" gives us only a very general idea of the person we're talking about. The adjective "six-month-old" gives the child specific age. What kind of "six-month old child"? The adjective "smiling" adds personality and temperament: "The smiling six-month-old child." The sentence's subject, "child" requires a verb: "The smiling six-month-old child enjoys." Enjoys what? Add a direct object, the object of the child's enjoyment: "enjoys food." What kind of food? Add more adjectives, to express the food's qualities: "soft, tasty, healthful food." Let's also add the possessive adjective "her," just to let our reader know that the child is female. In total, we now have "The smiling six-month-old child enjoys her soft, tasty, healthful food." Of that sentence's 12 words, 8 are adjectives, 2/3 or 67% of the sentence. Only 2 words are nouns, "child" and "food"—the extent of our material scene. The two remaining words are a verb ("enjoys") and a definite article ("The").

Remember that, like "her," possessive words are adjectives. They may originate as common or proper nouns, but with an apostrophe they become adjectives: teacher → teacher's desk (the desk possessed by, belonging to, of the teacher); city→ city's streets; pencil → pencil's eraser; cow → cow's calf; Salvador Dali → Salvador Dali's art; Broadway → Broadway's theaters and restaurants; Diet Rite → Diet Rite's carbonation. Like nouns, pronouns have a possessive form—"my," "your," "his," "her," "its," "our," and "their"—and therefore also are adjectives, because possessive words are adjectives. In the sentence "Her hair is red," the possessive "Her" functions as an adjective, as a defining quality or characteristic of "hair": hair that belongs to her. Similarly, in "The birds sewed Cinderella's gown," the possessive "Cinderella's" functions as an adjective modifying the direct object, "gown." What kind of gown? Cinderella's gown. "Cinderella's" is not a noun.

We can classify adjectives as six kinds:

Standard Adjective: tall giraffe, short gymnast, large house, small bug, big deal, little portion, good puppy, bad smell, right-wing conservative, wrong turn, lateral kick, liberal Democrat, lithe swimmer, effective plan, interesting issue

Ongiong-action or progressiveparticipial adjective: ripening banana, talking heads, freezing wind, entertaining comedian, fulfilling experience, seeing-eye dog

Completed-Action Participial Adjective: weakened defense, strengthened offense, divided nation, tossed football, interrogated prisoner, designated driver, impassioned orator, broken arrow, chosen official, frozen dinner, grown flowers, flown airplane, seen activity, spent money, kept promise

Prepositional Phrase Adjective: man on the moon, head in the clouds, above- average abilities, journey to the center of the earth, world beyond the sea, games for children

Possessive Adjectives: Milan's fashions, Pynchon's novel Gravity's Rainbow, the grapefruit's tartness, a wagon's wheel, the teacher's class, his class, my class, your class

Definite and Indefinite Articles: definite ("the"), indefinite ("a," "an")

Before a noun, we often use definite or indefinite articles. Use the definite article, "the," to indicate a specific person, place, or thing with which the reader may be expected to be familiar: "Did you consult the Oxford English Dictionary?" "Have you received the package?" "The corner store sells Pampers." "The economic strength of China is increasing rapidly." "Joe Crane is the doctor I recommend." "The general meaning of the book is best expressed in the chapter about butterflies." Use the indefinite article—"a" or "an"—when the noun you introduce is a generalization, not a specific person, place, or thing: "An apple will taste good." "I'm sucking on an icicle." "I have a hunch." "Richard Dawkins wrote a provocative book." "I will see a doctor Monday." "A nation's history is always revised." Note that the indefinite article sometimes can mean either "one" or "any": "A dictionary" = "Any dictionary"; "a hunch" = "one hunch."

You need no article when you are referring to an entire category or class: "I like books." "I eat food daily." "History usually is understood and appreciated more by older students than by younger ones." "Jim enjoys life." "Mary has interesting thoughts." "Diplomacy is an interesting subject." "Eleanor enjoys people for their peculiarities."

It follows from the preceding information about articles that you use "a" or "an" the first time you speak of something, whereas you use "the" the next time you state that subject or object: "I live in a house. The house is quite old and has four bedrooms." "I ate at a Thai restaurant. The restaurant has very good food." "Dr. Jones has a student whom he admires. The student is from Russia."

6) ADVERBS

An adverb also is a modifier expressing characteristics and qualities, types and kinds, but unlike the adjective it gives descriptive accuracy to verbs and also to adjectives and other adverbs. Multifaceted, single-word adverbs and adverbial phrases, like prepositional phrases, mirror the real world's complexities of location (where?), and time (when?), manner or way (how or why?), degree (how much?), and what. These are the questions whose answers in the real world, and therefore in grammar, we apply to actions (verbs), descriptive characteristics (adjectives), and other already existing manners or ways, degrees, locations, and times (adverbs). Examples in 1) through 4) illustrate adverbs' various uses, while 5) lists some frequently used adverbs:

1) Each of the following single adverbs modifies its sentence's verb: "The wind blows fiercely"; "Mary works hard"; "Uncle Bert arrived yesterday"; "The jury considered the evidence judiciously"; "Stefan drives fast"; "I am quite tired."

2) In the following sentences, one adverb modifies another adverb: "The wind blows fiercely here"; "Mary works tremendously hard"; "Uncle Bert arrived early yesterday"; "The jury considered the evidence very judiciously"; "Stefan drives very fast;" "I am inexplicably quite tired."

3) Here, an adverb modifies an adjective: "She looks stunningly [how?] beautiful"; "He is a very [how much?] nice man"; "Irrepressibly [how?] proud parents boast about their children"; "Jim is the fastest [how much?] sprint runner in his class."

4) Each of the following sentences contains a prepositional phrase functioning as an adverb that modifies a verb: "My mother went to the supermarket"; "She lives in Massachusetts"; "The cat walked on the roof"; "The clouds float through the air"; "We drove over the bridge."

5) Frequently used adverbs:
   - more ("She thinks more conceptually than he" = adverb modifying adverb) most("Most interesting are the foxgloves" = adverb modifying adjective) less "Some people are less tolerant" = adverb modifying   adjective)
   - least ("Of the three sisters, Jo ate least rapidly" = adverb modifying adverb) really ("Really happy, I want to share my contentment" = adverb modifying an adjective)
   - simply ("He speaks simply" = adverb modifying verb)
   - certainly ("I certainly didn't expect that" = adverb modifying verb)
   - very ("The basketball team, very disappointed by their game, went home forlorn"= adverb modifying adjective)
   - well ("She speaks English well" = adverb modifying verb) almost, never, always, rarely, sometimes, not

Review of adverbs: In addition to modifying verbs, adverbs also can modify other adverbs; this is true because in grammar, as in the real world, experience of all kinds can have compound characteristics. For example, we might have one adverb expressing the quality of "how" a verb's action exists ("Lana stretched lazily") modified by another adverb that expresses the "degree" of that laziness: "Lana stretched very lazily." Or, as other examples: "He needs to speak more clearly." "The house is undoubtedly magnificently furnished."

Adverbs also can modify adjectives, expressing the time, place, manner, or degree of a descriptive quality modifying a noun or pronoun. For example, in the sentence "Her writing is good," "good" is an adjective or the quality of the noun "writing" ("is" is a linking verb, or a linking verb is "is," so that X = Y, or Y = X). But possibly we want to emphasize how good her writing is: "Her writing is extremely good." There, the adverb "extremely" modifies the adjective "good." Such are the modifying structures in the following three sentences: "The perfectly organized explanation was logical and easy to read." "Martha was unexpectedly dizzy on the observation deck." "The brightly shining sun poured in the room like butterscotch."

Recall what you learned earlier about prepositional phrases: most often they express the physics of existence, the when (time) and where (space, place, location) of events and experiences. Thus, most prepositional phrases function as adverbs: "She works until midnight" (time, with "until midnight" modifying the present tense verb "works"); "I will see you on Saturday" (time, with "on Saturday" modifying the future tense verb "will see"); "He lived in Manhattan" (place, with "in Manhattan" modifying the past tense verb "live"); "In the penthouse on the seventy-ninth and eightieth floors of the Time Warner building at Columbus Circle near Central Park lives a wealthy man" (place, indicated in a series of five prepositional phrases).

As we've seen in some of the examples above, and as we know from life, actions expressed by verbs can have qualities. "She walks" is a complete sentence, but in that sentence the subject's action is very general, having no qualifying characteristic. First, it will be useful to refine our verb choice to a more specific kind of walk. Does she amble, limp, march, meander, pace, parade, proceed, promenade, sashay, saunter, shuffle, slink, stagger, stroll, strut, swagger, trudge, or waddle? We must choose which kind of walk comes closest to reality. Then, with our choice of specific verb, we can use an adverb to modify it, to give it additional physical and possibly psychological imagery whose defining characteristic the reader can see: "She ambles effortlessly . . . limps painfully . . . marches purposefully . . . meanders mindlessly . . . paces pensively . . . parades proudly . . . proceeds hurriedly . . . sashays happily . . . saunters dreamily . . . slinks surreptitiously. . . staggers aimlessly . . . struts confidently . . . swaggers sexily . . . trudges forlornly . . . waddles heavily." Bringing together a well-chosen verb and adverb can paint a small but lasting image.

7) CONJUNCTIONS

The only remaining part of speech to discuss is the conjunction, which means join together. Because so much exists and goes on in the actual world, and because what exists and occurs displays so many qualities and characteristics, grammar reproduces with conjunctions the actual world's compounded and complex realities.

As a part of speech, a conjunction can join together all functionally parallel sentence elements. When that happens, we refer to what is conjoined as being compound: nouns or pronouns functioning as subjects ("Bill and Tom walk"; "He and I work together); as direct objects ("I read fiction and nonfiction"); as indirect objects ("We mailed Mary and Bill an invitation"); or as objects of the preposition ("Joe travels in jets or on yachts"). We can conjoin verbs, making them compound ("Last night, I ate and drank too much"), or prepositions ("Hicham walked on the sidewalk and into a store"), single-word adjectives ("The fitness facility is modern, convenient, and affordable"), and adverbs ("He contemplated the issue broadly but not deeply"). Conjunctions also can link together two sentences, thereby making the resulting sentence compound: "I live in New York City, and I'm pleased by that."

In all examples from the preceding paragraph, the conjoined elements work together as equal parts of speech or of sentence structure: because in "Bill and Tom walk" the two subjects are equal and therefore can be reversed as "Tom and Bill walk," we call the conjunction "and" a coordinating conjunction. Coordinating means working together. The other common coordinating conjunctions are "but"; "or" and its negative form, "nor"; and "so" and "yet."

Thinking further about the boldfaced word "coordinating" in the preceding paragraph, we can say that it's an adjective. What kind of conjunction? Coordinating conjunction, the same grammatically as "coordinated athlete," someone whose muscles work together finely tuned to achieve the balance, speed, or propulsion required to perform well. As a noun, a "coordinate," pronounced "-et" at its end, refers to someone together with you and of equal rank or importance: "He is my coordinate." A "coordinator," (pronounced "-aytor"), also a noun-person, makes things work together harmoniously, and "coordinate" as a verb ("-Āte") is what coordinators do at work or for events. "Coordinate" is terminology also in math and chemistry.

The other kind of conjunction subordinates—puts on a lower level whatever it introduces—rather than coordinates on an equal level. Called a subordinating conjunction, it initiates all dependent clauses, whose logic cannot stand on their own and thus become dependent on the logic of an independent clause. If I were to say to you, "When I read quickly" or "Because you work hard," you naturally would want logic completed by something already independent and stable in formation, maybe "When I read quickly, I need relaxed eyes," or "Because you work hard, your boss and her clients benefit." Whereas "I read quickly" and "You work hard" are independent clauses and stand on their own, the introductory subordinating conjunctions, "When" and "Because," place those clauses on a 'lower' level— subordinate ("-Āte") them—and make their logic dependent on additional information. Common subordinating conjunctions include the following (note that some of these words also can function as prepositions): after, although, as, because, before, even though, if, since, that. though, unless, when, whereas, while

Note: a third kind of conjunction, the correlative conjunction, works with pairs: "either…or"; "neither…nor"; "whether…or"; and "not only…but also." I discuss these in the chapter about errors of logic in sentence structure.

ESSAY 7

"Rules" of English Grammar: Logic vs. Style, a Small Essay

Precise English grammar for business or academics and for anything else is easy to learn because its rules are few and either right or wrong, either correctly or incorrectly used. You'll learn some of them in the next chapter and later ones, explained and with examples, a set of practical grammatical rules to carry you through everything non-stylistic by which you must abide for workplace or classroom writing. These rules endure because of their incontrovertible logic, explicability, and socially purposeful standardization.

Beyond grammar's right/wrong logic, we enter the less defined world of style, an array of chosen, optional methods writers use to sound and appear however they prefer. Certainly we're all entitled to our style, but stylists sometimes forget that their stylistic standards and prescriptions aren't about actual rules but in fact are just choices, choices that may be logically incorrect, variably applied, and inconsistent in use.

As a 1962 public high-school freshman I learned among many grammatical requirements that it's wrong not only to use contractions, such as "it's," "you'll," or "shouldn't," but also to end a sentence with a preposition. Many people from my Baby-Boomer generation learned the same principle about the preposition and therefore never would write, "This is the table which my manual typewriter sits on." Instead, teachers required us to formalize our prose: "This is the table on which my manual typewriter sits." While both sentences contain exactly the same words, the latter indeed sounds more proper, superior, puffed up. However, linguists and grammarians know that this "rule" about not ending a sentence with a preposition is only a style-based requirement, a particular way to sound, not a logic-based grammatical necessity. Anecdotal history reports that Sir Winston Churchill, when told he had ended a sentence with a preposition, responded, "Madame, that is something up with which I will not put," to illustrate this stylistic "rule's" potential for the folly of tortured syntax.

Similarly, my English teacher told our class—and some teachers still tell their classes—that writers cannot begin a sentence with "Because" (or "But"). But why is a causal relationship called "cause/effect" if the cause—"be/cause"—can't come first?

Why philosophically hasn't been and isn't the duality called "effect/cause"? From many logical points of view in actual daily existence, the cause is more important to a viewer-thinker-writer than the effect, and so a writer emphasizes that reality by placing it first in the sentence. Certainly, sometimes, there's everything right about beginning with an effect ("I feel pleased") if my sentence plans to emphasize my pleasure and then to follow it by its cause ("because I was paid today"); however, if I were focusing on finance and if this sentence's priority intention were to emphasize today's new funds ("Because I was paid today, I am pleased."), then logic is fulfilled by that order of information. Or what if in an IM exchange one person writes," I can't believe this heat we've been having for two weeks," and the respondent says, "It's crazy! Because of these record highs I've been feeling fatigued," then the discussion is about weather, and the respondent's effect of fatigue exists principally as evidence caused by the high temperatures.

While it's true that using "because," a subordinating conjunction, makes the structure "Because I was paid today" a dependent clause and therefore makes its logic dependent on that of the independent clause "I am pleased," no one ever has prescribed that other subordinating conjunctions must be placed after the independent clause and cannot be placed before it: we say "If the weather permits, I will go," in accordance with the "If/then" hypothesis, or "Although she's a studious person, she never has earned an A." So why can't "Because" come first? Writers always have strategic purposes, which to be correctly realized may require logical dependence first ("Although," "Because," "If," "When," "Whereas"), before independent logic is stated.

Yet another stylistic "rule" which doesn't always make sense and can be illogical but which pervades business and academic writing instruction is that writers may not use the passive voice and must use the active. Of course as a general rule it makes sense to use an active construction, which allows readers to know the actual doer or subject of an action ("John designed the kitchen to be spacious and family- friendly") instead of taking the direct object, "kitchen," making it the subject, and passing over the active subject, John ("The kitchen was designed [by somebody, but who?] to be spacious and family-friendly"). Of special concern to public writing is the "institutional passive," which eliminates sentences' subjects or doers to avoid responsibility, to hide the names of whoever or whatever allowed an action to occur. Here are a few examples of the "institutional passive": "The little girl was hungry because she had been neglected." Somebody neglected the child, but that person or agency remains nameless in this sentence's passive construction. Another example of the institutional passive might be "The building's maintenance, especially its trash bins, has been overlooked during the past two weeks, so we are making strides to improve cleanliness." Who overlooked the maintenance? The writer intentionally has avoided "pointing the finger" at someone, thus eliminating the active doer of the overlooking. Similarly, academic arguments can be insubstantial when the passive is used: "Peace is believed to be attainable if…" Who believes this? Is this person a reputable academic or professional source? The reader never will know from the passive construction, unless the writer adds the prepositional phrase "by X" ("Peace is believed by Serenity Jones to be attainable if…" [10 words]); however, the better, more concise option is to stick to the active ("Serenity Jones believes peace is attainable if…" [7 words]).

Still, there are three instances in writing where a passive construction is preferable to an active one.

The first instance calls attention to the receiver of the action rather than to the active performer of it. This passive construction occurs when, for example, we read or hear on television that "Parental discretion is advised." The active construction might be "NBC advises parental discretion" or "Fox advises parental discretion," but NBC and Fox aren't nearly as important to the message as "parental discretion"; besides, we already know we're watching NBC or Fox. Here's another example of this first instance of acceptable passive constructions, which might occur in academic or business writing: "To help underdeveloped nations, new farming techniques could be used by our government." Here, the active construction would be "Our government could use new farming techniques to help underdeveloped nations," but the writer's emphasis is on "farming techniques" and the help they can offer, not on "Our government."

The second instance of acceptable passive is to emphasize the receiver of an action when the doer isn't known or is implied by the verb. In the sentence "The active voice needn't be used all the time," which is a passive construction, the doer is implied or understood: the active voice would be "You [or Writers] needn't use the active voice all the time." However, the active subject, "You" or "Writers," is understood or implied, and the sentence is more directly meaningful when its major focus is "The active voice." If the doer isn't known or is unimportant, then again we may use the passive acceptably: "On Friday the sign-up sheet will be posted." Whoever posts it isn't actually relevant, even if known; of greater importance is the sign-up sheet.

The final instance of acceptable passive constructions is when a writer wants to suggest objectivity—that is, nobody is involved—when one writes scientific experiments, analytical studies, or technical information. We read this kind of passive construction all the time: "The solution should be kept stirred while the dry ingredients are added," or

"The test tubes are heated to 185 degrees," or "The questionnaire will be administered at three different hospitals," etc. In these situations, usually we already know who will stir the solution, heat the test tubes, or administer the questionnaire, so the active agents or doers or subjects of stir, heat, and administer are omitted.

The problem with style-based "rules" isn't only that they can be illogical; equally problematic, they promote confusion among English writers and speakers, who of course want to be correct and who therefore are willing to follow "rules" from teachers who advocate style-based choices as absolute requirements.

If fact, most of grammar's right/wrong rules apply to one of just four categories: a pronoun's use as subject and object, and as a possessive adjective that expresses the characteristic of ownership and belonging; a pronoun's use as a reference to something else; the agreement of number—singular or plural—between a sentence's subject and verb; and comparative and superlative adjective endings. (If you don't yet understand the vocabulary in the preceding sentence—subject, object, verb, adjective—then you will want to read Essay #3.) Certain incidental rules of grammatical logic may arise, such as logical permission for writers to begin sentences with "And" or "But,"[1] but the four mentioned categories monopolize the kinds of grammatical errors writers are likely to make.

When we can explain a grammatical rule as incontrovertible, as absolute, as not to be argued about, then we can practice grammar assuredly because we know how to describe and defend its usage. Some of what we hear on the street or television today tries hard to sound in-the-know grammatically but in fact is dead wrong, as for example the incorrect pronoun usage of "I" in "Between you and I…" or "She sent it to my wife and I." In each instance "I" should be—must be—"me," because "I" is a subject and subjects must have verbs. So let's learn once and for all why logic-based rules make obvious sense and why writing grammar well cannot "center around" but instead must center on logic.

REFERENCES

[1] Beginning a sentence with "And" or "But" may seem informal, but there is nothing illogical or incorrect about doing this. In fact, each word may provide the emphatic heightening a writer desires at a sentence's beginning: "And as if that weren't enough evidence, let me add that . . ." "And with that understood, we will be prepared to . . ." "But the point here isn't to . . . " "But how can we pay serious attention to someone who . . ."

ESSAY 8

Grammar Between You and Me, Mostly About Pronouns

Remember when in grade school our teachers had us and the rest of class conjugate verbs? Together we pledged or maybe mumbled, "I talk, You talk, He/She/It talks, We talk, You talk, They talk." Whatever language we were learning, at whatever age, conjugation taught us proper use of verb "tenses," which in English are time distinctions grouped broadly by past, present, or future; also, each verb had to be connected to a personal pronoun acting as its subject, a pronoun functioning as doer either of the action verb, in this case "talk," or of a state of being ("I am," "You are," "He/She/It is"…). When conjugating "to talk" we didn't say, "Me talk…Him/Her/It talks, Us talk…Them talk," not only because that would have sounded silly and child-like, but because we knew that those personal pronouns, as used, are functionally illogical; they are not subjects but objects.

Objects receive action or are acted upon, such as "She likes me" (the object of her liking) or "I praised them," (the object of my praise), or "I split the money between us" (object of the preposition "between") or "She sent the invitation to my wife and me" (compound object of the preposition "to"). Already having a 50%/50%, either/or chance of choosing correctly—I or me? who or whom?—we shouldn't really have much difficulty learning what's correct.

In English, every personal pronoun and noun functions in one of two ways grammatically in sentences, either as a subject or as an object, because every person, place, or thing in the world can cause action and also can receive action or be acted upon, or can exist exclusively in a preposition's explanation of where ("in town") or when (by midnight"), how ("with passion") or what ("for peace"). In the sentence "Bob teaches classes," Bob is a subject or doer of the action "teaches," whereas in "Students appreciate Bob," Bob is the receiver of an action or the person acted upon, the object of the students' appreciation. Using a place rather than a person as a subject, we can write, "Central Park displays beautiful landscape architecture"; Central Park as an object might be, "I enjoy Central Park," the object of my enjoyment.

Below is a list of the personal pronouns in English and how they are used:

PERSONAL PRONOUN	SUBJECT	OBJECT	POSSESSIVE
First Person Singular	I	Me	My
Second Person Singular	You	You	Your
Third Person Plural	They	Them	Their
	Who(ever)	Whom(ever)	Whose(ever)

Later we will discuss possessive words and how to formulate them when a noun requires an apostrophe to show possession or ownership, but first we need to think further about the objective use of pronouns. Look at the pronouns listed below the heading "Object": me, you, him/her/it, us, you, them. Notice that if I am writing or talking about myself, then I use "I" as a subject ("I love my wife") but "me" as an object ("My wife loves me"); both words refer to the same person—one person, a singular person, Bob Davis—but the pronouns change if their function in a sentence differs, depending on whether that singular person, Bob, is performing an action ("I love my wife") or is receiving an action or is acted upon ("My wife loves me"). That's very straightforward, and most native speakers of English have no difficulty instinctively distinguishing between subject and direct object personal pronouns.

However, native speakers too frequently don't use the objective case properly when an object is the "object of a preposition." Every preposition in English must have an object and must answer at least one of these questions: when (time); where (direction, location, or source); how (manner or way); or what. In English, sometimes the same preposition can express different ideas when used in different contexts, but invariably it must have an object: "Will he arrive by midnight?" (when); "His exit ramp is by the concession stand" (where); "He will arrive by taxi" (how). The preposition and its object (above, the objects are "midnight," "the concession stand," and "taxi," respectively) become a prepositional phrase.

There are over 150 prepositions in the English language, but the following four groups contain the most common prepositions. Important for understanding other grammatical and syntactic principles, recognition of these prepositions will be easy if you read the list a few times; do that, noting that some prepositions are either two or three words, and realizing that a preposition alone makes no sense without an object—either a noun or a pronoun—to go with it:

    a. Often answering the question "When":
    b. after, as of, at, back to, before, beyond, by, during, from. . .to . . ., near, over, past, prior to, since, subsequent to, toward, until, up to, within

c. Often answering the question "Where":
d. above, across, against, ahead of, along, alongside, amid, among, apart from, around, at, atop, back to, before, behind, below, beneath, beside, between, beyond, by, down, excluding, far from, from, in, inside, inside of, into, near, near to, next to, off, on, onto, opposite, out from, outside, outside of, over, through, throughout, to, toward, underneath, up, up to, upon, within
e. Often answering the question "How":
f. according to, against, along with, apart from, around, as well as, because of, between, by, despite, except, excepting, for, from, in addition to, including, instead of, like, minus, opposite, out from, pursuant to, regardless of, unlike, up to, via, with, without,
g. Often answering the question "What":
h. about, as regards, concerning, for, instead of, minus, of, over, regardless of, with, without

Writers have no difficulty using a noun as the object of a preposition; choose any preposition from the preceding lists, and you'll find it easy to think of a noun that accompanies it, such as "among friends," "before dinner," "with foresight," "about politics," "of importance," "near noon," "after the debate," "from here," "to eternity," "beneath the sun," "on target," "at Target," " "like a paramecium," "under the microscope."

With pronouns as objects of prepositions, however, confusion still prevails in the U.S.: stylistic selection rather than logic informs most people's choices for what's "right and wrong." Instead of just understanding the language's requirements, and why whatever we use is right or wrong, Americans yield instead to value-brandability for how they think speakers and writers want to sound and should sound and write. Unfortunately, and too frequently, the sound of grammar is a speaker's or writer's determining criterion for correctness. "Marianne invited my wife and I to dinner" sounds very formal, and whatever is very formal would seem to be very correct, so of course it must be correct, yes? No, not correct. In fact, the two objects of Marianne's invitation are "my wife and me," or "me and my wife," or, if combined, "us." Notice that the first-person plural object, "us," combines "my wife and me"; therefore, if we were to combine "my wife and I" into a plural pronoun, then we would have to use the plural subject "we," or "Marianne invited we to dinner." Here, however, sound suddenly loses its grip on correctness: if we can say "Marianne invited my wife and I to dinner," then we should be able also say that she "invited we to dinner." Nah, we all know that it's "invited us to dinner," so, if we know that, then why don't we simply split the plural object "us" into the two singular objects it represents, "my wife and me," and write in full, "Marianne invited my wife and me to dinner"?

Further, let's consider the possibility that Marianne didn't invite my wife to dinner.

In that case, having eliminated "my wife," would you be willing to say "Marianne invited I to dinner"? I bet you wouldn't. You'd say, "Marianne invited me to dinner," correctly using the object "me," the object of Marianne's invitation. So what makes you think that "I" is correct with "my wife" when you definitely would say "me" by itself, in the singular? Any object can be either singular ("me") or plural ("my wife and me"). Whatever reason you may have heard or explained to yourself to justify phrasing such as "Between you and I," or "Marianne cooked dinner for my wife and I," or "The host greeted Joan and I" is wrong.

Taking this error one step further, people now are inclined to retain "I" in its possessive form. Recently I heard a man say on television, "My wife's and I's complaint was neglected," when speaking of the couple's report to an agency. Obviously he was talking about "my" complaint, not "I's," but again the sound of "I" seems to have been the determining factor for his grammar, not logic.

Properly using either a subject or its object form can be guaranteed by the following rule: all subjects must have a verb, because subjects either must be doers of an action ("He sleeps"; "The horses gallop") or can exist ("I am"; "She is"; "There were possibilities"). Consequently, it is incorrect to say "Me and my friends went to the movies," because "Me" is an object and because the past-tense verb "went" requires a subject, in this case "I"; therefore, the sentence should be "I and my friends went" or "My friends and I went," or, if the friends didn't go, then simply "I went." You wouldn't say "Me went to the movies."

Further applying the rule that all subjects must have a verb, we always will know when to use "who," which is a subject, or "whom," an object. In the sentence "She is the student who[m] won the election," we must choose "who," because the verb "won" requires a subject: "She is the student who won the election." In the sentence "She is the student who[m] I enjoy most in the class," we must choose "whom," because there is no verb for "whom," which is functioning as the object of my enjoyment: "She is the student whom I enjoy most in the class." Notice that in each sentence "student" is being replaced either by the pronoun "who" or by "whom"; called relative pronouns, "who" and "whom" relate two original sentences that can be combined, so that we might originally have written "She is the student. I enjoy her most in my class," with "her" being the object of my enjoyment. When we combine or relate those two sentences, the pronoun replacement for "student" must therefore be "whom," whereas the subject "who" replaces the student when we relate "She is the student. She won the election."

Used illogically, pronouns also can confuse a sentence's meaning. If I tell you, "My father told my uncle that he was beginning to bald," we never can know for sure whom "he" refers to. Called an ambiguous pronoun, "he" in that sentence can refer either to father or to uncle. To correct it, we can write either "My father told my uncle that he, my uncle [or my father], was beginning to bald," or "My father told my uncle, 'You are [or I am] beginning to bald.'" Also containing an ambiguous pronoun is the sentence "The SUV crashed into the pine tree, but luckily it wasn't damaged." What wasn't damaged, the SUV or the pine tree? It might seem that the sentence intends "it" to stand for "The SUV," but very possibly the writer is an eco-friendly tree-hugger or botanist whose priority interest is trees, not SUVs. Here's an additional sentence with an ambiguous pronoun: "Having removed the receipt from the plastic bag, Joan threw it in the garbage." The receipt or the bag? A writer's intentionality is irresolvable when a pronoun is ambiguous, so don't assume that your readers will know for sure what you mean.

A pronoun also will confuse a sentence's meaning when its reference is vague. With a vague pronoun reference, the pronoun is supposed to refer to someone, somewhere, or something that "comes before," its "antecedent"; however, the antecedent doesn't actually exist earlier in the sentence. In the sentence "When Senator Fretwell toured South America, they gave him a cold welcome," the plural pronoun "they" is vague. To whom does it refer? To South Americans, of course, but "South Americans" doesn't exist earlier in the sentence and therefore cannot be replaced by "they." In this case a writer must say. "When Senator Fretwell toured South America, South Americans gave him a cold welcome," or, if it wasn't all South Americans, then the writer should be more specific: "When Senator Fretwell toured South America, the urbanites of Argentina and Chile gave him a cold welcome." Here's a sentence with another vague reference: "Although John is intelligent, he never uses it." Because "intelligent" is an adjective (a quality, not a thing), the pronoun "it" cannot take its place; pronouns replace only nouns, so the corrected sentence should be "Although John is intelligent, he never uses his intelligence [or his brain]." Similarly, in the sentence "As John approached the hornet's nest, one flew directly toward him," we assume that "one" refers to a hornet; however, according to the sentence's expressed logic, "one" can refer only to "nest," because the possessive "hornet's" is an adjective and cannot be restated by a pronoun.

Possessive words in English are adjectives, expressing the quality of ownership or possession characterizing a noun, such as "Bob's essay" or "The man's essay" or "His essay." What's the quality of the essay? "Bob's," "The man's," or "His."

Let me restate that whenever a noun or pronoun shows possession—shows ownership, shows that something belongs to it—it automatically becomes an adjective, which is a quality or characteristic of that noun or pronoun ("Bob's class"; "my class"; "New York City's skyscrapers"; "its skyscrapers"; "this essay's grammatical principles"; "its grammatical principles"; "the woman's profession"; "her profession"). In the Romance languages—principally Spanish, French, Italian, Portuguese, Romanian—there is no possessive apostrophe; instead, those languages use the prepositional phrase "of . . ." (prep phrases are either adjectives or adverbs) to show ownership, for example "the wife of Bob" instead of "Bob's wife," or "the purpose of any mystery" instead of "any mystery's purpose." English developed the possessive apostrophe for simplicity; with English we can say, "the dog's tail's fur's knotted tufts" instead of "the knotted tufts of the fur of the tail of the dog."

Knowing how to use the possessive apostrophe correctly is simple, so long as you are able to determine in the first place that a word shows possession. Basically, to show possession, we take the original noun—"the student" (singular), "the students" (plural), "a bus" (singular), "the buses" (plural)—and then add the apostrophe to convert the noun into a possessive adjective: "the student's essay" (= the essay of one student), "the students' demands" (= the demands of more than one student), "one bus' passengers," and "the buses' routes." Because in English we usually add "s" or "es" to make a noun plural ("students," "buses"), the distinction between singular and plural possessive is easy to formulate. However, a few plural English nouns do not end in "s" or "es," in which instances we again add the apostrophe and "s" to the original plural noun: men's toiletries, women's clothing, children's toys, teeth's cavities, criteria's stipulations, geese's feathers.

Unlike possessive nouns, possessive pronouns do not require an apostrophe: my, mine, your, yours, his, her, hers, its, our, ours, their, theirs. Note that "its" is the possessive form of "it," such as "the bicycle doesn't have one of its pedals" or "the dog chased its tail"; with the apostrophe, "it's" is a contraction for "it is" or "it has," and there is no word in English spelled "its'."

There are two other rules regarding pronoun usage that you may want to know, although these rules generally remain only in formal writing. Granted, you may find that using these principles of logic sounds awkward, but that's because you may not be accustomed to hearing what's logically correct.

The first rule applies to subjective or objective pronouns and nouns used in comparisons. When using "as . . . as" and "than" to compare two (pro)nouns, be certain that both parts of the comparison are in the same case, both of them subjects, or both of them objects. Just as apples and oranges are two separate categories of fruit and therefore can't be fairly compared, so in the sentence "My father is as tall as I" the comparison's first half, a subject (which must have a verb, "father is"), requires that the second half also be a subject, in this case "I"; basically, we are saying that "My father is as tall as I am tall" or "…as I am." Although you might be inclined to say or write, "My father is as tall as me," the object "me" can't be compared logically with the subject "My father." Similarly, we would write, "She knows more about politics than he [knows about politics] [does]," not "She knows more about politics than him." Another example comparing subjects is "Yes, we're aware of the altercation that the Smiths had with their crazy next-door neighbors, the Joneses, but we believe that the Smiths are as crazy as they [are crazy]." Comparing objects is simpler, because we're accustomed to doing that accurately: "I like Pete better than him" is correct, because two objects are being compared, the direct object "Pete" and the objective pronoun "him."

The other formal logic-based rule for pronouns that you should remember concerns subjective-complement pronouns linked by forms of the verb "to be." When used by itself, "to be" is a "linking verb" in any tense (am. is, are // was, were // will be, would be // has been, had been); as a link, it establishes a subjective case equality ($X = Y$, or $Y = X$) between the subject and the pronoun linked to it. Called a "subjective complement," the word on the right side of the equation complements or adds information to the subject. Linked, both sides of the equation are equal and interchangeable.

Consider this use of the subjective complement: "For ten years, I have seen Dr. Phillip Drew as my primary-care physician." Then, I write, "He is my only doctor" ($X = Y$) or, if I prefer, $Y = X$, "My only doctor is he." Logically, "My only doctor is him" does not work. This same grammatical principle applies to situations with whose sound you may be familiar: ding-a-ling-a-ling, "Is Bob there?" "This is he [$X = Y$], speaking."

You may prefer not to apply these rules of logic when you speak, because conversation is a medium different from writing. However, when you write publicly, you want to be certain that you are following grammar's rules—and, again, there aren't that many rules—to guarantee that your prose is logical and not confusing.

Essay 9

Eliminating Wordiness, Eleven Simple Strategies

Writers often must explain their reports, critical analyses, and proposals within required spatial limits or word counts: journalists are allowed X-# of column inches to report their story; newspapers specify allowed lengths for editorials from the public; full-page magazine advertorials are allowed possibly 250 words to accompany their page's photographs; professional fundraisers usually have less than one page to convince their public to donate money to a cause; writing contests or competitions, college application essays, and professional cover letters explicitly or implicitly suggest page or word lengths; academic writing assignments often stipulate a maximum number of pages, possibly with 12-point Times New Roman font, and 1½" margins. Sometimes these requirements exist to set a standard within whose limits everyone must be comparatively evaluated, sometimes they're simply as much space as money can afford or an executive consensus wants, and sometimes they intend to impose conciseness.

Less can be more—fewer words can say more—when writers are thorough yet concise, by which we mean "free from superfluous detail." If a sentence is a flowered garden of thought, then eliminating wordiness and repetition is like removing weeds, the cluttering and useless vegetation which can starve the flowers' purposeful roots and detract from their stand-alone beauty. For the sake of my discussion here, let's assume—

and this is a very realistic assumption—that using strategies for eliminating wordiness (along with "sentence combining," in the next essay) will enable you to remove from your writing at least one word per line, without any compromise to the quality of your content. Let's also assume, again for the sake of this discussion, that you are writing a five-page report or essay. Each page has twenty-five lines, times five pages, for a total of 125 lines, thus 125 words eliminated from the original text. Because a standard typed page has between 250 and 300 words, 125 eliminated words allows you to gain free space of 40-50% of an additional page, perhaps for a conclusion with livelier thought in it, or for further development of a paragraph's topic whose investigation you hadcut back, or to add detailed evidence for argumentative proof throughout the essay. In effect, nearly a half-page of additional space provides numerous opportunities for strengthening your work's content. And it's free. And with practice it's easy to achieve.

Before the next essay discusses "sentence combining" as a way to eliminate repetition, I want to examine eleven single strategies here that help all of us to avoid wordiness in our phrasing. Operating from a larger theoretical base, "sentence combining" invites us to use possible clauses and phrases to help integrate and arrange an idea's parts, about a dozen separate options. *The Writer's Options*. 1982, the first published book explaining and exercising how "sentence combining" benefits writing's content, organization, and style, offers diverse and deep consideration of combining's multiple benefits. But no matter how we pursue combining, we must understand that it requires thinking about a whole idea's component parts, about the logistical variables when arranging those parts informatively, coherently, and transitionally, and about the stylistic enhancements from the combined sentence's resulting rhythmic syntax. Each of the following eleven strategies, however, works on its own, a single method which by itself helps to identify wordiness and whose benefits will come naturally with practice and visual attention to details. None of these strategies by itself is overly difficult to learn; it's when we try to remember to apply all of them simultaneously that we may become overwhelmed. So let's look at them one at a time and then consider how to use them advantageously when we edit.

1. **MAKE A SENTENCE'S SUBJECT PLURAL INSTEAD OF SINGULAR WHENEVER THAT SENTENCE'S GENERAL MEANING WILL REMAIN THE SAME**

Most singular common nouns—persons, places, things—acting as a sentence's subject require an article: "a," "an," or "the." We don't say, "Editor requires," so we add an article: "An editor requires . . ." Not "Bonfire burns," instead we say, "The bonfire burns." The point here is that each singular noun requires an additional word, an article, whereas plural common noun subjects don't, yet still retain the sentence's general idea. In place of "An editor requires" we can write, "Editors require . . ." Instead of "A plaintiff is entitled," it can be "Plaintiffs are entitled." Instead of "Hardy believes that a debt owed must be repaid," it's "Hardy believes that debts owed must be repaid." Instead of "A journalist is allowed X-#," I wrote at this essay's beginning, "Journalists are allowed X-# . . ."

2. **CHANGE ADVERBIAL PREPOSITIONAL PHRASES INTO SINGLE-WORD ADVERBS ENDING IN "-LY"**

Prepositional phrases function either as adjectives or adverbs. As adverbs they usually describe a verb, as in "paints *with passion*," "lives *in style*," "knows *from instinct*," or "saves *day by day*." What kind or quality or characteristic of painting, living, knowledge, and saving is answered by the adverbial prepositional phrase? Just be sure that your conversion from the adverbial prepositional phrase to the "-ly" adverb preserves your sentence's logical intention: it does work with "paints passionately," "lives stylishly," "knows instinctively," and "saves daily"; however, sometimes the "-ly" replacement may not accurately convey the psychology or physicality that the prepositional phrase does, as with "marches at attention" replaced by "marches attentively," so be your own best judge of appropriateness when you apply this strategy.

3. **CHANGE ADJECTIVE PREPOSITIONAL PHRASES SHOWING OWNERSHIP OR POSSESSION—PHRASES USUALLY USING "OF . . ."—INTO SINGLE WORDS USING THE POSSESSIVE APOSTROPHE**

The Romance languages—Spanish, French, Italian, Portuguese, Romanian—do not use a possessive apostrophe and therefore must show possession or ownership or belonging usually by using the prepositional phrase "of . . ." Instead of "Bob's house," the French must say or write, "La maison *de* Robert." Instead of "Isabel's clothes," the Spanish must say or write, "La ropa *de* Isabel." German, to show possession, attaches the genitive suffix without an apostrophe, as do the Finno-Ugric languages, which include Hungarian. .Obviously this isn't a big deal, since all languages can express possession regardless of form; however, realities represented by language symbolism sometimes indicate multiple possession, as for example "The Senator's wife's press agent's grammar's inaccuracies," which unfortunately in a Romance language must be "The inaccuracies of the grammar of the press agent of the wife of the Senator" (15 words → 8 words); in cumbersome situations such as that, clearly it's preferable to use the English possessive apostrophe.

    a. Not all phrasing adds to the meaning *of a sentence*. → Not all phrasing adds to a *sentence's* meaning. (10 → 8)
    b. The purpose *of plot* in any story is to structure the understanding *of all readers*. → *Plot's* purpose in any story is to structure all *readers'* understanding. (15 → 11)
    c. The interruption *by the referee* impeded the fight *of the boxers*. → The *referee's* interruption impeded the *boxers'* fight. (11 → 7)

4. **USE SINGLE-WORD VOCABULARY ("SELF-CONCEPT WORDS") TO EXPRESS THE SAME MEANING AS NEEDLESS PHRASING DOES**

Sometimes, using phrases to define what a single word means can contribute to wordiness; when possible, replace those phrases by their single-word vocabulary, a self-concept word, which itself expresses your idea.

    a. The accountant must *put all of* the receipts *together*. → The accountant must *assemble* the receipts. (9 → 6)
    b. The team *makes the most of* its skills when it works as a group. The team *maximizes* its skills when it works as a group. (14 → 11)
    c. *Purposefully determined not to be harsh or strict*, the judge sentenced the defendant to a year of community service instead of *putting him in jail*. → *Resolutely lenient*, the judge sentenced the defendant to a year of community service instead of *incarceration*. (25 → 16)

Over five hundred self-concept words are listed at http://alexandriaes10.lausd.k12.ca.us/Staff_Pages/Henry_Anker/Lesson_Plans/acrostic_adjectives.pdf. Just reading the list will familiarize you with how to think about and to apply this principle for eliminating wordiness.

5. **ELIMINATE UNNECESSARY DETERMINERS AND MODIFIERS**

Writers sometimes stuff their prose with extra words or phrases that seem to add to a sentence's meaning but actually don't. Although such words and phrases can be meaningful in the appropriate context, they often are used as "filler" and easily can be eliminated.

a. Any *particular type of* dessert is fine with me. → Any dessert is fine with me. (9→ 6)
b. Balancing the budget by Friday is an impossibility without *some kind of* extra help. → Balancing the budget by Friday is impossible without extra help. (14 → 10)
c. *For all intents and purposes,* American industrial productivity *generally* depends on *certain* factors that are *really* more psychological *in kind* than technological. → American industrial productivity depends more on psychological than technological factors. (22 → 10)

6. **DON'T OVERUSE EXPLETIVES AT A SENTENCE'S BEGINNING**

Expletives are phrases using either the form "*It* + conjugated *to be*" ("It is" or "It was" or "It will be") or the form "*There* + conjugated *to be*" ("There are [or is]" or "There were [or was]" or "There will be"). Such expressions in some situations can be rhetorically effective for emphasis, but often they are useless. In the sentence "*It is* imperative that we find a solution," the expletive is useful. Although the same basic meaning could be expressed more succinctly with "We must find a solution," the expletive construction allows the writer to emphasize the situation's urgency with the word *imperative*. Still, you generally should avoid excessive or unnecessary use of expletives.

The most common kind of unnecessary expletive construction involves an expletive followed by a subjective complement ("It is the governor . . . ") and then a relative clause beginning with *that, which,* or *who* ("*It is* the governor *who* sent me a thank-you."). In most cases, you can create a more concise sentence by eliminating the expletive opening, making the noun ("governor") the subject of the sentence, and eliminating the relative pronoun ("The governor sent me a thank-you.").

a. *There were* many factors *that* affected the situation. → Many factors affected the situation. (8 →5)
b. *It is* the governor *who* signs or vetoes bills.→The governor signs or vetoes bills. (9→ 6)
c. *There are* four rules *that* should be observed:→Four rules should be observed: (8 → 5)
d. *There was* a big explosion, *which* shook the windows, and people ran into the street. → A big explosion shook the windows, and people ran into the street. (15 → 12)
e. *It is my belief that* learning grammar is useful. → I believe learning grammar is useful. → Grammar is useful. (9 → 6 → 3)
f. *It was* Mary *whom* I nominated for the award. → I nominated Mary for the award. (9 → 6)

7. CHANGE UNNECESSARY RELATIVE CLAUSES INTO PHRASES

Using a relative clause to convey meaning that could be presented in a phrase or even one word contributes to wordiness.

a. The report, *which was released recently,*… → The recently released report (6 → 4)
b. I am subscribing to *Coilhouse, which is* an alternative magazine devoted… → I am subscribing to *Coilhouse,* an alternative magazine devoted…(11 → 9)
c. All students *who are interested in the job* must… → All students interested in the job must . . . (9 → 7)
d. The system *that is most efficient and accurate* → The most efficient and accurate system (8 → 6)

8. WHEN APPROPRIATE, USE ACTIVE RATHER THAN PASSIVE VERBS

Every sentence has a verb, usually an action of some kind. Every verb must have a subject, the doer of that action. Using the "active voice" means that the doer of the action is identifiable and actively functions as the subject. In "Ben assigned the project," we know that Ben is the subject enacting or doing the assigning. However, were we to use the "passive voice" and write, "The project was assigned," we lose the actual doer of the action; "Ben" no longer exists in the sentence. Thus, the passive voice transvalues the active sentence's direct object, "the project," by converting it into its sentence's subject; now, the actual subject, "Ben," either is eliminated altogether or becomes the object of a preposition ("The project was assigned *by Ben*"). Note that the verb in all passive constructions has a helping verb—an additional word—before the participle ("*was* assigned [by someone]" or "*is* spoken [by someone]" or "*will be* purchased [by someone]" or "*had been* stolen [by someone]").

   a. Your figures *were checked by* the research department. → The research department checked your figures. (8 → 6)
   b. The ball *was thrown by* George. → George threw the ball. (6 → 4)
   c. *It was mentioned to* Alan that he might be excused. → Alan heard he might be excused. (10 → 6)
   d. *Yesterday it was brought to the awareness of* our department that travel will be on a per diem basis. → Our department learned yesterday that travel will be on a per diem basis. (19 → 13)
   e. An account *was opened by* Mrs. Simms. → Mrs. Simms opened an account. (7 → 5)

9. REPLACE CIRCUMLOCUTIONS BY USING DIRECT EXPRESSIONS

Circumlocutions, or roundabout expressions, take several words to say what can be said more succinctly. We often overlook circumlocutions because many such expressions are habitual *figures of speech* from business, advertising, and law. In writing for conciseness, though, you should avoid them, since they add extra words without extra meaning. For rhetorical effect you occasionally may decide to use a circumlocution, so please consider these guidelines as recommendations, not as absolute rules.

Here are some common circumlocutions that you can compress into just one word. Circumlocutions are in the left column, while their more direct equivalents are in the right:

despite the fact that
notwithstanding the fact that   →   although
regardless of the fact that

being as		
being that		
due to the fact that	→	because, since, why
for the reason that		
owing to the fact that		
in light (or view) of the fact that		
on account of		
on the grounds that		
the reason why is because		
considering the fact that		
the reason for		
for the reason that	→	because, since, why
at such time as		
on the occasion of		
in a situation in which	→	when
under circumstances in which		
during the time that	→	while
at the present time		
at this point in time	→	now
if it should happen that		
in case		
as to whether	→	if
if conditions are such that		
in the event that		
provided that		
it is crucial that		
it is critical that		
it is necessary that	→	must, should
there is a need/necessity for		
it is important that		
cannot be avoided		
is able to		
has the opportunity to	→	can
has the capacity for		
is in the position to		
has the ability to		
is capable of	→	can

be in a position to possible that		
there is a chance that it could happen that the possibility exists that	→	may, might, could
considered to be happens to be has been proved to be is found to be serves the function of being	→	is
so as to in order to for the purpose of	→	to
a majority of a preponderance of large numbers of significant amounts of a sufficient amount of	→	most, many, enough
along the lines of not dissimilar to	→	like
by means of	→	by
as regards in reference to with regard to concerning the matter of where _____ is concerned	→	about
in proximity to in the neighborhood of in the vicinity of	→	near
manner in which	→	how
in many cases	→	often
in many instances	→	often
in most cases	→	usually

| in no case | | |
| in no instance | → | never |

| there can be little doubt about | → | likely, probably |

10. OMIT REPETITIVE WORDING OR REDUNDANT PAIRS

Many pairs of words imply each other. The phrase *completely finished* is redundant in most cases, because *finish* implies *complete*. The phrase *scratchy in texture* also is redundant, because scratchy IS a *texture*.

Nouns Modified by Adjectives

actual experience	advanced planning
basic fundamentals	close proximity
competent manner	damaged condition
each individual	end result
final outcome	free gift
future plans	large size
major breakthrough	most unique
past history	past memories
personal opinion	sudden crisis
terrible tragedy	total sum
true facts	unexpected surprise
various differences	

Prepositional Phrases

at an early time	close in proximity
general consensus of opinion	few in number
heavy in weight	honest in character
in a confused state	of cheap quality
rate of speed	red in color
rough in texture	round in shape
shiny in appearance	visible to the eye

Verb Phrases

appear to be	assemble together
cancel out	continue on
cooperate together	lie down
penetrate into	prioritize in order of importance
progress forward	refer back
return back	separate out
split apart	stand up
start over again	watch over

Modifying Phrases
each and every

Watch for phrases or longer passages in your writing in which you repeat words with similar meanings.

a. During that *time period*, many buyers preferred cars *that were pink in color and shiny in appearance.* → During that time, many buyers preferred *pink, shiny cars*. (17 → 9)
b. Before the travel agent was *completely able to finish* explaining the *various differences* among *all of the many very unique* vacation packages his travel agency was offering, the customer changed her *future plans*. → Before the travel agent finished explaining the differences among the unique vacation packages his travel agency was offering, the customer changed her plans. (33 → 23)
c. The microscope revealed a group of organisms *that were round in shape and peculiar in nature.* → The microscope revealed a group of *round, peculiar organisms*. (16 → 9) → And how important is "a group of"? (16 → 9 → 6)

11. <u>AVOID NOMINALIZATIONS</u>

Use verbs when possible rather than noun forms of those verbs, known as *nominalizations*, which, if used, require you to add a replacement verb. Many English nouns originate as verbs: "commitment" comes from "commit"; "appearance," from "appear"; "discovery," from "discover"; "decision," from "decide"; "failure," from "fail." Practice transforming nominalizations into action verbs, to create more engaging prose and to eliminate at least two words:

a. Defense counsel *made an objection* to the question asked by the prosecution. → Defense counsel *objected* to the prosecution's question. (12 → 7)
b. I *have a suspicion* that she will not attend. → I *suspect* that she will not attend. (9 → 7)
c. This note *is a reminder* to you that the essay is due. This note *reminds* you that the essay is due. (8 → 5)
d. Remember that this advice *is an expression of* my concern for your future. → Remember that this advice *expresses* my concern for your future. (13 → 10)
e. *To get an assessment of* his abilities, I tested him. → *To assess* his abilities, I tested him. (10 → 7)
f. A sentence's length *must be in accordance with* the life of its idea. → A sentence's length *must accord with* the life of its idea. (13 → 11)
g. They did not *give an explanation for* the fire. → They did not *explain* the fire. (9 → 6)
h. The surgeon *will perform an operation* later today. → The surgeon *will operate* later today. (8 → 6)
i. *Make a decision about* what you want to do. → *Decide* what you want to do. (9 → 6)
j. The professor *provided students with an indication of* what's important. The professor *indicated to students* what's important. (10 → 7)
k. The group's *failure was the result of the chairman's resignation*. → The group *failed because the chairman resigned*. (10 → 7)
l. *My intention is to give an illustration of* how to eliminate wordiness. → *I intend to illustrate* how to eliminate wordiness. (12 → 8)
m. Tonight, Lady Gaga will *give a performance* at the club. → Tonight, Lady Gaga *will perform* at the club. (11 → 9)

Most nominalizations end with the following letters:

- **-ANCE** (e.g., acceptance, allowance, appearance, avoidance, compliance)
- **-ENCE** (e.g., coherence, insistence, persistence)
- **-ERY** (e.g., delivery, discovery, recovery)
- **-MENT** (e.g., accomplishment, acknowledgement, arrangement)
- **-NESS** (e.g., blessedness, happiness, homeliness, resourcefulness,)
- **-SION** (e.g., admission, conclusion, discussion, emission, erosion)
- **-TION** (e.g., acquisition, calculation, characterization, communication)
- **-URE** (e.g., disclosure, exposure, failure)

To practice eliminating wordiness, use a short, maybe one- or two-page text that you've written in the past, and review it. First, choose just two of the eleven strategies discussed here. With both in mind, look exclusively for their particular kind of wordiness; practicing with a limited set of two skills will enable you to restrict your focus and to find it easier to detect your wordiness. Next, do the same thing by using another two strategies, and so forth. The first few times you do this will require additional patience, but in short time, through focused reinforcement, you naturally will avoid adding needless noise to your pure thoughts.

Essay 10

Sentence Combining

Encouraging writers to allow different clauses and phrases to play their working parts in sentences, sentence combining considers and actualizes four necessities of sentence structure: elimination of repeated subjects or objects and of wordiness caused by implied repetition; a clearer, improved vision—literal vision and intellectual seeing—of what an idea's or image's functional parts are in a sentence; strategic, logical arrangement of those parts in the sentence's body, so that how you organize and engineer those parts creates an optimal information architecture and so that your reader doesn't have to piece those parts together; and, an auxiliary benefit of those first three improvements, enhanced syntactic style.

First, sentence combining eliminates not only needless repetition of subjects or objects, but also wordiness caused by implied repetition. Frequently, side-by-side sentences use the same subject: "Jim is my neighbor. Jim is a banker." = "Jim, my neighbor, is a banker." or "Eloisa has an advanced degree in finance. She works at a Midtown corporation." = "Having an advanced degree in finance, Eloisa works at a Midtown corporation." Frequently as well, an object in a first sentence becomes the subject of the next: "I like Jim. Jim is my neighbor." = "I like Jim, my neighbor." or "I placed the candelabra on the piano. The piano now looks formal." = "I placed the candelabra on the piano, which now looks formal." Sometimes, in side-by-side sentences we state similar ideas that don't require restating: "He began the trek home. The distance was three miles." Here, "distance" already is implied by "trek" and by "three miles," so those two sentences = "He began the three-mile trek home."

Second, sentence combining helps you, the writer-educator, to identify in your mind the essential, related parts of one idea or one visual image, parts which if disconnected into separate sentences must be pieced together by your readers rather than by you, the educator; don't allow your readers to educate themselves. Consider the following example, written here in five sentences: "The membrane helps make DNA. DNA is a substance of nucleotides. The substance contains information. The information is necessary for all things to reproduce. The things are living." Although it's not likely your writing's structure allows that much repetition, it is likely that sometimes you may not realize that you are disconnecting related points of information that will attain full, cohesive meaning only when combining occurs: "The membrane helps make DNA, a substance of nucleotides containing information necessary for all living things to reproduce." Reducing the original five sentences' twenty-eight words to the combined sentence's eighteen, without any loss of meaning, sentence combining also integrates logically all of the idea's parts into an understandable whole. Sentence combining thus provides a genuine intellectual service by freeing your reader, as a reader, not only from having to start and stop and start and stop and so on, but also from repeatedly tripping over the dead weight of repetition, and then having to assemble the intellectual puzzle laid out in a series of sentences,

Third, then, is the assembly or organization of the sentence. Because sentence combining requires that you be familiar with the grammatical purpose and structure of different clauses and phrases, you'll be better able to think about how and where to position the parts of a sentence's idea. Keep in mind that the parts of a sentence's idea also must be organized according to a governing logic and strategy; some organizations are better than others, especially when you must present an idea's component parts in their best educational order. Depending on your intentions, your emphasis of an idea may occur at the sentence's beginning or, conversely, at its end: "Having won many dance competitions, Ronen and his partner are famous tango artists." OR "Ronen and his partner are famous tango artists, having won many dance competitions." The first sentence prioritizes the winning of dance competitions, while the second prioritizes the couple's famous tango artistry. But then you realize you should incorporate a third section in that sentence's intellectual structure: "Ronen and his partner's style is perfectly matched." You might combine the sentences this way: "Having won many tango competitions, Ronen and his partner are famous dance artists, their style perfectly matched." OR "Their style perfectly matched, Ronen and his partner are famous tango artists who have won many dance competitions." And certainly there are other arrangements you might prefer. For the moment, just remember that every sentence ought to be its own living organism: as a complete body, each sentence contains a set of parts whose information's organizational structure you must think carefully about.

Fourth, sentence combining improves your sentences' style by making you use different kinds of sentence structures. All clauses and all phrases contain their own particular rhythmic energies; varied and juxtaposed rhythms can yield interesting and appealing sentences, which improves style. Sentence combining's benefit here is that you don't even have to think about enhancing style; the varied rhythms will come on their own, because they are what they are and will give a separate syntactic vitality to each sentence.

I hope it's clear that sentence combining is a serviceable intellectual process and not about creating long cumbersome sentences just to make them seem weighty; instead it's about the intellectually supervised and concise best presentation of ideas and images. Keep in mind that long sentences aren't a problem and probably won't even seem long if their information is managed. Conversely, a "run-on" isn't about length but about not knowing when to stop your sentence. Concise 100-word sentences exist, and run-on 15-word sentences exist.

Every sentence has a main idea to whose body a writer adds or appends related parts, intellectual outgrowths providing greater meaning to the main idea. Generally, we place a sentence's main idea or most central part in its independent clause, which is the sentence's stand-alone structure or main body; to that, we can and almost always do add appendages. In fact, most sentences have just two to four words in their independent clause or main body of thought; all else grows from that. In the thirty-five word sentence "On Tuesday afternoons, for three hours, Bob teaches a class exclusively about grammar's logical requirements and stylistic variables to both international and American students who are interested in learning to manage the English language precisely," only four words are the independent clause: "Bob teaches a class." Everything else in the sentence grows out of and is attached to that clause's words' meanings. Take any other clause in the sentence ("who are interested") or any phrase ("On Tuesday afternoons," "to manage . . ."), and it will make no sense on its own, because its logic is seeded in and grown from the independent clause.

In advance, therefore, writers should determine what and where they want a sentence's main idea to be. For example, assume that you will write a sentence that combines these four ideas:

1. My sister is a renowned editor.
2. She is highly skilled with language.
3. Her talents extend beyond words.
4. Her talents are diversified.

Do you want to emphasize a) the sister's job as editor? b) her skill with language? c) her diversified talents other than those linguistic? If a), her job as an editor, then the combined sentence might be this: "My sister is a renowned editor highly skilled with language, although her diversified talents extend beyond words." If b), her skill with language, then this: "A renowned editor, my sister is highly skilled with language, although her diversified talents extend beyond words." If c), her talents other than those linguistic, then this: "My sister has diversified talents other than those linguistic, despite being a renowned editor highly skilled with language."

As a), b), and c) illustrate, whatever we place in the independent clause gives greater independence to that part of an idea, because the independent clause is the only part of the sentence that can stand on its own. All other structures—other clauses and all phrases—are subordinate to or dependent on the existence of the independent clause, or main body of the sentence.

Sentence combining will be easier for you if, when it's possible, you avoid the habit of always making your subject the sentence's first word. Sometimes, of course, we want our subject to be the sentence's first word—but not always. For example, in the sentence "Mandy, mud-covered and shivering, sat at the table, where she sipped hot chocolate," the subject comes first, then is described, and next receives its verb with an adverbial prepositional phrase from whose object, "table," grows a dependent clause ("where . . ."). Although the sentence is acceptably constructed, you may want to rearrange its information not only to make the sentence less choppy (multiple commas can chop up a sentence), but also to emphasize Mandy's condition—especially if Mandy already has been introduced in preceding sentences: "Mud-covered and shivering, Mandy sat at the table, where she sipped hot chocolate." In that combined sentence the independent clause, "Mandy sat at the table," is not an especially important point of information; however, containing the subject and object to which the other information is attached, it is the most central and only autonomous part of the sentence, thus allowing dependent growth around it.

This idea of a sentence's parts' placement requires us to be certain that every sentence is "context sensitive." Because a context is a passage's entire meaning, every sentence's intellectual purpose and structural arrangement of information will depend on the context—the larger or surrounding meaning—in which it is located. When we write, our documents express a series of contexts based on concepts and theories, facts and information, scenes and images, so we always first must think of the context in which all individual sentences sit, and then decide the order in which to lay out that sentence's information. Also think of a sentence's context sensitivity with this in mind: except for the first and last sentence in any document, all other sentences are transitional, growing out of what precedes them and developing into what follows them. To guarantee that each sentence's transitional "flow" is maintained, you will want to organize it so that its beginning reflects something about the former sentence and its end anticipates the next one.

Assume that you have a conceptual term—"analytical cubism"—which requires this long definition: "an early twentieth-century art movement which, as a philosophical reaction against fixed views of nature, analyzes people and spatial objects in basic geometric parts and then depicts them from multiple and mixed perspectives." Unlike the example describing Mandy, above, here it will be an intellectual problem to place this hefty definition at the sentence's beginning if your readers have no idea what you're talking about in the first place. In that case, the sentence will be better if you place the subject first, this way: "Analytical cubism, an early twentieth-century art movement . . . , was created by Pablo Picasso and Georges Braque." However, if contextually your preceding sentences already have introduced the subject of analytical cubism, then the reader can connect the already-identified term with your next sentence's immediate definition of it: "An early twentieth-century art movement . . . , analytical cubism was created by Pablo Picasso and Georges Braque."

As with paragraphs, sentences must provide an intellectual organization of parts so that their sequencing is coherent and structured to educate, providing the best possible system delivering information. How an idea is organized can make its presentation more persuasive, too. Which of the following three sentences do you think is most persuasive?

1. "Television reporters, often evaluated by their facial attractiveness, are pawns in the ratings game."
2. "Often evaluated by their facial attractiveness, television reports are pawns in the ratings game."
3. "Pawns in the ratings game, television reporters often are evaluated by their facial attractiveness."

Most of us would agree that the first sentence is the least persuasive, because it prioritizes or gives dominant focus to the subject, "Television reporters," and thus de-emphasizes, in steps, the facial evaluation and the sentence's claim that these reporters are "pawns." More persuasive, the second sentence begins with a phrase that prioritizes the facial evaluation but still buries the aspect of "pawns." The third, however, begins with the most salient, most percussively ("p") harsh word in the sentence, "pawns," and then lets us know who those pawns are and why they are pawns. You may disagree with my reasoning, and context sensitivity may require reformulation, but your disagreement nevertheless illustrates that a sentence's organization is open to options and that you as the person who best knows your intentions can write the sentence according to your own priorities.

    My guiding strategy here is that you shouldn't assume your sentence is complete after first having written out its idea's parts; you may have expressed all of those parts, but they aren't necessarily expressed in the way you want your reader to understand your idea best as a whole. Sentences also require codified thinking, and sentence combining is an excellent way to help you achieve that.

    I want you to learn and experience sentence combining, but in one essay I must limit the theory and the practice I can provide. If you think sentence combining can benefit your writing and if you want more than what I've included, then I encourage you to pursue any of the books cited here[1], books whose discussions extend beyond those I provide. What I do provide, however, are useful syntactic structures with which you may not be familiar or still may need more introductory explanation. Because I can define and identify each structure only by using "parts of speech"—noun, pronoun, verb, adjective, adverb, preposition, conjunction—you may want to refer to Essay #3 for clarification of them.

Dependent Clauses
    All clauses and therefore dependent clauses must have a subject and a verb with tense. However, the dependent clause cannot stand on its own, as its name suggests, because its logic depends on the completed logic of an independent clause; as such, any dependent clause is an incomplete sentence or sentence fragment. If I were to say to you, "Although I read," a clause because it has a subject ("I") and a verb with tense ("read"), you still would anticipate and be poised for the remainder of my information; the subordinating conjunction "Although" subordinates that clause, placing it on a 'sub-' or 'lower' level and making its logic dependent on additional information.

    Dependent clauses are important to know for sentence combining because their subordinating conjunctions signal specific intentions of logic. As soon as we hear a subordinating conjunction—most commonly, after, although, as, because, before, even though, if, since, though, unless, until, when, whereas, while—we know what intent the sentence's logic will pursue. Obviously indicating time are after, before, since, until, and while (these also can function as prepositions). Suggesting an exception to something are although, even though, though, and while. Alternatives and contrasts are most clearly indicated with whereas. Unless expresses exceptional circumstances. Hypothetical and speculative situations are signified by if, and causes or explanations by as, because, and since.

When you read the following examples using the most common subordinating conjunctions, notice that the dependent clause can occur at a sentence's beginning, at its end, or in its middle:

a. "After I went shopping, Jeff came to my apartment."
b. "Our buzzer rang persistently, although I have no idea who rang it."
c. "As you learn more, you realize how much there is to know."
d. "I will work hard on your behalf, because I like you."
e. "I will prepare dinner before my wife comes home."
f. "Even though participating in a triathlon is demanding, Phil commits to doing it."
g. "If you want to succeed in life, be a good person."
h. "He's been consulting since he lost his permanent job." ("since" as time)
i. "Since polar icecaps are melting, oceans are rising." ("since" as cause)
j. "The referee knows that this player is not a sportsman."
k. "[Al]Though I'm a Yankees fan, I sometimes still root for the Boston Red Sox."
l. "I'll stay, unless you want me to go."
m. "Until I hear to the contrary, I'm staying."
n. "The weather, when conditions are dry and not too hot, is agreeable."
o. "South Korea is a republic, whereas North Korea is a totalitarian dictatorship."
p. "While Nero fiddled, Rome burned."

Relative Clauses

Frequently used by writers, relative clauses must have one of English's five relative pronouns: who, whom, that, which, or whose. Like all other kinds of pronouns, the relative pronoun restates a noun; however, the relative pronoun is able to relate its new clause's information and logic to the preceding clause containing the restated word.

who   (relates to a person and functions as the relative clause's subject)
a) "He's the person who gave me money." (= "He's the person. He gave me money.")
whom (relates to a person and functions as the relative clause's object)
b) "He's the person whom I like." (= "He's the person. I like the person /him.")
that   (relates to a place, thing, or common-noun person ["teacher," "student," "superintendent," "nurse"] either as subject or object)

      c) "The Left Bank is an interesting part of Paris that [OR which] I enjoy staying in." (= "The Left Bank is an interesting part of Paris. I enjoy staying in that part of Paris.")

---Note: the relative clause "that I enjoy staying in" ends with a preposition. If you need to write more formally, change "that" to "which" and write, "in which I enjoy staying." We cannot put a preposition in front of the relative pronoun "that": "The Left Bank is an interesting part of Paris in that I enjoy staying."

      d) "Do you see the statue that [OR which] Rodin sculpted?" (= "Do you see the statue? Rodin sculpted the statue / it.")

      e) "He's the man that [or whom] I most admire." (= "He's the man. I most admire the man / him."]

which (relates to a place or thing)

      f) "Paris is the European city which I love most." (= "Paris is the European city. I love Paris / it most.") (Note: restrictive construction)

      g) "Paris's architecture, which I admire, is visually compelling." (= "Paris' architecture is visually compelling. I admire Paris' architecture / it ." (Note: non-restrictive construction)

whose (relates to a person, place, or thing in its possessive form)

      h) "Amy, whose ability to play the violin is excellent, recently auditioned at The Juilliard School." (= "Amy recently auditioned at The Juilliard School. Amy's [Her] ability to play the violin is excellent."

      i) "The Juilliard School, whose president is Joe Polisi, attracts some of the world's finest cultural performers." (= "The Juilliard School attracts some of the world's finest cultural performers. The Juilliard School's / Its president is Joe Polisi.")

      j) "Less than ten years old is the Juilliard Jazz program, whose student body is small in quantity but large in quality." (= "The Julliard Jazz program is less than ten years old. The program's / Its student body is small in quantity but large in quality.")

You'll notice that relative clauses can't occur at a sentence's beginning, because they restate something that comes earlier. These clauses are especially useful when their pronoun has its own verb in the clause: "She bought a used car. The car performs extremely well." = "She bought a used car, which performs extremely well."

Participial Phrases (Ongoing Action OR Completed Action)[2]
      All participles are called "verbals," which means that the participial word expresses the action of the verb it comes from but does not function as a verb; instead, it's always an adjective—a quality, characteristic, or kind of a person, place, or thing.

Gerunds, which always end in "-ing," and infinitives, which precede a verb with "to," also are verbals, but they won't require a formal lesson here since most writers seem to have mastered these structures' use, by instinct, by behavioral conditioning, or by a combination of both. Whether you use the gerund-noun ("Writing requires hard work") or the infinitive-noun (To write requires hard work") as a subject, or as an object ("I like eating" or "I like to eat"), the actions of "write" and "eat" are retained, even though both verbals in those sentences are a noun, specifically a thing.

Two kinds of participles exist: the progressive or ongoing action, which always ends in "-ing" ("stimulating lecture" as a single word; "Gesticulating with his hand, he hailed the waiter" as a phrase) and the completed action, which ends most commonly in "-ed" ("divided nation"), "-n," ("blown glass"), "-en" ("frozen yogurt"), and "-t" ("kept letters"). Participial phrases used in sentence combining are particularly advantageous when we want to convey an action inherent in our adjective or adjective phrase, and when we also need to describe the status of that action as still ongoing or completed.

  To understand participles more fully, we should look first at actual verbs that contain them. If we write or say, "I am laughing today" or "I was laughing yesterday" or "I will be laughing tomorrow," the "laughing" part of the verb, which is the participle, expresses the ongoing nature of the laugh, regardless of when it occurs; in fact, it does not occur in time, because "laughing" has no tense. When it occurs is indicated by the "helping verb" or "auxiliary" part of the verb—"am," "was," "will be"—which gives tense or time to the participle's ongoing laughter. Every verb must have tense, which is why the past, present, or future indicator in the verb "helps" the verb attain time. But when we remove "laughing" from its helping verb or auxiliary, then it loses time, becoming instead an adjective. There's a cheese named "The Laughing Cow" (what kind of cow, her quality? laughing). In a participial phrase, "laughing" might be used in "Laughing with Jon Stewart, the audience appreciated the senator's gaffe," where it's a quality and characteristic of the audience, or in "I ignored the student laughing in the back of the class," where it's a quality or characteristic of the student. Taking any verb that comes to mind, I'll add the progressive participial "-ing" to it and then use it first as a single-word adjective, next as the basis for a phrase: "inquiring minds" and "Inquiring about Antonio's marriage to Melanie, the reporter asked the press agent for details"; "waltzing Matilda" and "Waltzing with my wife in Melbourne, I felt very nineteenth-century"; "winning Olympian" and "I felt pleased for the Americans winning Olympic medals"; "sitting duck" and "The pianist, sitting erect but relaxed, began the concerto." Using the following single-word completed-action participles for assistance, write sentences with completed-action participial phrases (e. g., "Increased to offset higher city taxes, our monthly maintenance fee is like a second mortgage"): "increased inflation";

"inflated increases"; "known variables"; "spun straw"; "chosen contender"; "forgotten candidates"; "spilt [or spilled] milk"; and "burnt [or burned] toast." Keep in mind that participles are adjectives and, because of that, express the quality of an appropriate person, place, or thing. English's completed-action participial endings are diverse[3], so you may want to review some of them.

When you combine sentences using participial phrases, there's one additional fact you must know. Let's assume that to eliminate repetition and to integrate two parts of one idea we should combine "Ellen walked into the gym, with optimism. She enjoyed working out." How do you get to use a participle when there is no participle in the original two sentences? Take either of the past-tense verbs, "walked" or "enjoyed," and convert it into an ongoing, "-ing" participle, either "walking" or "enjoying." Making one of the verbs an adjective that expresses ongoing action is not a problem, because tense—in this case, past tense—still remains in the verb kept in the independent clause and thus indicates that the entire sentence occurs in the past: ""Enjoying working out, Ellen walked into the gym, with optimism." OR "Walking into the gym, with optimism, Ellen enjoyed working out." And I've placed a comma between "gym" and "with optimism" because optimism characterizes not the gym but Ellen.

When we don't need to convert a verb with tense to its "-ing" ongoing-action participle, then for participial phrases we just drop the helping verb from one of the original sentences: "Pilates was created for World War I veterans who needed physical therapy. Pilates now is taught at most fitness centers." Notice that both sentences' verbs have helping verbs plus a participle—"was created" and "is taught"—which will allow you to choose either for conversion into your participial phrase: "Created for World War I veterans who needed physical therapy, Pilates now is taught at most fitness centers." OR "Now taught at most fitness centers, Pilates was created for World War I veterans who needed physical therapy." How you organize this sentence's two parts depends on what you want to emphasize and also the purpose—exercise history? what contemporary gyms usually include?—of your paragraph's larger context within which this sentence occurs.

To further identify single-word participles and also participial phrases, look at the italics in the following passage: "Walking down the paved sidewalk ["paved" is a completed-action participle within the ongoing-action participial phrase], Jim saw a young woman dancing on the street corner ["dancing on the street corner" is the adjectival characteristic of "woman," a direct modification, so we use no comma]. As if blown by a gentle breeze, she undulated her body, her arms like two leaves swirling slowly through the air. Mesmerized by her own dance and seemingly by the accompanying music in her head ["accompanying" is an ongoing-action participle within the completed-action participial phrase], she never ceased for the entire time she was within Jim's view. Most passersby, like Jim, pleased by her pleasing innocence ["pleasing" is an ongoing-action participle within the completed-action participial phrase], just went about their business as the self-preoccupied young woman continued to gyrate.

Appostive Phrase

An appositive is a noun phrase that provides defining information about a noun or pronoun. Meaning "in the position next to," apposition requires the appositive phrase to sit directly before or after the noun or pronoun it defines. The appositive phrase is easy to use, so long as we remember to use it. For example, here's a possible set of sentences requiring combining: "Bob Davis is explaining appositives. He is an author of essays about writing." Noticing that the second sentence restates "Bob Davis" with the pronoun "he," we can eliminate "he" and the necessary verb that every subject requires, in this case "is"; that then leaves us with "an author of essays about writing," a noun phrase—"an author . . ."—defining who Bob Davis is. In effect, combining the original two sentences by using an appositive could produce, "Bob Davis, an author of essays about writing, is explaining appositives." OR, if we want to position the defining appositive before "Bob Davis," we could write, "An author of essays about writing, Bob Davis is explaining appositives."

Appositives can occur anywhere in a sentence—beginning, middle, end—because nouns and pronouns can occur anywhere in a sentence and, wherever placed, may require definition. Let's assume that we begin again with "Bob Davis is explaining appositives" but then realize that it will be useful for readers to know what appositives are. Instead of repeating "Appositives" and that subject's required verb—"Bob Davis is explaining appositives. Appositives are noun phrases that provide defining information about a noun or pronoun."—we can place the definition directly after the direct object that it's defining: "Bob Davis is explaining appositives, noun phrases that provide defining information about a noun or pronoun."

It's worth repeating that if the noun or pronoun to be defined is a subject at the sentence's beginning, then its definition will be at the sentence's beginning or in its middle, directly after the subject: "A chef, John serves coq au vin" OR "John, a chef, serves coq au vin." If the noun or pronoun to be defined is a direct object at the sentence's end, then its definition will be at the end: "John serves coq au vin, a French braise of chicken cooked usually with Burgundy wine and mushrooms." We can use appositives to define any object of a preposition, too, regardless of where it's placed: "She is studying at Cornell, a northern New York university." or "In New York City, capital of the world, productivity never ceases and the city never sleeps." or "She enrolled for Macroeconomics II, an advanced seminar in global economic models, as the final course of her curriculum."

Be confident that you may use more than one appositive if two of a sentence's nouns or pronouns need to be defined: "For Valentine's Day, I gave to my wife, Izzy, the perfect gift, a heart-shaped necklace." OR "I gave to her, my wife, a heart-shaped necklace, the perfect gift for Valentine's Day."

Absolute Phrase

Its structure unusual, an absolute is the least frequently used phrase in written English, although you may not find it that unusual if "Its structure unusual"—itself an absolute phrase—seemed and sounded acceptable to you. A significantly useful structure, the absolute is the only phrase that has its own subject; implied, its verb doesn't explicitly exist and so the absolute cannot be a clause and must be a phrase. The meaning of the absolute's subject always relates logically to the main clause, usually particularizing one aspect of the main clause's more general announcement; that occurs in this paragraph's first sentence, whose main clause's subject is "an absolute" and whose absolute's subject is "structure," a particular aspect of an absolute.

In the short article "The 'Absolute' Advantage" (The Writer, V. 119, Issue 2, February 2006), Arthur Plotnick reminds writers of the stylistic and functional value of the absolute phrase. Stylistically, using an absolute "offer[s] a lyrical way to vary sentence structure" (15), notes Plotnik, who adds that "When editors see absolutes used competently, they are reassured that the writer has a feel for sophisticated, economic writing" (15). Functionally, "Absolutes often contain the real headlines of a sentence . . . because the device provides such a condensed, telegraphic way of imparting the news" (15-16).

Following an absolute's subject will be one of five possible structures, four of them functioning as adjectives—regular adjective, ongoing-action participial phrase, completed-action participial phrase, and prepositional phrase—and one as a subjective complement.

As seen in all of the italicized absolutes illustrated in the following examples, absolute phrases require you either to delete the existing form of the verb "to be" or, if the verb isn't a form of "to be," to change that verb to its ongoing-action participial form. That, then, leaves a subject followed by one of the four adjectival options or a subjective complement.

1. Regular Adjective

   a. "The news dreadful, I stayed home."
   b. "Joan threw down the newspaper, her frustration total."
   c. "Ex-President Bill Clinton had a quadruple heart bypass a few years ago, the outcome of his surgery successful."
   d. "Its structure the least familiar to you, an absolute is the only phrase containing its own subject."

2. Ongoing-action Participle

   a. "His head nodding every three seconds, Ed was nearly asleep."
   b. "Many runners have been unable to finish the Boston Marathon, their strength diminishing on Heartbreak Hill."
   c. The power of the Chinese economy, its global growth developing from cost-effective productivity and capitalist incentives, already is having a significant international impact—and will continue to, because China has over two billion people.

3. Completed-action Participle

   a. "All things considered, I don't think I'll buy that stock."
   b. "The subject of an absolute, its meaning related to that of the main clause, is followed by one of four adjectival possibilities or a subjective complement."
   c. "Toni Morrison, her Nobel Prize for literature given in 1993, is without doubt one of the world's best novelists."
   d. "Strategies are reviewed, product promotions determined, potential story ideas considered, and target media outlets identified."

4. Prepositional Phrase

   a. "The entire department against my goals, I feel as if I must leave the corporation."
   b. "His head in the clouds, Bob wandered through the streets of Manhattan."

c. "The homeless man, his shivering body without an overcoat, always makes me sad."

5. Subjective Complement (form of "to be" as a linking verb is dropped)
   a. "His mind a tornado of unrest, Jim couldn't think straight."
   b. "Tessa was getting ready for dinner, her dress a designer rip-off that looked as good as the original."
   c. "The geology professor, his expertise in strata formations, taught students about the core of planet Earth."

For additional examples of all five kinds of absolute phrases, go to this chapter's end.[4]

The two clauses (dependent and relative) and the four phrases (ongoing-action participle, completed-action participle, appositive, and absolute) presented here are different from one another in three ways: their intellectual purpose, their syntactic or structural function, and their rhythmic or stylistic identity. Practicing with these structures will help you to differentiate among them, to recognize instinctively which one(s) will satisfy your immediate needs, and to incorporate them correctly into your combined sentence. Let's work with an example, which I'll walk you through:

   a. A man in my building is unfriendly.
   b. He lives on the ninth floor.
   c. His attitude is belligerent.
   d. His negative attitude is a trait apparent to everyone around him.

Immediately we notice that a) and b) are about "a man" and c) and d) are about "His attitude." Both sets contain repetition, so first we'll combine a) and b), then c) and d). Remembering that a sentence's independent clause usually contains the sentence's most important or at least most essential information, we realize that a) is more important and that b) is incidental information that we can combine with a). We also realize that the information of c) and d) develop from "unfriendly" in a), which therefore logically connects the end of a) with c) and d). To combine the leftover b) with a), we can turn b) into an adjective phrase characterizing "A man," which will allow us to eliminate the repetitious pronoun "He." Of the four phrases presented here, only the ongoing-action participle will work as an appropriate adjective, so we can turn the verb "lived" into a verbal (the "-ing" ongoing-action participle): "Living on the ninth floor, a man in my building is unfriendly . . ." Because c) and d) have a new subject, "His attitude," we will have to use an absolute phrase, the only phrase that has its own subject, being certain to eliminate "is" (the form of "to be") in both sentences and thereby making them phrases: "his belligerent attitude a trait apparent to everyone around him." Notice that I chose to eliminate "negative," since "belligerent" is negative, as is "unfriendly" in sentence a). Now we can piece together what remains: "Living on the ninth floor, a man in my building is unfriendly, his belligerent attitude apparent to everyone around him." As always, you may opt for a different syntactic arrangement of information. Is the juxtaposition of "unfriendly" and "belligerent" a good strategy of reinforcement, or would you prefer to keep those two words separated? Would you opt to retain "negative," for the sake of further emphasis? How important is the ninth floor? Might it be better placed at the sentence's end? Please remember that sentence organization, like paragraph organization, like essay or report or memo organization, is not a matter of simple right and wrong; instead, it's about better and worse, which means that writing well requires us to think about the context within which the sentence sits and then to organize that sentence's parts for premium logical and educational value.

If you're willing, take a look at another example of combining, which as above I will explain fully:

a. I really care for my dog.
b. My dog is a mixed beagle and spaniel.
c. I walk her in the park.
d. In the park she gets exercise.
e. Her name is Muffet.

Looking at these five sentences, we see that there are different parts belonging to one controlling subject, "my dog.... My dog ... her ... she ... her name." Combining will help to unite these parts and, as always, to eliminate repetition, but first we must establish the sentence's governing logic and then its independent clause. As always, there is no right or wrong way to do this, rather one's own governing priorities. I've decided that there is a causality here, or a cause/effect relationship: I walk Muffet in the park because I really care for her. Therefore, I'm going to begin my sentence with a dependent clause whose subordinating conjunction is "Because": "Because I really care for my dog..." Next, notice that "My dog" is defined in sentence b) as "a mixed beagle and spaniel." Defined? An appositive, which functions as a noun phrase, is what we use to define another noun, in this case "my dog," so now we have "Because I really care for my dog, a mixed beagle and spaniel..." Yet another definition of "My dog" comes in sentence e), where we learn that her name is Muffet. If I want to, I can put all of my defining information together: "Because I really care for my dog, Muffet, a mixed beagle and spaniel..." By doing this, I can eliminate "Her name is." Having now arrived at c) and d), we see that both of those sentences are about "the park"; therefore, eliminating the repetition, I can add the prior dependent clause and appositive to the sentence's independent clause: "Because I really care for my dog, Muffet, a mixed beagle and spaniel, I walk her in the park for exercise." Notice I've changed "where she gets exercise" for the much simpler but still understandable "for exercise"; however, I also could have written, "I walk her in the park, where she gets exercise," adding another dependent clause to the independent clause. Also, had I preferred not to place "Muffet" next to "a mixed beagle and spaniel," I could have substituted her proper name for the pronoun "her": " . . . beagle and spaniel, I walk Muffet in the park for exercise."

Again, it's important to remember that you have options when you combine and that those options depend on your own priorities for the sentence's organization. So long as your syntax is structured logically, you should feel free to create each sentence according to what you decide is the best educational and persuasive sequence of information. For further practice, try combining into one sentence each cluster of sentences identified by a capital letter in the footnote section at this essay's end.[5]

REFERENCES

[1] Here are three useful books about sentence combining:

Altman, Pam and Mari Caro, Lisa Metge-Egan and Leslie Roberts. Sentence-Combining Workbook, 3rd Ed. Beverly, MA: Wadsworth Publishing, 2010.

Morenberg, Max and Jeff Sommers. The Writer's Options: Lessons in Style and Arrangement, Edition 8. New York: Longman, 2007.

Strong, William. Sentence Combining: A Composing Book, Edition 3. New York: McGraw-Hill Companies, Inc., 1994.

[2] Although participles do not have time (they require a helping verb to give them time), standard grammatical terminology refers to them as either a "present participle" or a "past participle." I find this illogical and misleading, so I refer to the "present participle"—e.g., "believing," "thriving," "talking," "helping"—as "ongoing action" and the "past participle"—e.g., "dimpled," "broken," "grown," "spent"— as "completed action." Remember: the participle's "action" isn't the action of a verb but that of a verbal, in this case an adjective.

[3] Here are some of English's irregular and commonly unknown completed action participles:

to abide → abode, abided	to leave → left
to arise → arisen	to lie (recline) → laid
to awaken → awoken	to lie (be untruthful → lied
to begin → begun	to ride → ridden
to bite → bitten	to ring → rung
to bleed → bled	to seek → sought
to break → broken	to sell → sold
to buy → bought	to sing → sung
to catch → caught	to sink → sunk
to choose → chosen	to speak → spoken
to creep → crept	to speed → sped
to drink → drunk	to spin → spun
to eat → eaten	to stand → stood; under-; with-
to fight → fought	to swear → sworn
to find → found	to sweep → swept
to flee → fled	to swim → swum
to fly → flown	to swing → swung
to forget → forgotten	to think → thought
to freeze → frozen	to weep → wept
to get → gotten	to win → won
to hold → held	to wind → wound
to keep → kept	to write → written
to lay → laid	
to lead → led	

⁴   All of the absolute phrases below are shaded in gray. Each absolute's subject is italicized but not boldfaced. Each specific adjective or subjective complement following the absolute's subject is italicized and boldfaced. Notice that each absolute phrase can become a full sentence if you add a form of "to be," either as a helping verb or as a linking verb (e.g., #1 below = "her voice was hollow in the stairwell"); however, to save words and to join related parts of the same idea, we preferably can delete the form of the verb "to be," thus creating an absolute phrase.

I've taken these absolutes from three novels: Dan Brown's The Da Vinci Code*, Toni Morrison's Paradise**, and Pete Hamill's North Shore***.

Noun + Standard Adjective

"I'm going back up," Sophie declared, her voice hollow in the stairwell.*

The room is messy, its bed invisible under a hill of clothes.**

For twenty minutes they traveled, Soane cautious at every rise or turn of the road.*

His hand clumsy with sleep, he lifted the black telephone on the night table.***

McNiff laughed, his teeth brown and splintery.***

A hundred yards ahead, the intersection was blocked by a couple of DCPI police cars, parked askew, their purpose obvious.*

The agent's head tilted to one side, his skepticism evident.*

They were silent through most of the meal, the food too delicious for chatter.***

The clicking of Teabing's crutches approached in the hallway, his pace unusually brisk.*

Noun + Ongoing-Action Participle

Langdon reacted with surprise, his excitement over the code giving way to a sudden ripple of concern.*

Heart racing, Sophie ran to the woodshed and got the spare key her grandfather kept hidden under the kindling box.*

She also saw the bloody cilice around his thigh, the wound beneath it dripping.*

The back room was warmer, radiators knocking with steam heat.***

The man advanced, his white fists gripping the iron stand.*

The wife stood over a washtub in the yard, wisps of hair irritating her forehead.**

Outside the window, the glass pyramid shone, its reflection rippling in the windswept pools.*

. . . two crystal glasses sat beside an opened bottle of Perrier, its bubbles still fizzing.*

"My Teacher is very wise," the monk replied, inching closer, the gun shifting between Teabing and Sophie.*

Collet wheeled, anger brimming.*

Noun + Completed-Action Participle

Inside were two thick stacks of bonds, each embossed with the Vatican seal . . .*

Sophie deleted everything they had just typed in and looked up at Langdon, her gaze self-assured.*

Most of the space was taken by Delaney's Arrow bicycle, its pedals and gears wrapped tightly in oiled cloth.***

Vernet was taking dead aim, standing on the ground behind the rear bumpter, his gun outstretched into the cargo hold now.*

She smiled in an odd way, then swung the bat sharply through the air, upper teeth clamped over her lower lip.***

Noun + Prepositional Phrase

Box in hand, Langdon moved across the hold to the open door.*

Delaney sat in the old worn chair by the fireplace, the pages of the letter on his lap.***

Carlito stopped walking, the snow near his knees, and watched. . . . Carlito blinked, his eyes like a camera shutter, as if freezing each new thing he saw into memory.***

On the floor above, two men walk the hall and examine the bedrooms, each with a name taped on its door.**

Delaney got off the El at Twenty-third Street, hurrying down the rickety steps, Carlito's bundle under his good arm.***

Steward waited at the piano, his steel-gray hair and innocent eyes in perfect balance.**

The woman stood beyond the gate, snow on her wool hat and shoulders.***

. . . Rose took her place at the table, her back to the yard.***

Noun + Subjective Complement

"Does this kid have a union card?" he said, his voice a growl.***

Then Frankie Randall came in, his face a pale yellow.***

"You got some pair of *****, coming here," Botts said, his mouth a slit.***

Compound Absolutes

Eyes closed, hips grinding, she circled her arms to enclose the neck of a magic dancer.**

The door opened and a pair of St. Vincent's interns came in, overcoats buttoned tight over green uniforms, their eyes frazzled and hungry.***

The young men were all smiling, perhaps preening, their suits pressed, their shoes glistening with polish.***

Rose was seated on her bed, back against the wall, her legs extended, big downy slippers on her feet, reading the Daily News and marking it with a red pencil. . . . Delaney watched the boy and glanced at Rose, her back to him, her waist more defined by the belt of the housecoat.***

[5] Experiment with sentence combining in each cluster of sentences that follows. Remember that each cluster should become only one sentence. Locate the repetition, examine the idea's parts, think about how best to organize those parts, and, if necessary, review this essay's discussion of dependent clauses, relative clauses, the two kinds of participial phrase, appositives, and absolutes. Take your time and be patient: as with all skills, sentence combining requires practice.

A)

1) The cooling northeast wind swept through our bedroom windows.
2) That happened almost every night in June last year.
3) The wind made air conditioning unnecessary.
4) It even required us to use a light blanket.

B)

1) Eleanor is successful.
2) Her success is as an entrepreneur
3) Eleanor now is CEO of her company.
4) The company is her own.
5) Eleanor began her company six years ago.
6) She began it with only two employees.
7) Now her company employs one hundred people.

C)

1) She was born in Atlanta, Georgia.
2) She now serves as the corporation's legal officer.
3) As legal officer, she investigates many marketing policies.
4) She was educated at Duke University.

D)

1) The Autobahn was built by Hitler to transport tanks and troops to Germany's borders in W.W. II.
2) The Autobahn is one of the world's finest highway systems.
3) The Autobahn sometimes is called "the crossroad of Europe."

E)
1) The bodies of the two wrestlers were glistening with sweat.
2) The two wrestlers struggled together.
3) Each of the two wrestlers was intent on victory.

ESSAY 11

EASILY CONFUSED OR MISUSED WORDS AND PHRASES

Grading students' essays and editing professionals' written English can reveal amusing errors in all categories of writing. Even misspellings can be innocently humorous. An irate student told me I was wrong to correct his spelling of "possess," which he'd written as "posses," because Spell-Check had accepted it; he didn't understand that what his computer recognized as a legitimately spelled word was the plural noun denoting a group of sheriff deputies, most commonly associated with America's late-nineteenth-century Wild West. A freshman college student recounted in a descriptive essay how he'd ripped his pants on a "Bob-wire fence." Beyond misspellings, lists of entertaining punctuation, grammar, and sentence structure errors fill books, journal articles, and Websites, and, because none of us is perfect, sometimes it's fun to see the troubles we inadvertently invite with language. Recently I found disseminated through the Internet this sign posted by a church: "Don't let worries kill you: let the church help."

But the purpose of serious educators and editors isn't to look for and to make fun of writers' errors; rather, knowing that language can be devious, we want to emphasize precision and to help eliminate tricks and confusions so that communication needn't be haphazard and can fulfill a writer's genuine intentions. Therefore, nothing cataloged that follows in this essay is or is intended to be about humor. A decades-long compilation, this alphabetized list is a serious endeavor, because I have witnessed and realize that its items are, through time, still the most commonly confused and misused English words and phrases. Misspellings, difficult verb tenses, illogical phrasing, non-existent words—yes, they may seem devious and certainly can be tricky, but there's nothing humorous about misapplying them.

accept / except
accept is a verb meaning "to agree to," "to adapt to," or "to receive":
    "Gabrielle needs to accept Xena's dark side."
    "This store has not accepted Canadian coins for five years."
except is a preposition or conjunction meaning, roughly, "unless" or "if not":
    "All Xena's enemies are men, except Callista."

affect / effect
effect is usually a noun that means a result or the power to produce a result:
    "The sound of the falling rain had a calming effect, nearly putting me to sleep."
affect is usually a verb that means to have an influence on:
    "His loud humming was affecting my ability to concentrate."

Note: as a verb, *effect* means to bring about or to execute:
    "The teacher's somber tone effected a dampening of the students' general mood."
    "Frank Lloyd Wright effected what architecturally is known as the Prairie Style."

all ready / already
all ready means that everything is ready:
    "The class is all ready for the test."
already means "by this time":
    "Joan already is seated at her desk."

    "Are you already all ready to quit?"

all right / alright
Although *alright* is widely used, especially in movie subtitles, it is nonstandard English. As the *American Heritage Dictionary* notes, it's "not all right to use alright."

all together / altogether
all together is applied to people or things that are being treated as a group:
> "We put the pots and pans all together on the shelf."

all together is the form that must be used if the sentence can be reworded so that *all* and *together* are separated by other words:
> "We put all the pots and pans together on the shelf."

altogether is used to mean entirely:
> "I am altogether pleased to be receiving this award."

allusion / illusion
allusion is a noun that means a direct or indirect reference to something else:
> "The speech made allusions to Shakespeare's *The Merchant of Venice*."
> "Perplexed about how to apportion his fortune in his will, the elderly CEO alluded to *King Lear*."

illusion is a noun that means a mental or physical misconception:
> "The policy is designed to give an illusion of reform."
> "They decorated the store to create the illusion of holiday festivity."

a lot
This isn't yet an acceptable, standardized spelling; use *a lot*.

altar / alter
altar is a table or stand upon which religious ceremonies are performed:
> "The minister ascended the steps to the altar, where the newlyweds stood."

alter means "to change":
> "Have you altered your diet to restrict the intake of bad carbohydrates?

alternately / alternatively
alternately is an adverb that means in turn, one after the other:
> "We alternately spun the wheel in the game."

alternatively is an adverb that means on the other hand:
> "You can buy a large bookcase or, alternatively, you can buy two small ones."

beside / besides
beside is a preposition that means next to:
> "Stand here, beside me."

besides is an adverb that means also:
> "Besides, I need to tell you about the new products my company offers."

between / among
between refers to what occurs with two people, places, or things:
> "There was a television ratings war between *Star Search* and *Survivor*."

among refers to what occurs with more than two:
> "Ivy League competition is intense among Princeton, Harvard, and Yale."

capital / capitol
capital is the city or town that is the seat of government:
> "The capital of the United States is Washington, D.C."
> "The capital of New York is Albany."

capital also can refer to an accumulation of wealth or to a capital letter:
> "I have decent capital, but that doesn't make me rich with a capital 'R.'"

capitol is the building in which a legislative assembly meets:
> "Television's *Boston Legal* sometimes showed the Massachusetts capitol building."

center on / revolve around
Both of the above phrases are proper usage. However . . .

. . . Logic tells us that it is *inconceivable to "center around"* anything; a center is *not* a circumference or perimeter, thus not around, but rather is the point equidistant from all sides or boundaries. Therefore, we *center on* singular points of interest, or our discussions or analyses *revolve around* them. Often, the distinction between the two phrases is a matter of degree: *center on* for one point, *revolve around* for more than one.

cite / site / sight
cite is a verb that means to quote as an authority or example:
> "I cited several eminent scholars in my study of water resources."

cite also means to recognize formally:
> "The public official was cited for service to the city."

cite also can mean to summon before a court of law:
> "Last year, the company was cited for pollution violations."

site is a noun meaning location:
> "They chose a new site for the factory just outside town."

Note: Don't forget *sight*, yet another spelling:
> "My sight tells me that this site is beautiful; I think I'll cite it in my book."

complement(ary) / compliment(ary)
complement is a noun or verb that means something that completes or makes up a whole:
"The red sweater is a perfect complement to the outfit."
"Complementing one another, the two angles are called complementary."
compliment is a noun or verb that means an expression of praise or admiration:
"She received compliments about her red sweater."
"The teacher was very complimentary about my essay."

connote, connotation / denote, denotation
connote is a verb that means to imply or suggest:
"The word 'espionage' connotes mystery and intrigue."
connotation is a secondary meaning, one that is implied or suggested but not literal:
"Two pejorative connotations of 'pig' are a sloppy eater and a policeman."
denote is a verb that means to indicate or refer to specifically:
"The symbol for 'pi' denotes the number 3.14159."
denotation is the literal meaning of a word, its first definition in the dictionary:
"The denotation of 'pig' is a barnyard animal that goes oink-oink."

council, councilor / counsel, counselor
councilor is a member of a *council,* which is an assembly called together for discussion or deliberation.
counselor is a person who gives *counsel,* which is advice or guidance. More specifically, a *counselor* can be an attorney or a supervisor at camp.

continual / continuous
continual means frequently repeated:
"The dog's continual yapping whenever it hears a noise is driving me crazy."
continuous means without any interruption:
"Writing improves from continual practice, but practice cannot be continuous unless you want to drive yourself insane."

data / datum
data is a Latin plural, like *curricula [-um], strata [-um], phenomena [-on].*
"The data are inconclusive; the phenomena were strange."

desert / dessert
desert is a dry, sandy place
dessert is the sweets we eat at the end of a meal

discreet / discrete
discreet is an adjective that means prudent or modest:
> "Her discreet handling of the touchy situation put him at ease."

discrete is an adjective that means separate or individually distinct:
> "Each company in the conglomerate operates as a discrete entity."

disinterested / uninterested
disinterested is an adjective that means unbiased or impartial:
> "We appealed to the disinterested mediator to begin the negotiations."

uninterested is an adjective that means not interested or indifferent:
> "They seemed uninterested in searching for an apartment."
> "My nephew is uninterested in my wife's stamp collections."

> "All effective judges must always remain distinterested but never uninterested."

e.g. / i.e.
e.g. means for example (from Latin *exempli gratia*):
> "Her talents are varied (e.g., deep sea diving, speed reading, bridge, and salsa dancing)."

i.e. means "that is" or "in other words" (from Latin *id est*):
> "The joy of my existence (i.e., my wife) imbues my life with meaning."

elicit / illicit
elicit is a verb that means to draw out, often to draw out a meaning:
> "They elicited from today's news the ongoing political confusion in Iraq."

illicit is an adjective meaning unlawful:
> "No matter how hard I tried to elicit a few scandalous stories from her, she kept all knowledge of illicit goings-on discreetly to herself."

farther / further
farther is used to express calculable, measurable distances:
> "We drove fifty miles today; tomorrow, we will travel one hundred miles farther."
> "From New York City, it's farther to Boston than to Philadelphia."

further means at a greater extent or degree and is used to express immeasurable distances:
> "We won't be able to suggest a solution until we are further along in our e valuation of the problem. The committee will consider the proposal further."

further also can mean in addition or moreover:
> "They stated further that they would not change the policy."

fewer / less
fewer is used with countable objects and must modify a plural noun:
>"This department has fewer employees."

less is used with objects of incalculable mass and modifies a singular noun:
>"Because the classroom has fewer students, there is less noise."
>"Less crime means fewer arrests."

>less hair, fewer strands; less money, fewer dollars; less nutrition, fewer nutrients; less rain, fewer drops; less music, fewer notes

foreword / forward
foreword is a noun that means an introductory note or preface:
>"In my foreword I explained my reasons for writing the book."

forward is an adjective or adverb that means toward the front:
>"I sat in the forward section of the bus."
>"Please step forward when your name is called."

forward is also a verb that means to send on:
>"Forward the letter to the customer's new address."

hanged / hung
hanged is the past tense and past participle of hang when the meaning is to execute by suspending a body from the neck:
>"They hanged the prisoner for treason."
>"The convicted killer was hanged at dawn."

hung is the past tense and past participle of hang when the meaning is to suspend from above with no support from below:
>"As I hung the painting on the wall, she hung the clothes to dry."
>"The painting was hung at a crooked angle."

healthy / healthful
healthy is a positive physical condition of someone or something alive:
>"All of Bill's children are healthy."
>"The growing tomatoes look healthy on the vine."

healthful promotes a positive physical condition:
>"Granola can be a healthful cereal."
>"Regular exercise promotes a healthful way of life."

(Technically, the brand name "Healthy Choice" is grammatically incorrect and ought to be "Healthful Choice," because choices cannot have health or be healthy.)

historic / historical
historic, in general usage, refers to what is important in history, while *historical* applies more broadly to whatever existed in the past—whether or not it was important:
>"An historic summit meeting between the prime ministers occurred."
>
>"Historical buildings torn down because of redevelopment, particularly those that have historic significance, can make me angry."

imply / infer
A writer or speaker *implies*:
>"The lecturer implied that the textbook is inadequate, although he said nothing explicitly negative about it."

A reader or listener *infers*:
>"The students were able to infer from the lecturer that the book is inadequate."

Noun forms are *implication* and *inference*.
>"His implication was negative; the class's inference therefore also was negative."

Adjective form of "imply" is *implicit*.

irregardless
Doesn't exist. *Both* "ir" and "less" mean "without," thus stating "without-regard-without," so that the prefix and suffix cancel out themselves. The correct word is *regardless*.

it's / its
it's is a contraction for *it is* or *it has*:
>"It's been a long time since I last saw you; it's a shame."

its is the possessive form of *it*:
>"Because the plan is good, it's troublesome to me that the company ignores its merits."
>
>"The dog chased its tail."
>
>"It's been a difficult month, but its difficulties are subsiding."

Note: *its'* doesn't exist.

lay / lie
lay means to put or to place; it must have an object:
> "The hen *lays an egg* today [present tense], *laid an egg* yesterday [past tense], and *has laid four eggs* this week [past participle, with helping verb]."
> "I *lay the book* on the table now, *laid it* there yesterday, and *have laid it* there many times before."
> "Now I *lay me* down to sleep . . . "

lie means to recline and cannot have an object:
> "I *lie down* today [present tense], *lay down* yesterday [past tense], and *have lain down* often [past participle]."
> "'Lie down,' he said to the dog." (*Not* "lay down.")

lead (v.) / led (past tense v.) / lead (n.)
lead means to show the way by going in advance; its past tense and past participle are
> *led*
> "'I will lead you to your seat,' the usher said. Then, she led me there."

lead, pronounced the same as *led*, is a metallic element:
> "Lead paint has caused poisoning."

lend / loan
lend is a verb
> "Can you *lend* me a quarter?"
> "I'm tired of *lending* [not loaning] you money."

loan is a noun, not a verb. A loan is the money lent.
> "I received a $5,000 *loan* from the bank."

loose / lose
loose means "not tight" and is an adjective:
> "His head's screwed *loose*!"

lose is a verb that means to misplace (e.g., a watch), to be defeated (e.g., a game), or to eliminate (e.g., weight):
> "I hate *to lose* any game I'm playing in."
> "Because I've been *losing* weight, my skin is *loose*."

oral / verbal:
oral means "by mouth"; therefore, when concerning words, whatever is oral can be heard:
> "She read her paper orally at home, just to hear how it sounded."
> "His dentist suggested a few lessons about oral hygiene."

verbal means "in words," whether or not the words are spoken:
> "Both oratory and writing are verbal forms of expression."

passed / past

passed is the past tense and past participle of *pass*:
> "I passed the test."
> "He passed me the football".

past refers to time gone by; it is also a preposition meaning beyond:
> "In the past decade, I passed over countless opportunities; I was determined not to let them get past me again."

premier / première

premier is an adjective meaning first in importance or status; chief; foremost

première is a noun and a verb meaning the first public performance, as a movie or theatrical production:
> "We attended tonight's première of Meryl Streep's latest movie."
> "Meryl Streep's latest movie premièred tonight."

principal / principle

principal is a noun that means a person who holds a high or major position or who plays an important role:
> "The school principal has twenty years of teaching experience."
> "As the investment's principal, she is undertaking a major task."

principal is a noun also meaning financial capital that is distinct from the interest derived from it:
> "Initially with just $2000 in principal, he managed to invest smartly and to earn himself large amounts of money."

principal is also an adjective that means chief, leading, or main:
> "The necessity of moving to another city was the principal reason I turned down the job offer."
> "I'm principally concerned about his behavior, not his appearance."

principle is a noun that means a rule or standard:
> "They refused to compromise their ethical principles."
> "On principle, I'm inclined to agree with her point of view."

renown / renowned
renown is a noun; *renowned*, an adjective
> "His renown among doctors is high." "His best-seller brought him high renown."
> "He is a highly renowned doctor."
> "Renowned for his best-seller, he became a frequent guest speaker."

rise / raise:
rise, rose, risen means to get up:
> "Every weekday morning I rise a 7 a.m., but yesterday I rose at 6 a.m. On the weekends, however, I have risen as late as noon."

raise, raised, raised means to lift up:
> "The principal raises the school's flag each morning. To him, it's an important principle."

roll / role
roll, as a noun, is a small piece of bread, a list of people in a group, or a cylindrical formation; as a verb, it denotes turning over and over:
> "Before she made the roll, she had to roll the dough."
> "Having just left the bank, his roll of cash was large."
> "I love to roll down the hill when it snows outside."

role is a part in a play or, more loosely, the function you perform in a certain group:
> "As head chef, it's my role to call the roll of employees before the bakers make the dinner rolls."

stationary / stationery
stationary is an adjective that means fixed or unmoving:
> "They maneuvered around the stationary barrier in the road."

stationery is a noun that means writing materials:
> "We printed the letters on company stationery."

than / then
than is a comparative term. Use it only when you're making a comparison between two or more things:
"I am shorter than over half of the world's adult male population."
"There are more cherries in my bowl than in Gabby's."
"She is better than I [am] at cooking." (see Essay #7)
then denotes a duration of time. Use it to indicate that something happens after something else, often with a cause-and-effect relationship:
"I explained the principle and then illustrated it."
then also is used in conditional statements (after "if" clauses):
"If A, then B."
"If a government proves itself to be despotic and tyrannical, then it is the people's right and duty to overthrow it."

their / there / they're
their is the possessive form of they:
"They demand their tax return."
there can be an adverb, adjective, noun, or pronoun, in all instances referring to place, stage, moment, and concrete or abstract point:
"I'll sit there."
"Stop there before you make any more mistakes."
"Pedro didn't agree with Yo-Der there."
"There are 1700-sf in her apartment. You will find 1700 sq. ft. there."
they're is the contraction of *they are*:
"They're going to Paris, and their mother insisted that they become familiar with French while there."

this kind / these kinds // that sort / those sorts
Without exception, the *singular* demonstrative pronouns *this* and *that* accompany the singular words *kind* or *sort*; the *plural* pronouns *these* and *those* go with the plural words *kinds* and *sorts*:
"This [or that] kind [or sort] of rule creates these [or those] sorts [or kinds] of syntactic constructions."

to try to
English speakers often mistakenly substitute "and" for "to" when expressing what they will try to do. Instead of "I am going to try *and* convince you to respect learning grammatical principles," the phrasing should be ". . . going to try *to* convince you . . ." In effect, you are performing not a compound action ("to try *and* convince") but a single one ("to try to convince"). The infinitive that expresses trying modifies/belongs to and is not separate from (or coordinated by) the other infinitive.

who's / whose
who's is the contraction of *who is* or *who has*:
    "Who's got the tickets?"
    "He is the candidate who's most likely to win."
whose is the possessive form of other relative pronouns:
    "Who's going to figure out whose job it is to clean the stables?"
    "Meet The Donald, whose Trump Towers continue to rise."
    "I recommend Paul, whose abilities I think are superior to all others'.
    "I'd like to purchase the coffee whose taste tastes like coffee."
    "Maura is searching for the zoo, whose animals are well tended."

-wise
Avoid the ugly attachment of "-wise" to make words adverbial, such as "behaviorwise" or "informationwise." In most instances, adding "-ally" will suffice ("behaviorally" or "informationally"). If the "-ally" construction cannot work (e.g., with "fashion" or "travel"), then revise your phrasing: "She knows a lot about fashion"; "They're as smart about travel as anyone we know."

your / you're
your is the possessive form of you:
    "Is that your coat?"
you're is the contraction for *you are*:
    "If you're planning on swimming, then be sure to bring your life vest and flippers."

In addition to the misspellings in the preceding list, the following words—correctly spelled here—often are misspelled:

accidentally	**judgment**
accommodate	**liaison**
acquire	**maneuver**
apparent	**medieval / Medieval (Middle Ages)**
argument	**memento**
calendar	**millennium**
category	**miniature**
changeable	**minuscule**
collectible	**mischievous**
committed	**misspell**
conscience	**noticeable**
conscientious	**occurrence**
conscious	**pastime**
discipline	**perseverance**
embarrass(ment)	**personnel**
exhilarate	**playwright**
exceed	**possession**
existence	**privilege**
fiery	**publicly**
gauge	**questionnaire**
grateful	**referred**
guarantee	**relevant**
harass(ment)	**schedule**
height	**separate**
ignorance	**sergeant**
independent	**supersede**
indispensable	**threshold**
inoculate	**weird**

Essay 12

Punctuating Points to Remember

Your Writing Well would be remiss without an essay about punctuation—for your writing well. But I don't intend to steamroll you with hundreds of rules; instead, I'll bring up only those logic-based principles of punctuation that I know most writers may not be aware of or fully understand and thus require explanation of. Some of those principles, for commas, are what I call "better safe than sorry rules," used with cases in which it's better to be safe by using the comma(s) than sorry by not using it (them), as my examples will illustrate. Also, I've found that most writers still need to learn when to include commas for non-restrictive logic, and when not to include them for restrictive logic; I'll spend more time explaining and illustrating that principle than any other, because it occurs so frequently yet may take time to make sense and "click." My final principle for whether or not to use a comma concerns coordinate and non-coordinate side-by-side adjectives. Other forms of punctuation, such as the semicolon, colon, and em dash, require thorough but simple clarification so that you can use them assuredly.

Punctuation is writing's set of graphic signs and signals used to guide readers through sentences. As road signs and signals do for drivers, punctuation directs and instructs readers when to look ahead, when to move ahead, when to yield, when to slow down, and when to stop. Just as road signs and signals help to guarantee passenger safety, so punctuation promotes reader safety as each sentence journeys across the page. Based on logic, just as grammar is, punctuation attempts to use safe, consistently applied road-rules. Please keep in mind that punctuation *cannot* be driven and steered principally by breath control or by stylistic preference according to I-like-the-way-this-looks inspirations. Logic always should drive and steer your sentences.

There are **four "better safe than sorry" rules for commas** that I want you to think about, because for your reader they will eliminate potential confusion and misreading. Sometimes these "rules" aren't required, and to that extent they aren't really "rules" at all, but applying them will be a guaranteed prevention against potential errors if logically they *are* required; furthermore, you never will be incorrect if you do use these commas, so better safe than sorry pays off.

First, for compound sentences—independent clauses connected by a coordinating conjunction—you may not always want or need to use a comma between the two independent clauses. Each of the following examples is acceptable, because its logic is not compromised by the lack of a comma: "I like bacon but I hate eggs."; "Cleon plays the zither and Morpheus plays the accordion."; "You can meet me in St. Louis or you can stay home." In those sentences, were we to place a comma before English's three most common coordinating conjunctions—"but," "and," and "or"—our sentences never could be considered incorrect, but the comma does *not* have to be included. Yet in the following two examples, taken from a Website about the Punjab region of India, confusion results from the comma's absence: "The Punjab civilization was a highly developed urban one and two of its towns, Mohenjodaro and Harappa, represent the high watermark of the settlements" (Punjab, 52). When I first read that sentence, for a moment I was thrown off by "a highly developed urban one and two . . ." And three and four and five? No, this compound sentence's second independent clause begins after the coordinating conjunction "and," and the sentence reads properly and more logically with a better-safe-than-sorry comma: "The Punjab civilization was a highly developed urban one, and two of its towns, Mohenjodaro and Harappa, represent . . ." Potential confusion is even greater in this sentence: "There was a fairly clear division of localities and houses were earmarked for the upper and lower strata of society" (Punjab, 52). Innocently, readers are likely to read that "There was a fairly clear division of localities and houses . . . ," as if "localities and houses" were compound objects of the preposition "of"; however, "houses" actually is the subject of the sentence's second independent clause, and, to make that clear, a comma must be placed after "localities." Using a comma may not seem like a big deal, but as a writer-educator you do not want impede your readers, slowing them down and making them return to your sentence to understand what it actually says.

Second, using a comma after introductory dependent or subordinate clauses will keep you safe and never sorry. As I mentioned before, there are instances where no comma is necessary, as in the following three sentences: "Because I was paid yesterday

I'm happy today"; "Although Jim was born on November 5 he doesn't have the traits of a Scorpio"; "If it's acceptable I'll visit tomorrow." The absence of a comma does not affect those three sentences' logic or readability, but in the following sentence its absence does: "After the construction workers finished eating rats emerged to look for the scraps." There, "rats" is the subject of the independent clause, not what the construction workers finished eating. Similar in confusion is the following sentence: "As you can see the profits peak around 10-12%."; in that sentence the writer appears to be directing the reader to view a graph ("As you can see"), while "the profits" is not the object of the reader's seeing but the independent clause's subject of the verb, "peak." Here are three more "sorry" examples: "Six of us worked on the award-winning film *Revenge*. Before we began to shoot the director had everyone read about the psychology of retribution." "Because I object to products made of paper napkins at my house are made of cloth." "As layoffs continue demand for space will persist in falling."

Third, it's safer to place a comma after introductory prepositional phrases whose object should be separated for clarity from the independent clause's subject. Exceptions to this "rule" once again exist, when no comma is absolutely needed: "On Sunday I plan to see a movie."; "For fun in the sun let's travel to Rio."; "At the rainbow's end you will find a pot of gold." However, writers frequently write themselves into trouble if they avoid using a comma after the introductory prepositional phrase: "Under the car tools are scattered everywhere."; "On top of the mountain snowcaps remain unmelted all year."; "About flying Robert has interesting comments."; "On Friday night dances are held either at the school gym or in the cafeteria." "From Malawi Ndere Ubani is sending unique African art."

My fourth and last "better safe than sorry" rule is about prudent use of the serial comma. A series is a list of three or more items, and anything in a sentence can be serialized: subjects ("Jim, Tom, and Joe [played poker]. . ."); verbs ("[Jim] shuffles, deals, and later calls."); direct objects ("[Jim likes] Brunello, Pinot Noir, and Shiraz."); prepositional phrases ("[Today my dog walked] down the steps, out our building's door, and onto the street."); adjectives ("[She is] congenial, intelligent, and funny."); and adverbs ("[He spoke] authoritatively, articulately, and calmly.") In a sentence, to guarantee that your reader understands that each part of your serial list is distinct from the others, the serial comma occurs between the next-to-last and last item, before the concluding "and," if in fact there *is* that "and." Much wasted printed space has been and is given to disputation over whether or not to include the serial comma,[1] as if its existence were a right/wrong, either/or binary opposition; in fact, not using the serial comma sometimes isn't a problem, but sometimes it is. So before we understand the safety of using it, its logic requires some historical background, which should help to educate any contemporary writer who has inherited the bad habit of always disregarding its use, in compliance with those who rule against using it.

During the twentieth century, abandoning the serial comma occurred because it saved column space and, with newspapers and magazines, therefore added money for advertising. Notice the two information blocks that follow. Both contain exactly the same words in the same order, but the first omits the serial comma between "Raimersin and Wilkinson":

> Waider, Raimersin and Wilkinson are in Bains County Jail, each held in custody on $1.5 million bail. The Laffeys' daughter is being held in neighboring Granite County's detention hub. Traylor says he isn't aware if attorneys have been contacted yet.

> Waider, Raimersin, and Wilkinson are in Bains County Jail, each held in custody on $1.5 million bail. The Laffeys' daughter is being held in neighboring Granite County's detention hub. Traylor says he isn't aware if attorneys have been contacted yet.

In block 1, line 1, omission of the serial comma allows "on" to sit at the line's end. However, in block 2, the added space used by the serial comma forces "on" to spill onto line 2 and "County's" to spill onto line 3, resulting in the necessity of line 4. When column lines are even narrower, as in newspapers, more spillage occurs, thus taking up more space. Although omitting the serial comma may be financially profitable for advertising-supported publications, and although sometimes there is no need for the serial comma when no ambiguity exists, there definitely are instances where it's better to be safe than sorry.

Absent serial commas occur regularly in professional public writing and can create problems for readers, as this and the next paragraph illustrate. A publisher received a dedication page that said, roughly, "With enduring gratitude, I dedicate this book to my parents, Jim Gill and Diane Freeberg." Is the writer dedicating the book to two people or to four? Without a final comma between "Jim Gill and Diane Freeberg," those two people can be considered an appositive phrase defining who the writer's parents are. But are they the parents? Or are they two separate people in addition to the parents? You, as a writer-educator conveying facts and realities, know what is true and must express that truth safely; therefore, if the dedication sentence addresses four people, then the serial comma is required, but, if only two, then the reversal of " . . . Jim Gill and Diane Freeberg, my parents" would be an easy solution. Recently I read this real estate advertisement, online: "This condo is a full-service building that has a gym, pool, sauna, parking garage and laundry room on every floor." Parking garage on every floor? Even with an added "and" before "parking," the problem remains if no comma is placed after "garage." Here is *Newsweek's* quoted transcription of a Bill Gates statement: "As intellectual property became increasingly important to businesses, and personal computers started appearing on every desktop, employees morphed into knowledge workers, companies began to focus on knowledge management and key information was stored in knowledge bases connected via knowledge networks" ("Road Ahead"). Without the serial comma after "management," it seems at first as if "companies began to focus" not only on "knowledge management" but also on "key information," which logically they might have done; however, "key information" is the subject of its own clause, not the second object of the preposition "on."

Although the serial comma's omission may not seem to be *that* important, remember that it can mislead readers and require them to review a sentence to gain the logic which you, as writer, originally should have provided for them. Technical and legal writers are reminded that they "are not in the civilian world. The serial comma is always more precise. Because precision is essential in legal writing, you should always use the serial comma. You'll never offend anyone by using it and, in the legal world, a single comma can be worth a million dollars" (Buckley). For example, legal history reports that a very wealthy woman had her lawyer write part of her will as paraphrased in the following quotation; the lawyer died before the woman, so when she died there was no one but the judge to interpret the will: "Beneficent Will leaves her money to Sally and Fred Smith, Margaret and John Williams, Betty and Harold Spivey and all their children." If Beneficent had intended to leave money to the children of all three couples, then there should have been a serial comma after "Spivey," but, because there wasn't, the judge had to read the will strictly, according to "the letter of the law": only the Spivey children—"Betty and Harold Spivey and all their children"—received any money, while the Smith and Williams children did not.

My guiding point about all four "better safe than sorry" rules is simple: sometimes, without the comma, a sentence's meaning will confuse your readers, which obviously is not writing well. So you have two options: either think judiciously if you need to include commas whenever one of these four "better safe than sorry" situations occurs, or just always include the comma to guarantee correctness.

Probably the most intellectually demanding decision about whether or not to use comma(s) is **the non-restrictive or all-inclusive category (with comma[s]) vs. the restrictive or subset category (without comma[s])**. Part of the intellectual demand results from writers having to decide whether or not to use comma(s) with four different units of syntax: relative clauses, participial phrases, appositive phrases, and prepositional phrases.

A non-restrictive construction means you are writing about a total or all-inclusive category, whether it is singular or plural, whereas a restrictive construction means you are writing about a subset of a category, one restricted part of that category. For example, I must write, "My wife, Izzy, is my best friend" and must set off "Izzy" with commas, because "wife" is a non-restrictive category: according to legal logic, I can have only one wife, so my sentence logically cannot restrict or offer a subset to the category of wife. I am and can be married *only* to Izzy, not also to Ellen and Joan, so "wife" is an all-inclusive category immediately followed by a comma. If I write, "My wife Izzy is my best friend," then I have signified that I am at least a bigamist, possibly a polygamist, and that Izzy is my best friend but that my other wives aren't, since there can be only one "best." Conversely, I must write, "My friend Jeff lives on the Lower East Side" and use no commas there, because I am restricting the category of friend to one of my many friends, my friend Jeff. Were I to write, "My friend, Jeff, lives on the Lower East Side," I'd be saying in that non-restrictive or all-inclusive category that I have only one friend (with the comma, the category is singular, "friend"), that his name is Jeff—and that I'm one sorry guy.

For your additional familiarity with these constructions, this paragraph examines examples in pairs and, for each pair, will present a restrictive or subset category and also a non-restrictive or all-inclusive category. On the one hand, we must write, "Shakespeare's play *Macbeth* is about unrestrained ambition," without commas, because Shakespeare wrote thirty-seven plays and here we are restricting the logic to a subset of those thirty-seven, in this case a subset of one, *Macbeth*; on the other hand, we must use commas if we write, "Shakespeare's final play, *The Tempest*, is set on an island," because Shakespeare can have written only one final play, and thus the category is all-inclusive, or non-restrictive. We must write, "In *The Wizard of Oz* Dorothy's dog, Toto, is stolen by the Wicked Witch of the West," because we know that Dorothy has only one dog; therefore, the non-restrictive or all-inclusive category, with commas, is correct. Conversely, in the sentence "In *The Wizard of Oz* the witch Glinda is good, not wicked," is a restrictive category of "witch," because we know from the preceding sentence that there are at least two witches in the film and that Glinda therefore is a subset of the category. Last year on the New York City subway I saw the sign, "Teach math to students who need it most." Correct, that sentence also is a subset or restrictive category and therefore uses no comma, because the message is talking about a particular group of students, those who need math most—as opposed to those who don't. If the sign had been written using the comma, "Teach match to students, who need it most," then it would incorrectly have stated that the category is "students," *all* students, and that it is they who need math most; naturally, not all students need math most, so this cannot logically be an all-inclusive or non-restrictive category.

Sometimes, your choice of an all-inclusive (commas) vs. subset category (no commas) will be determined contextually, by information in preceding sentences. For example, consider the following sentence, in which I have put the non-restrictive, all-inclusive commas in brackets, so that *you* must determine whether or not to use them: "For the gymnastics competition, the U. S., Russia, China, and Japan sent three competitors apiece to the event, or twelve competitors in total. The Japanese competitor[,] who won the event[,] was outstanding." Commas, or no commas? The answer is no commas, because the Japanese sent three competitors, only one of whom could have won the competition; therefore, the winner is a restrictive subset, one out of three. Similarly, try this one: "My apartment building hires three doormen, each daily working a different eight-hour shift. The late-night doorman[,] Argus[,] spends much of the night reading." Commas, or no commas? Here, the answer is commas, an all-encompassing or non-restrictive category, because three doormen work different eight-hour shifts during the day's twenty-four hours, each doorman thus by himself during his shift, with Argus being the only late-night doorman; the category of "late-night doorman" is all-encompassing or non-restrictive, and the commas are required.

Try the following examples on your own; after you have decided where and where not to use commas, go to the following paragraph for an explanation of what is correct:

1)
    a. Drivers who have been convicted of a DUI offense (Driving Under the Influence) should lose their license.
    b. Drivers, who have been convicted of a DUI offense (Driving Under the Influence), should lose their license.

2)
    a. Katami's CEO Bruce Kao lives in New Jersey.
    b. Katami's CEO, Bruce Kao, lives in New Jersey.

3)
    a. My father whom I write regularly lives in Lexington, KY.
    b. My father, whom I write regularly, lives in Lexington, KY.

4)
    a. Animals, frightened by thunder, often try to hide.
    b. Animals frightened by thunder often try to hide.

5)
    a. The film director, Spike Lee, has made an excellent five-part movie about Hurricane Katrina, which caused incalculable damage to New Orleans.
    b. The film director Spike Lee has made an excellent five-part movie about Hurricane Katrina which caused incalculable damage to New Orleans.
    c. The film director Spike Lee has made an excellent five-part movie about Hurricane Katrina, which caused incalculable damage to New Orleans.
    d. The film director, Spike Lee, has made an excellent five-part movie about Hurricane Katrina which caused incalculable damage to New Orleans.

For 1), there can be no commas around "who have been convicted of a DUI offense (Driving Under the influence)," because, if you use commas, the sentence says non-restrictively or all-inclusively that all drivers, categorically, are convicted of a DUI offense *and* that all drivers should lose their license; obviously, this is a restrictive, subset construction about a particular group of drivers. For 2), we want commas around "Bruce Kao" because logically there is only one Chief Executive Officer—officer, in the singular, end of category. The same logic applies to 3), in which commas go around "whom I write regularly," because I can have only one father; I may have a step-father or a father-in-law, but only one father, end of category, thus the comma. Sentence 4), using a completed-action participial phrase ("frightened by thunder"), should have no commas, because not all animals are frightened by thunder and therefore this is a restrictive, subset category pertaining only to those animals that are frightened, as opposed to those that aren't. Last, letter c) is the correct sentence for 5). Because Spike Lee is one of thousands of film directors, this sentence is restricting its logic to him, thus not using commas around his name; further, because there has been only one Hurricane Katrina, which in the sentence is restated by "which," the category is non-restrictive or all-inclusive and requires a comma after "Katrina."

Side-by-side adjectives—"extensive[,] beneficial "—also require writers to choose **whether or not to use a comma**. If we place a comma between side-by-side adjectives, we call those adjectives coordinate; if not, non-coordinate. Most important is remembering that any comma placed between two side-by-side adjectives is equivalent to saying "and," which is why we refer to the adjectives with a comma between them as coordinate; recall that "and" is a coordinating conjunction. As such, coordinate adjectives can be reversed, without any loss to the sentence's logic. For example, the sentence "She is a *tall, beautiful* woman" expresses that the woman has two separate qualities, tall *and* beautiful; with the comma, the sentence conveys no relationship between the woman's height and her beauty. Independent of one another, yet coordinate in the sense that they both equally modify "woman," the two adjectives can be reversed and we could write, "She is a beautiful, tall woman," the only difference being which of the two adjectives we prioritize. Conversely, in "She is a *tall beautiful* woman," the adjective "tall" directly modifies "beautiful woman" and therefore interconnects her two physical qualities in a way that the other sentence does not; this sentence suggests that unlike beautiful women who may be short or mid-height, this woman is a tall beauty. When no comma is used between the adjectives, the structure is non-coordinate; principally important here, however, isn't that you learn the terminology but that you understand the logic that differentiates coordinate from non-coordinate.

It's because the same set of adjectives can assume a different logic with or without the comma between them that we need to think carefully about what we're trying to express. Here are some additional examples: if we write, "Today we have a *bright blue* sky," then we are saying that the blue sky has the characteristic of being a bright blue—as opposed to possibly a dusky blue. If, however, we write, "Today we have a *bright, blue* sky" and use the comma, we are stating that the sky has two unrelated characteristics: it's illuminated by the sun and it's also blue. Consider these two options: "Her *new yellow* raincoat keeps her dry" and "Her *new, yellow* raincoat keeps her dry." Again, both sentences are logically possible, but the first tells us that the female has had at least one older yellow raincoat prior to her new one, whereas the second states only that the raincoat is new *and* yellow. Here's a final example of sentences with the same sequence of words that make different sense, depending on whether the adjectives are non-coordinate or coordinate, respectively: "The *frightened lost* child whimpered," and "The *frightened, lost* child whimpered." The former sentence has "frightened" directly modifying "lost child"; logical, a "frightened lost child" possibly implies that the child is frightened because she is lost, that for her it's scary to be in an unknown environment. The latter sentence, with the comma, has both adjectives modifying "child," thereby separating "frightened" from "lost"; there, we cannot infer from the words' syntax that the child's fright is caused by her being lost.

Examples only of coordinate side-by-side adjectives, which require a comma, are in this paragraph: "Sally is an *energetic, mischievous* girl," a girl with two separate characteristics; from that sentence we cannot deduce that there is any causal relationship between her mischief and her being energetic. In "Myles prefers reading in a *bright, comfortable* library," we learn that Myles wants a library that has two separate qualities conducive to his reading well. And in "The dog's *muddy, scruffy* coat will need to be washed," there are two separate reasons or qualities requiring the dog's coat to be washed.

And here are examples only of non-coordinate side-by-side adjectives, which do not require a comma: "The pilot followed the *odd low-flying oblong* object," in which "oblong" directly modifies "object," "low-flying" directly modifies "oblong object," and "odd" directly modifies "low-flying oblong object." "Last year he saw the Broadway play *Dirty Rotten* Scoundrels," a group not just of rotten scoundrels, but of dirty rotten scoundrels. "We found an *old wicker* basket in the basement," the characteristic of the wicker basket being old. "Georges Seurat's *luminous Pointillist* paintings are a joy to behold."

Like a period, a **semicolon** is *terminal punctuation*, which means it ends or terminates a complete sentence; as terminal punctuation, semicolons and periods also are followed by complete sentences. Thus having two complete sentences, the entire structure in which the semicolon is used is called a compound sentence. The difference between the semicolon and the period is that unlike the period, the semicolon indicates a closer, more inseparable logical relationship between the two sentences it divides and is not followed by a capital letter. There is one exception to the rules just stated, an exception substantiated by logical necessity.

Standard use of the semicolon occurs in two ways. First, it's used between two sentences not connected by a coordinating conjunction: "Many people question why Elle works so hard; I think she needs to feel productive." "My wife and I try to do our food marketing every Saturday morning; she markets for fish, chicken, and bread, and I search our neighborhood for the best fresh produce." "Gaining entry into the Chinese marketplace is not a guarantee of success; the penetration of the many segmented markets within China is the real challenge." The three preceding sentences show the close logical connection between their two parts, before and after the semicolon; because readers see the lower-case letter after the semicolon, as with the word "because" in *this* sentence, instinctively they know that the idea hasn't yet been completed, even though a new sentence presents that idea's new part.

Second, the semicolon often is used before a second sentence beginning with a conjunctive adverb or conjunctive adverbial phrase[2]: "Some students dislike grammar; consequently, they avoid learning its logic." "Bill excels as an athlete; on the other hand, John excels as a student." "Some people vote as a Democrat; however, sometimes they act as if they were Republican." "Over a decade ago, the seat belt law went into effect; therefore, more people now drive with their seat belts on." "As I write this sentence, Michael Phelps is the best-known, most prominent swimmer on planet Earth; nevertheless, despite his global fame and twenty-two Olympic medals, he's a fairly modest man."

The one exception with semicolon use occurs either in a series after a colon or in a series of objects or subjective complements at a sentence's end—but *only if* the information within some of the listed parts of the series contains internal punctuation. First, let's see the semicolon used after a colon: "There are three new officers in our class: Rose Bloom, President; Biennial Plant, Vice-President; and Fern DuBois, Treasurer." Notice how confusingly cluttered with commas the sentence would be if each semicolon weren't used; the semicolon allows writers to keep their information ordered and neatly packaged. Here are two more: "I put different flowers in the vase: daffodils, because they are spring-like; other flowers produced from bulbs; and roses, my wife's favorite kind of flower." "I decided to earn a Ph.D., despite its hard work, for three reasons: I enjoy living in an academic environment, whose intellectual and cultural stimulation attracts me; I wanted to continue to teach, a personal and not just professional opportunity allowing me to interact with new groups of people; and I needed to learn more and to think better." What follows are examples of the semicolon used at a sentence's end, in a series of direct objects, inverted subjects, and subjective complements. Here's an example of a serial, compound direct object: "*The Man Who Made Lists* outlines the 'chronic mental instability' of Roget's maternal grandmother; the 'psychotic trance' in which his mother spent her last days after a life of neurotic 'neediness'; the breakdowns undergone by Roget's sister and daughter (he married late and was widowed early); and the grief-driven, throat-slashing suicide of his uncle, the great British civil libertarian Samuel Romilly, who expired in Roget's blood-soaked arms" (*Times Book Review*, 9). Here's an example of a compound subject coming after the sentence's verb: "Among the many additions are a full-room assembly of "The Wisteria Dining Room," a French art nouveau interior designed by Lucien Lévy Dhurmer shortly before World War I that is the only complete example of its kind in the United States; Henry Lerolle's enormous *The Organ Rehearsal*, a church interior of 1885; a group of newly accessioned nineteenth-century landscape oil sketches; and a selection of rarely exhibited paintings by an international group of artists" (Metropolitan Museum). And here's a series of subjective complements: "London is one of the world's major cities, both in economic influence and in population; an amalgam of diverse races and ethnicities; a cultural cache of historical sites, architecture, and sightseeing opportunities; and host of the 2012 Olympics, sixty years since its previous hosting."

One rule and two reminders are all you need to know about a **colon**: the rule is that the colon must follow a complete sentence, as it just did in *this* sentence. A sentence such as "Many items: pencils, pens, paper clips, and erasers are on his desk" is structurally awkward and must be changed to "Many items are on his desk: pencils, pens, paper clips, and erasers." The first of the two reminders is that we always use the colon to move a sentence's information from the general to the particular or from a broad understanding to a more specific one; given that function, we can think of the colon as a pair of binoculars lying on its side, a clarifying tool which, after readers see something broadly, then allows them to view it up-close. The second reminder is that *any* kind of sentence structure may come after the colon: compound and complex sentence, simple sentence, phrase of any kind, and single word.

In all three of the colon's common uses—to list, to elaborate on an idea, and to indicate a quotation as supporting evidence—writers can offer greater precision or clarification of a thought or image that precedes it; this more specific focus is why you may want to think of the colon as binoculars.

The colon's most common use is for listing, after the general introduction has been made about what's being listed: "Piles of correspondence lay unsorted on his desk: bills, credit card solicitations, marketing appeals, personal letters, and printed e-mails." "Mass education in the nineteenth century consisted of three courses: punctuality, obedience, and rote, repetitive work." "Each of Jake's sisters plays a musical instrument: Emma, piano; Sarah, violin; and Maggie, drums."

To elaborate specifically on a general idea introduced before the colon is the colon's second use: "They also found a correlation between Website quality and e-business activity: the Website with the highest quality produced the highest business performance." "After a few weeks, an interesting phenomenon occurs within the flask: a brown soup appears, containing a large number of molecules more complex than the ones originally put in." "We now find in contrast to the scapegoat psychology that the exact opposite in happening: people are internalizing vicarious suffering, with an 'I feel your pain' purpose." "The central idea I shall make use of was foreshadowed by A. Weissman in pre-gene days at the turn of the century: his doctrine of the 'continuity of the germ-plasm'" (Dawkins, 5). "After years of false assertions, fearful hyperbole, and self-righteous propaganda, the Bush administration's principal purpose for invading Iraq became clear: oil."

The colon's third useful function introduces quoted evidence validating a claim that requires proof: "Everything about Shakespeare's tragic hero Macbeth, including his self-destruction and his own soliloquized beliefs, suggests that he is a nihilist: 'Life's but . . ./. . . a tale/Told by an idiot, full of sound and fury,/Signifying *nothing*'" (italics mine)

(V, v). "Hamlet's tragic flaw is his indecision: 'To be, or not to be' (III, i) is the most famous example of his inability to reach a conclusion."

Having greater horizontality than any other form of punctuation, **em dashes** can be used either mid-sentence on both sides of an interrupting clause or phrase, or at a sentence's end for delayed emphasis. In mid-sentence, em dashes appear to lift an idea off the page, highlighting important editorial comments, memorable thoughts, lists, and definitions whose significance cannot be postponed; in such situations, they function structurally just as two commas do around an interrupting clause or phrase. To set off a definition, for example, commas are fully acceptable in "Creators of fractal art, computer-generated designs that sometimes use post-processing techniques, believe it is a new artistic genre for the twenty-first century." More boldly, however, em dashes heighten readers' attention to the definition: "Creators of fractal art—computer-generated designs that sometimes use post-processing techniques—believe it is a new artistic genre for the twenty-first century."

Basically, using either commas or em dashes mid-sentence is a matter of stylistic choice; as writer-educator, you have the right to choose which option better accomplishes your intentions. In some instances, when there are internal commas in a definition, set-off list, or editorial comment, you may find that the em dashes are preferable to commas. For example, whereas the sentence "Throughout human history, all cultures, primitive, agricultural, industrial, technological, and informational, have used energy" becomes bothersome with additional commas surrounding the list of "cultures," the em dashes keep that list neat and tidy: "Throughout human history, all cultures—primitive, agricultural, industrial, technological, and informational—have used energy." (Certainly one also could write, "Throughout human history, primitive, agricultural, industrial, technological, and informational cultures have used energy," but that revised sentence loses the original sentence's immediate emphasis on "*all* cultures.")

Although there is no em dash on the Word™ keyboard, you can create it by putting two hyphens *directly after* the last letter of the word before them—such as the "m" in "them"—and then continuing your sentence's next word ("and," here) *directly after* the two hyphens; thus, you use no spaces. But when you hit the space bar after that next word ("such" and "and" in the preceding sentence), Word™ automatically connects the two dashes and creates the graphically sizeable em dash. Do the same to set off delayed emphasized information at a sentence's end.

More and more the em dash is being used in newspaper, magazine, and general business writing, so you may be certain that it is a common, professionally recognized form of punctuation. Perhaps the most common professional use of em dashes is to set off interrupting editorial thoughts or significant ideas pertinent to a sentence's main idea, as illustrated in the following sentences: "In response to Cross' remarks about teaching, we believe it is a fallacy—incidentally, a very common one—to assume that teachers teach only because they 'cannot do.'" "Perhaps the greatest rewards of higher education—and this is something that most students ultimately realize—is learning how to think for oneself." "Iceland's prolonged nights—sometimes there are only 4.5 hours of sunlight daily—are an attraction to vacationers looking for extensive indoor partying, drinking, and snuggling." "Again this year, the city's increased taxation—property taxes will be the most radically affected—continues to force average-income dwellers to relocate to suburbia."

Em dashes also are useful for isolating lists, which usually help to define something further, and for definitions themselves. We see how added attention is given to a list in "The division of the human psyche into two archetypal traits—the *anima* and the *animus*—remains one of Carl Jung's important psychological theories." Highlighting a definition is apparent in "Archetypal traits—innate universal psychic dispositions—are energies forming the substrates of personality and actualizing basic symbols or representations of unconscious experience."

For delayed stress given to an idea at a sentence's end and presented as if that idea were an afterthought worthy of separate consideration, one em dash can be stylistically useful because its visual extension postpones the reader's encounter with the afterthought: "In a culture of specializations disseminating fragmented data, synthesis is not merely useful—it is crucial." "In the spring of 1968, a Florida cargo pilot named Robert Brush discovered what looked like a sunken building off the coast of Bimini—exactly where Edgar Cayce said such a formation would appear." "A brain-dead patient clinically diagnosed as being in a vegetative state can be kept alive for years by a life-support system—but what's the point of that?" "Altruism is a myth conceived by humans to feel good about themselves—or at least that's what sociobiologists believe."

Entire books are written just about punctuation, but so many of its matters and concerns are based on common sense and reasonable intuition. Naturally we want to know how to punctuate properly, to be assured that our writing isn't careless and won't confuse, but punctuation's "rules" often are style-based preferences and not mandatory requirements (see Essay #6). Given the plethora of prescriptive but not necessarily logic-based "rules," this chapter has discussed only those instances when logic can be injured and compromised by inappropriately used or absent punctuation. Just remember that your writing well always *must be* governed by logic as you codify your thinking's content, organization, sentence structure, grammar, word choice, and punctuation.

My recommendation of the book that best manages not only punctuation (in less than fifty pages), but also all of writing's other mechanical principles, plus researching and documentation, is Diana Hacker's *A Writer's Reference*. Comparatively inexpensive and bound in an almost indestructible plastic, this is an excellent single reference source for answering whatever questions you may have about principles of punctuation, grammar, diction, and spelling, and about citing and formatting.

REFERENCES

[1] Too much huffing and puffing still occurs about the dedicated inclusion or the dedicated omission of serial commas; this is not an exclusively two-sided controversy—in fact, not a controversy at all. Common sense, which doctrinaires sometimes lack, indicates that each serial situation must be evaluated by its own informing logic and punctuated, or not, accordingly. Said evaluation aside, my "better safe than sorry rule" offers writers a "no-brainer" opportunity to be always logical and structurally precise by using the serial comma.

[2] Indicating the transitional logic that conjoins a compound sentence's two parts, conjunctive adverbs and conjunctive adverbial phrases follow the semicolon and themselves are followed by a comma. Here are the most common single-word conjunctive adverbs:

- "therefore" and "thus," for a conclusion or consequence, which in different contexts also is indicated by "hence," "consequently" and "accordingly"
- "however" and "instead," for an exception
- "nevertheless," "nonetheless," and "still," for whatever overrides earlier declarations
- "furthermore," "moreover," "also," and "additionally," for supplementary information
- "comparatively," "likewise" and "similarly," for comparisons
- "contrastingly," "otherwise," "instead," and "rather," for contrasts
- "indeed," for acknowledgement of the preceding idea
- "first," "second," "next," "meanwhile," "last," "finally," etc., for sequence-related information

Conjunctive adverbial phrases usually begin with prepositions, whose object marks the transitional logic: "for instance," "for example"; "in contrast," "on the other hand," "on the contrary"; "as a result"; "in fact," "in effect," "after all"; "at the same time," "in the meantime"; "at any rate," "in other words,"; "in addition," "even more"

Dawkins, Richard. *The Selfish Gene.* Oxford: Oxford University Press, 1976.

http://mariebuckley.com/2012/01/19/lets-get-serious-about-the-serial-comma/

Metropolitan Museum Newsletter. Sept. 2008.

http//www.punjabonline.com/servlet/library.history?Action=Page&Param=52

The New York Times Book Review 16 March. 2008: 9.

"The Road Ahead," *Newsweek* 25 Jan. 2006.

ESSAY 13

Evidence

Any investigative analysis, appraisal or evaluative survey, proposition or proposal, and argument that you make will require evidence, a support system to reinforce your unique position or point of view. Evidence accompanies and augments your "warrants," your own logical reasoning that explains and makes sense of your position's or point of view's claims. The product of analysis, a warrant "tells" readers what is true when the writer declaims an idea or belief as a well-founded or defensible opinion, whereas evidence "shows" and helps to prove by illustrating and demonstrating what the writer tells.

Writers frequently are admonished not to over-tell, as in "Find a Job," an AOL article that states, "In the cover letter [for a job application] . . . . Show, don't tell. 'Share a good story about what you've accomplished. Stories show why you're the best candidate'" (Rachel Zupek) and indeed can illustrate how and why you're a "goal-oriented" "self-starter," "hard-working" "go-getter," and "team player," the generalized traits that all other job applicants probably have told the prospective employer they are. Showing therefore always is useful when you write, if only because it wdifferentiates you from the rest of the pack. But exclusively showing and never telling is almost impossible and certainly ought not be a rule; rather, "to show, not tell" is a reminder that writers also should give illustrative specificity—give evidence—to their announced opinions. When you persuade a reader about anything, a combination of telling and showing is inevitable; only the balance of the two—**75-25% /50-50% /25-75%**—remains uncertain and requires you to determine how much proof your opinions require.

Opinions are a mainstay of thinking in the professional and academic worlds, which is why we have think-tanks, brain-trusts, workshops, boards, and committees to generate ideas from multiple people and perspectives, to sift through them, to combine what's best from them, and ultimately to resolve all kinds of situations and to advance all aspects of knowledge. As a writer, you are expected to offer and then to resolve opinions, because as logical conclusions they often are the foundations of whatever case you intend to construct. However, to state opinions is only to "tell" them; they remain general, just as "Mary is vastly intelligent" is a general assertion that doesn't show or give examples of her intelligence. Supporting or backing up your general opinions requires that you persuasively defend them with a show of proof or evidence: statistical data, quotations or paraphrases of corroborative evidence from expert sources, academic knowledge from all disciplines of study, illustrative examples, and anecdotal information. When you tell readers that Mary scored 179 on her LSAT, quote parts of a superlative recommendation from her college multivariable calculus professor, and mention that as a high-school senior she won the 2007 U. S. Chess Federation's North Carolina competition for her age group, then you have shown her vast intelligence. But let's think about the show/tell principle using a "told" opinion whose defense is more demanding than Mary's.

Telling your reader that India's overpopulation is a problem creating other problems certainly is an acceptable opinion; however, it remains a generalization. The list of problems caused by the problem of India's overpopulation also is "telling": India's children's well-being is affected, environmental pollution is created, and a decrease in India's collective quality of life results. Those three topics give greater analytical precision to the opinion—but again remain generalized and, as such, still are unsubstantiated opinions requiring proof or evidence. Basically, any document's or essay's conceptual framework results in "told" pronouncements; as you analyze or break down a complex generalization into its operative parts, you still are announcing the "telling" generalized principles of that larger generalization from which they come. Given that, you will want to examine where it may be useful "to show" how and why your claimed opinions are induced from facts and truths beyond your personal point of view.

Let's return to India. Statistics certainly are evidentiary aids demonstrating the claim that India is overpopulated. In March, 2012, 1.22 billion people lived in India (http://www.indiaonlinepages). By itself, that statistic may appear to suggest overpopulation, but using comparisons to it and deductions from it always will give greater understandability to your statistical evidence. First, therefore, it would be useful to note that 1.22 billion is 17.4% of the world's 7-billion population—between

1/5th and 1/6th of the world, which lends magnitude to the statistic's meaning. Second, you might add that India's population is four times greater than that of the United States, just to "bring home" the statistic's meaning and to put it in relative perspective. Third, to dramatize your point even more, you might mention that India's 17.4% of the world's people exist on 2.4% of the world's land mass. This simple arithmetic using public domain[1] statistics "shows" convincingly in an introductory manner the extent of India's "told" overpopulation, helping with evidence to prove your belief.

Still working just with statistics, a writer could "show" more evidence in the hypothetical body's first topic of investigation, about how India's overpopulation contributes to affecting the country's children's well-being. The writer could note factually that about 300,000,000 of India's population go to bed hungry every night, while 50% of all Indian children are "undernourished" (India Together). Furthermore, again 300,000,000 people or 25% of India's population live in urban areas, in which 38% of children under three years are underweight and more than 35% are physically "stunted" (Food Insecurity Atlas of Urban India). To "show" an idea from different perspectives—statistics describing the children's condition both nationally and in urban areas—often features and helps to prove the "told" idea even more meaningfully.

Alongside statistics to "show" the problems of India's overpopulation might be a significant quotation from a UNICEF report or from the U.S. Embassy in New Delhi, or, for the topic of environmental pollution, a quotation about how overpopulation's vast amounts of human waste are being discarded into and "killing India's rivers," for example New Delhi's Yamuna River, 50% of whose daily received sewage is ineffectively treated (Hindustan Times).

Notice that statistics and well-chosen quotations—evidence that "shows" what you "tell"—can have large emotional and ethical impact in addition to their logic.

The quoted single word "stunted" two paragraphs ago, for example, is powerful emotional evidence that will require readers to feel more deeply one effect of malnourished children. Balancing your show and tell depends on your document's or essay's purpose and the degree to which you think you need to prove your claims. Just keep in mind that all sweeping generalizations require proof or evidence.

GUIDELINE IDEAS FOR USING EVIDENCE

1. Discovering Who and What Are the Most Reliable Sources of Ideas and Data

To persuade your readers of the credibility in all parts of your essay, you must cite authoritative data from reputable sources and quote useful ideas from respected experts. Knowing who or what is authoritative, respected, and reputable is part of good research. Whatever claims you make that are essential to your position or point of view must be proven or at least made persuasive with reliable evidence. Naturally, added strength comes from your use of diversified multiple sources of evidence. Like inbreeding, similar emphasis on the same kind of evidence—nothing but quotations, nothing but statistics, nothing but historical documentation—can weaken the intelligence and lessen the strength of what you produce.

2. Evidence is the Support System of Your Essay, Not the Basis of It

Regardless of your profession or field of study, the universal purpose of persuasive writing is to think originally, to generate revised or alternative convictions based on a creative synthesis of existing knowledge. Therefore, evidence helps you elucidate and authenticate your own original thoughts and alternative ideas—serves as a means to an end, not as an end in itself. Think of evidence always as your support system. To paste together a collage of other sources' data and ideas may display the breadth of your collected research, but it reveals no unique intellectual contribution from you and is not what good thinking and thus writing well are about. Scholarship certainly does and must include excellent evidence, but you use that evidence the way original Gothic architecture used flying buttresses for cathedrals: to support, stabilize, and also call further attention to an already magnificently planned, composed, and executed structure.

3. **Multiple Evidence in Quick Combinations Can Have Intellectual Impact, Maybe Even Persuasive Influence on Readers**

Not just multiple hard evidence—e.g., "17% of the world's population on 2.4% of the world's land indicates India's overpopulation"—grabs and holds your reader's attention; also, descriptive evidence's multiple imagery—e.g., "legally polished and brilliant, with street-smart assuredness"—can have impact and influence. Keep in mind that you do not want to overwhelm your reader with too much evidence; instead, look for usefully advantageous combinations of two or three evidentiary points.

4. **Using Your Skeletal Outline of the Essay's Body, Approximate How Much Space Each of Your Topics Will Require; Then, with that Approximate Spatial Allowance in Mind, You Will be Better Able to Decide How Much Evidence Your Discussion can Accommodate**

It is very possible that because of spatial limitations you will be unable to use all of your compiled evidence. Therefore, you must decide judiciously which points of evidence, together, offer the strongest, most all-encompassing support for each part of your discussion. In addition to including your strongest evidence, think also about including diverse evidence—a variety of proof that confirms or exemplifies a broad range of ideas. You can accomplish this more easily if you make an evidence chart, as explained in #5, below.

5. **Make a Chart of Your Evidence**

To help you to use diversified sources of evidence and to be able to discover how different supporting ideas can be creatively combined for greater persuasiveness, I strongly recommend that you create a chart or spread-sheet of your evidence. Very simply, classify your evidence into labeled categories, as below, and then in priority order list the appropriate evidence for each category. You will begin to learn how the juxtaposition—the side-by-side placement—of certain kinds of evidence can yield additional force to your beliefs. Also, prioritizing evidence in each category will guarantee best choices if you cannot use everything you have compiled.

Statistics / Quotations / Paraphrases[1] / Hard / Illustrative / Anecdotes / Background, / Science, / Causal[2] / Facts Examples / Biographical   Other /Historical Fields

After you have compiled your evidence, look for relationships—again, as I advised when discussing organization, always think "relationships"—among all that you've listed, and discover complementary points of evidence that add power to your proof. For example, assume you have a quotation indicating that "Of the 10 lifestyle health risks considered [by the Journal of Occupational and Environmental Medicine], obesity"—body weight 20% or more above the "ideal" or actuarial norm—"was by far the most costly—accounting for approximately 14 percent of lifestyle-related health costs for men, and 25 percent for women" (http://www.hr.cch.com/news). The quotation contains useful statistics, but they will attain heightened significance if the writer combines them with the hard factual evidence from the Centers for Disease Control and Prevention that "a whopping 78 million adults—more than a third of the U.S. population—are obese" (Schupek, 1), evidence whose calculations don't even include children. Given that "whopping" statistic, readers can better understand why obesity radically affects employment costs. And obesity-caused employment costs are likely to continue into the next generation, because, a writer might add, "Childhood obesity has more than tripled in the past 30 years. The percentage of children age 6 to 11 in the United States who were obese increased from 7 percent in 1980 to nearly 20 percent in 2008. The percentage of adolescents age 12 to 19 who were obese increased from 5 percent to 18 percent over the same period" (http://www.cdc.gov).

6.   Do Not be Disinclined to Cite Multiple Sources as Proof of the Same Idea

If you use in-text citations—also known as parenthetical references—you list the multiple sources as follows: (Jones, 52; Moray et al., 189-94; Balcon, xix). Notice that the entire three-source citation is only half a line, not at all cumbersome; also, an in- text citation, unlike a footnote, doesn't distractingly send your readers to the page's bottom and then back up to find where the interrupting footnote is. Providing multiple evidence in an in-text citation to support your position has benefits: first, it lets your reader know that your research is thorough or at least expansive; second, it shows directly and conclusively the recurrence of important ideas and beliefs, which gives them added intellectual strength; and third, possibly it can prove the ongoing validity of an idea or belief if the dates of your multiple sources span a significant period of time.

7.   In Addition to Your Logical Warrants and Factual Evidence, Remember That You Can Depend for Evidence on Socially Beneficial Ethics and Wise Emotions to Expand Your Own Persuasion or to Bolster Your Position Against the Opposition's

Ethics are morals and values applied behaviorally and thus enacted in life; as such, your appealing to readers' ethics can bring theory to the real world and can illustrate how that theory, when applied, is or is not individually and collectively beneficial. Ethical and emotional evidence that reinforces your point of view can be very helpful in any persuasive context but especially so when your own logical reasoning isn't or can't be significantly more persuasive than the opposition's; all logic being close to equal, you then can augment your persuasiveness by emphasizing how your position is more ethically beneficial or more emotionally satisfying, or both, than that of the opposition. Basically, all effective persuasion relies not just on logic but also on desirable ethical values and practices along with pleasing emotions which at a gut level may move and influence your readers towards your point of view. Classical rhetorical persuasion is divided among logos, ethos, and pathos—logic, ethics, and emotion—because persuasion in life requires all three categories to convince people. Often, ethics and emotions are a "package deal," linked and mutually reinforcing, as for example the advocacy of an educational program that benefits children or a product that's both ecologically responsive and thus emotionally appealing.

Seen another way, theoretical logic sometimes exists only as an abstraction, as a premise that has no validity, no substance, beyond its own rationalized boundaries; consequently, the direct, urgent realism of ethics can assume powerful and persuasive leverage when you affirm your position or defend it against the opposition's. Take time, therefore, to assess ethically and emotionally your own governing theories or principles—on their own, or relative to your opposition's—when they are applied to real-world situations: clinical, medical, environmental, and ecological; legal, political, and international; financial, marketing, and lifestyle quality; psychological, familial, and humanitarian. What ethical and emotional benefits are strikingly apparent? Or, if necessary, can you find weaknesses in any of the opposition's theories when those theories are applied to life? In how many important facets of the real world do your own theories reveal their strengths, and, again if necessary, your opposition's their flaws? How so, and what are the repercussions? Incorporate your explanations either as offensive or as defensive evidence.

8. Using Your Evidence Defensively is a Natural, Often Necessary Part of Persuasive Strategizing

When learning about your subject or when reading researched material, you may discover dissenting points of view and arguments opposed to your own positions—contrary information you'd prefer to overlook and ignore. Such is the case with many positions we hold and defend in life: not everyone agrees with them, and sometimes that's aggravating. But don't disregard their existence: by ignoring them, you may appear to be ignorant of them or may seem, conspicuously, to be hiding them. So it may be good advice for you to follow these three steps: evaluate and prioritize, from strongest to weakest, your opposition's arguments and evidence; next, decide what on that prioritized list is weak enough to be disregarded altogether; and, then, determine how in self-defense you can gain persuasive advantage over whatever from your opposition's argument must be acknowledged because it has enduring force and logical value.

Call attention to the opposition's high-priority positions, and triumph persuasively over them as best you can. Keep in mind that to ignore the opposition's strongest defenses blindsides and undermines your own argument's legitimacy, because educated readers are likely to know the issues and expect you to know the issues, to know what's at stake for whoever is involved when controversy complicates those issues, and to establish openly your argument's superiority over the opposition's.

Towards that end, attempt any of the following:

Prove the opposition's major points to be wrong, or at least logically unsteady, or lacking useful evidence; by doing that, you simultaneously will promote your own position while nullifying or weakening theirs.

Examine and explain the relative weaknesses of each of their strongest points when placed against your own parallel opposing points of view, and, if necessary, add to your argument any supplemental evidence that works well for you at that point, even if you had intended to use it elsewhere.

Remember that supporting evidence often applies to multiple contexts and that you may feel free to use the same evidence more than once if a new context adds new meaning to it.

Quote one of your own strongest primary- or secondary-source supports to weaken the opposing perspective(s).

Using the opposition's concepts as your building-blocks, construct and then critically evaluate a worst-case scenario by showing how the opposition's logic diminishes its argument's credibility, or how its ethics are undesirable, or how its emotional affects and effects are a turn-off.

9. Publication Dates

Any subject requiring contemporary, up-to-date background information, theory, investigations, and statistical data obviously requires that your research focus on current publications. Let common sense direct your decisions about which sources are outdated, if indeed your evidence depends on current knowledge; if you cannot decide on your own, it's often best to rely on whatever are the most recent publication dates, whose up-to-date content is likely to have digested the material of earlier work.

There are instances, however, when a combination of old and new sources will be valuable to an argument or presentation of ideas. If you want to prove that a problematic situation for which you will propose solutions has been ongoing for a significant span of time, find evidence from a past source and a present source that addresses the same situation; then, in your essay, juxtapose the two, thereby conclusively establishing the recurring nature of that problem. The same approach applies to any recurring belief or "mind set" and to any institutional practice or social mode of activity which has prevailed through time and for which your document or essay proposes changes.

10. Warning Against Overuse of the Internet

Because source reliability isn't or can't always be established and verified online, writers risk receiving information that misguides or misinforms them if they rely solely on online research; in contrast, sources published in copyrighted journals, books, and data reserves—many of which are not reproduced online—will be significantly more reliable. While I think that to categorically disallow online use is nonsense—particularly because there are some very useful primary and secondary sources online—I nevertheless advise you to choose Web sources whose sites, authors, and content you know you can rely on as acceptable.

REFERENCES

[1] As a writer using evidence, for citation purposes you will need to distinguish between information and data that are "public domain" and that which must be quoted and cited because it comes from private sources. If something is known publicly and is locatable in various publicly available sources, such as encyclopedias and almanacs, then it does not have to be cited because it is not the intellectual property of an individual author, group of authors, think-tank, research team, journal, specific book, or institution. A part of the public's cultural heritage, public domain information does not contain an author's byline (many online sources do) and is not copyrighted, trademarked, or patented (many online sources are). Public domain information includes facts of biography, history, geography, and science: e.g., Bill Clinton, America's 42nd President, was born in 1946; Ronald Reagan has been the only divorced U.S. President; Johannes Gutenberg invented the movable type printing press in 1440; in the sixteenth century, Spain was the wealthiest Occidental nation; China is the most populated country in the world today; there are 206 bones in the adult human body; there are 118 elements in the Periodic Table. If you're uncertain whether information is public domain, then err on the side of caution and cite a source. There's nothing lost by being safe.

[2] When paraphrasing, you take one author's or group of authors' original idea(s) or information and summarize or reduce it in your own words. Frequently you may not want to quote an entire paragraph or more from a source, knowing that you can reduce it for our own purposes to much less than its original size. Paraphrasing always is acceptable—so long as you still cite the source immediately after your paraphrase ends, thereby giving credit where credit is due.

[3] Causal evidence, which helps to prove either causes or effects, offers evidentiary causes if an effect needs to be proven, or, conversely, offers evidentiary effects if a cause needs to be proven. Consequently, you might claim as an alleged cause that "global warming is negatively affecting planet Earth" and for evidence use as many diverse effects as you can discover.

Bhattacharyya, Dipayan et al. Food Insecurity Atlas of Urban India, M.S. Swaminathan Research Foundation [MSSRF] and the World Food Programme [WFP], 2002.

Hindustan Times, 9 October: 2008.

India Together; The News in Proporation. 9 October: 2008.

Schupak, Amanda. "Body-Fitness." http://www.youbeauty.com/body-fitness/obesity-diagnosis. April 25, 2012. Zupek, Rachael. AOL. October 8, 2008.

http://www.cdc.gov/healthyyouth/obesity/facts.htm http:hr.cch.com/news/hrm/042106a.asp
http://www.indiaonlinepages.com/population/india-current-population.html

ESSAY 14

Thesis Statement, and Introduction and Conclusion Strategies

Only after you know the complete content and organization of your document's or essay's body will you be prepared to write an introduction. Although the introduction comes first in your essay, its creation should not come first. Why? Because you cannot know with certainty what you're introducing until after the body fully exists; only then can you identify exactly how to prepare your reader for what's to come. Too many writers, myself included, have tried to introduce a document or essay before knowing the total background for, scope or extent of, and interconnections among what they're introducing. Therefore, don't write the introduction until you either have completed your skeletal outline or have written a final draft of the body. Then, for the introduction, be sure that you have considered all three of the following:

1) Introduce and define vocabulary essential to and used repeatedly throughout your entire subject. For example, the documents with the subjects "Revising the Eighty-Twenty Rule," "Safe Harbor Lease for Fortunaste," and "DAGMAR strategies for Vitaflow," and the essays titled "The Importance of Green Hotels," "Short-term Memory Reduction in Octogenarians," and "No-Risk Investment in Emerging Economies," will require an introductory definition of "the Eighty-Twenty Rule," "Safe Harbor Lease," "DAGMAR," "green," "short-term memory," and "emerging economies," respectively. Because each of those six concepts frames and clarifies the focus of its particular document or essay, readers must know immediately what those concepts mean. However, important vocabulary sometimes belongs only to one paragraph topic of your subject's investigation, not to the entire body; in such cases, define that vocabulary when you get to it in the body. Always define important new terminology as soon as you introduce it; if you don't, subsequent contexts using it won't make complete sense.

2) If you do not intend in the body to discuss necessary background information—actual history; previous systems for whatever now requires replacement or improvement; existing contextual understandings; underlying conceptual theories— then focus on them in the introduction, to provide the intellectual foundations upon which

your document or essay will build or from which it will depart. Only after you realize the general scope and particular analyses of the body's information will you be able to provide the right amount of background information, not too much, not too little, just whatever is sufficient and efficient enough to frame the foreground of your discussion. Even memos or brief messages may require contextual background, as seen in this 2005 bulletin from Harvard's FAS Dean William Kirby:

Dear Students, Faculty, and Staff: The devastating effects of Hurricane Katrina have stunned us all. The loss of life, destruction of property, and unimaginably severe conditions that remain in parts of Louisiana, Mississippi, and Alabama are profoundly saddening. Our thoughts, prayers, and sympathies are with all those who have suffered from the storm and its aftermath. How can we as a university help? Let me outline several ways (http://www.h-net.msu.edu).

3) Now that you fully grasp your document's or essay's purpose and understand the full range and meaning of its content, it's time to write your thesis statement, preferably towards the introduction's end so that it will serve transitionally into the body. Not to be confused with an entire "thesis," such as a "Master's thesis," a thesis statement is the academic term used to denote a general summary statement—one sentence only, or (this isn't cheating) two sentences in a compound sentence with a semicolon between them—that frames the entire intellectual picture portrayed in the document's or essay's body. Because early in your discussion the reader must know your overall purpose, you should locate the thesis statement in the introduction: it is an indispensable part of what you're introducing. And if the thesis statement equals what the document's or essay's body is about, and if what the body is about equals all the paragraphed topics, then the thesis statement equals a concise summary, abstract, précis, or digest of the topics.

Think of your thesis statement as the introductory road-map that your readers need and want to have before taking the unknown tour that you are about to lead them through. With that road-map, they will understand in advance what to expect generally—what territories (or topics) you will be exploring. You won't detail any of that tour's specific site-seeing until the body, but seeing the road-map in advance allows readers to better understand what each part of the journey is and how it connects with the others, giving the reader a cumulative awareness of your itinerary and its strategic purposes.

If your document or essay has too many topics to present in a list, use conceptual terms or even broader labels to group those topics. For example, a report's separate topics about sexual discrimination in job hiring, job pay, politics, religion, medicine, education, and the media—in total, seven different topics of investigation—can be referred to in the thesis statement as "forms of professional, cultural, and intellectual sexual discrimination," with "professional" blanketing the first two topics, "cultural" the next three, and "intellectual" the final two. If conceptual terms or labels (e.g., "initiative") still seem insufficient, modify them with adjectives ("national initiative"), or, if your verbs (e.g., "initiate") express some of the thesis statement's intentions, modify those verbs with adverbs ("initiate nationally").

Likening a document or essay to the biological metaphor of body, bones, etc., we may think of your thesis statement as the central nervous system of your writing's body (see beginning of Essay #5). Suffused through every part of that body, your thesis governs the document's or essay's entire intellectual operations and coordinates all of its organized movements. Like a human's central nervous system, your thesis statement is the brains behind and the motor stimulation for everything the document or essay is and does. For your writing to reveal information purposefully and to move coherently, you must guarantee that the thesis statement inheres in and activates the case you are attempting to build about the document's or essay's subject.

At every topic of investigation or paragraph, explicitly address and develop the case that you are building—if strategically you think the reader could use a reminder of the body's governing purpose. Because each topic necessarily adds to the strength of that case, remember to explain to your readers how or why each topic's information contributes to that governing purpose. You want your readers to assume that the investigation and its analyses are moving one step at a time towards a 'conclusive conclusion' that is persuasively educational.

When writing a thesis statement, assume your readers are aware that the document's or essay's thoughts come from you, the writer; consequently, there's no need for you to use the first person "I" to indicate your intentions. Using the third-person "This essay [or document]" also is unnecessary.[1] Instead, declare immediately the persuasive intellectual purpose: "Tolerance is essential to world peace," a declaration that readers know comes from you and that they also know the document or essay (thus you) will "attempt to prove." By the way, don't say you'll "attempt to prove," which suggests you don't yet know if you'll be able to provide adequate proof.

Keep in mind these three introductory requirements—definitions, background, thesis statement—for any document or essay you write, even for memos; although a thesis statement always is needed, the other two may not be, but don't overlook them as possible requirements. In longer expository writing, say three or more pages, you also will want to be sure that from the beginning you grab and hold the reader's interest: this is your writing's first impression, which has formative influence. What follows here are seven introductory strategies that can help you to create interest for your reader and to construct a logical framework within which to introduce your subject. You may find that your writing's body is best introduced by a combination of these strategies, not necessarily by only one.

A.   Funnel Movement

Like a funnel, whose broad form at top progressively narrows toward the bottom, an introductory funnel movement begins with broad, general understandings and develops more and more specifically toward the document's or essay's thesis statement. This developmental pattern allows for a gradual transitioning from the reader's familiarity with your thoughts to the potentially unfamiliar thesis statement.

Using the funnel movement will require of you some creative conceptual thinking, to the extent that you will need a broadly familiar conceptual framework to contain the thesis statement's particular picture. To illustrate the funnel movement here, I asked my wife to give me any subject for which I'd need to write an introduction; she happened to be reading an article in The New York Times about cryonics, the freezing and storing of diseased bodies until a future time when medical advances can cure them, so she responded with that subject. Here's my introductory funnel outline for a discussion of cryonics:

Death as life's ultimate enemy = broad generalization in the first sentence that any reader can understand

↓ = (Each downward arrow represents a move toward greater specificity or funnel

↓ narrowness, which for this introduction I created with a chronological discussion ending with contemporary "anti-death" schemes, including cryonics)

Human wish to counteract death, to extend life, to attain immortality, seen in all ancient cultures throughout the world

↓ = Introductory discussions also require persuasive evidence; a quick series of global examples is sufficient proof for my claim.

↓

Spiritual → world religions, afterlife of the soul

Physical → legends and myths, such as Sumerian Epic of Gilgamesh, Hindu Amrtramanthana myth, Egyptian belief in physical eternity, Fountain of Youth, even vampirism

↓

Particularly during the past three hundred years, medical advances have increased human longevity → examples and statistics

↓

Contemporary focus on physical eternity, applied and theoretical Added "youth" → plastic surgery, nutrition and diets, exercise, yoga Theories → mind/computer interfacing

→ "extropian futurism," belief in eventual uploading of consciousness

→ quantum immortality

→ "Something is impossible only if it violates a physical law. This is a basic tenet of science. Living for hundreds, even thousands of years does not violate a physical law, so it has always been possible." — Ana Tomas, M.D.

↓↓

Tomas's belief is now being tested with cryonics

→ cooling process

→ metabolism and decay almost completely stopped

→ ideally, allows clinically dead people to be brought back to life in the future, after cures to patients' diseases have been discovered and when aging is reversible

→ Thesis Statement

B. Fictive Account or Story, Anecdote

An introductory tale or anecdote can dramatize, introduce, and persuasively illustrate situations related to the thesis statement. Be sure your tale or anecdote is short, to the point, and relevant to your document's or essay's subject.

Yesterday Billy Barnes came home at 3:30 and let himself into his house with the key he carries to school every morning. After fixing himself a snack of five Oreo cookies and a glass of grape Kool-Aid, Billy watched television (MTV) for two hours. When the doorbell rang, Billy didn't answer it. Instead, he peered out the window from behind the living room curtains and waited anxiously until the stranger on his front porch walked away. At 5:30 Billy remembered that he was supposed to call his mother when he got home from school, but when he telephoned her office she was in a meeting and couldn't talk to him. Billy is eight years old; he represents a growing number of latchkey—home alone—kids who pay the price for their parents' changing lifestyles.

Effectively conceived and efficiently presented, this tale of Billy highlights the nutritional-physical, intellectual, psychological, behavioral, and obviously parental limitations imposed on children home alone after school, without supervision. Neither didactic nor preachy, the tale realistically "brings to life" the principles of limitation that the writer will investigate in the body.

C. Presentation of a Methodology

If the content of whatever you are writing presents your own conclusions from a procedural investigation—in business, IT, hard science, social science—which offers technical, systematic, or schematic research, then the reader must know up-front what your methodology is. Without your methodological approach made known, all else is nonsense: your conclusions, products, and data are arrived at by a methodology or process, whether inductive or deductive, so it must be brought into focus. Because your controlling purpose is your investigation's results, its ends, you must inform readers of your means to those ends. Here's one example which I use only to illustrate this strategy, not to advocate any conclusions from it:

In 1980, we reported large sex differences in mean scores on a test of mathematical reasoning ability for 9,927 mathematically talented seventh and eighth graders who entered the Johns Hopkins regional talent search from 1972 through 1979. One prediction from those results was that there would be a preponderance of males at the high end of the distribution of mathematical reasoning ability. In this report we investigate sex differences at the highest levels of that ability. New groups of students under age 13 with exceptional mathematical aptitude were identified by means of two separate procedures. In the first, the Johns Hopkins regional talent searches in 1980, 1981, and 1982, 39,820 seventh graders from the Middle Atlantic region of the United States who were selected for high intellectual ability were given the College Board Scholastic Aptitude Test (SAT). In the second, a nationwide talent search was conducted for which any student under 13 years of age who was willing to take the SAT was eligible. The results of both procedures substantiated our prediction that before age 13 far more males than females would score extremely high on the mathematical part of the SAT (Benbow, 1021).

D. Review of a controversy

An introductory review of a controversy's history examines both sides—or many sides—of a problem, briefly explaining the different perspectives on the controversy and then establishing with the thesis statement whatever position—or departure from existing positions—the writer believes should be propounded. Here's an example that I wrote for an instructor's manual for Conversations: Readings for Writing.

The arbitrary subjectivity and thus the impossibility of moral standardization in distinguishing between acceptable and unacceptable treatment of nonhuman animals reinforces the all-or-none positions held by the opposing sides of the animal-rights controversy. The animal-rights movement, brought to public awareness and moral recognition in Peter Singer's 1975 Animal Liberation, argues that humans must leave alone all nonhuman animals, and that to do otherwise shows callousness. Using Singer's coined term "speciesism," animal-rights activists deny that we humans are inherently superior to other life on earth and, as such, may not use nonhuman animals to our own advantage. Viewing speciesism as hubris, animal-rights activists oppose what they consider unnecessary or inappropriate acquisition and maintenance of animals for laboratory use, arguing that there are existing alternatives such as simulators and computer models that are not only more humane, but also more economical and efficient. Conversely, many scientists and scientific and pharmaceutical institutions favor the use of living nonhuman animals, none excluded, in medical research and laboratory testing. These people charge animal-rights activists with scientific ignorance, sentimentality, and equal callousness toward human welfare. They argue that animals are indispensable to the prevention of human disease and to the perfection of new surgical, therapeutic, and electronic devices for disease diagnosis and treatment. And not just humans benefit: because both humans and other animals suffer from many of the same diseases, millions of domestic animals are saved annually in the U. S. by prophylactic vaccinations resulting from laboratory experimentation on nonhuman animals. Furthermore, say the anti-rights activists, the words "unnecessary" and "inappropriate" are relative terms and can be used arbitrarily with respect to animal acquisition and maintenance—depending on one's moral agenda. [→ A possible thesis statement might say, "Between the extreme white and black oppositions in this controversy is a vast gray area which, given wise thought and prudent applications, can satisfy both sides of the controversy."] (Davis, 280-81).

E. Critical Overview

If you need readers to know immediately that your document or essay surpasses the scope and depth of existing information written about an issue, then providing a review or synopsis of your subject's critical trends and knowledge can be a useful introductory strategy. The following introduction begins with a superscription, an opening quotation whose idea(s) serve as a sturdy or at least sturdily believed premise for the introduction and body.

We may no longer make a cleavage between organic pathology and psychopathology, following the old Cartesian division between physical and mental. Everything matters to soul and expresses its fantasies, whether ideas in the head or bones in the body. The body has its home in the soul, and every organic pathology is cooperation between pathogenic agent and the human person as host (Hillman, 80).

Like its protagonist, Des Esseintes, common critical assessment of Huysmans's À Rebours displays a "blank incomprehension . . . of science" (18) and an unwillingness to acknowledge the author's relentless Darwinism. It is true that critics have noted, inconsequentially, that we can neither "dismiss the hero's physical degeneracy as extraneous" (Weinreb, 224) nor discount his value as "the Naturalist Child of the Naturalist Times" (Thomas, 58). But no one yet has fully appreciated the fact that the entire novel is determined by Des Esseintes's congenitally syphilitic and scrofular body (Davis).

F. Question

By posing a question, a writer directly encourages the reader to begin considering possible answers; the writer's thesis statement, presenting an answer, will be a satisfying response or at least a needed resolution to the opening question. Here, I've imagined a question I might ask if I were writing my own essay about gender mathematical performance and another about computer thinking:

Are males genetically predisposed to be better at math than females, having superior natural talent and proficiency with numbers by the time they reach junior high school, or is it possible that females are equally gifted with math but still have not received the sociological incentive and educational encouragement to perform better and to advance further?

AND

Can a computer think? Can a computer have conscious thoughts in the same ways that you and I have, or as the computer Hal did in Stanley Kubrick's 2001, A Space Odyssey? Over a decade after Hal, today's computers still cannot think: they can work with thoughts to the extent that they are programmed by humans to work with them, but they lack the complex ability to learn, to socialize, to be sentient and to gain sensory knowledge, to comprehend the abstract meanings and implications of emotions such as hope, trust, and friendship, and to have and to appreciate humor. Given recent progress with computers' intelligence, however, we cannot say that future computers won't be able to think by themselves.

G. Quotation

When presented as a superscription (see #4, Critical Overview), a quotation can alert the reader to your central issues and conceptual beliefs. In business and academic writing, the superscripted quotation usually comes from a recognized expert; the document's or essay's writer then proceeds to the larger discussion. An attention-grabbing quotation also can be incorporated into the introduction, as below, motivating your discussion toward agreement or disagreement and further investigation.

Michael Harris was a member of our school committee last year, 2010- 2011, in which capacity he made the following remark: "Neither our broad curriculum nor any of our teachers provides inferior education at Hypothetical High. What we have been getting is an inferior type of student." The remark is easy to ridicule, but close examination uncovers ways in which it is credible and must be heard by educators, parents, and students themselves.

The poet T. S. Eliot's "The Hollow Men" concludes with two lines about a conclusion: "This is the way the world ends/Not with a bang but a whimper." The "end" of which Eliot speaks reminds us that a world of hollowness, a "Paralysed force," concludes with the "dried voices" of a whimper, whereas its opposite, solidity with substance, concludes with a "bang." I've read countless documents and essays whose introductions and bodies were everything they ought to have been but whose conclusions, like Eliot's men, also were hollow, their "quiet and meaningless" worlds also ending with a whimper, as if they had no energy left and, bereft of options for continuing, exited with a final impression of intellectual oblivion, dying, feebly, in front of me. Don't let that happen in your own conclusions: end your documents or essays with a bang, generating continued interest and maintaining intellectual vitality.

Whatever approach your conclusion uses, it must shed new light on and add perspective to the subject just discussed in the body; therefore, it should be an organic extension of the essay's body, an appendage that grows naturally from it. As the name of this section of your document or essay suggests, you must draw conclusions here. What does the investigation that you just presented add up to? What are the implications or the significance of what you've investigated and explained in the body? What are your readers to make of it all? Or, what do you make of it all?

Especially with longer documents or essays, you may want to summarize quickly for your readers what the essay's principal points are; however, use that summary not as an end in itself, not as obvious repetition of what the body just proved, but instead as a useful means to further ends, as a launch into conclusive beliefs, suppositions, or possibilities that you can deduce from that summary. If your writing's body is principally informational and, as such, more objective—and it's likely that it will be—then the conclusion is where you may want to express subjective, personal opinions about what the body presents. Those opinions may require some persuasion of their own if their claims take you beyond the already defended thesis statement, but nonetheless the conclusion is your opportunity to be speculative. In general, just be sure that you leave your reader thinking about your concluding comments and that they suffice as an interesting, intellectually engaging, and possibly challenging last impression.

Any one or any combination of the following eight strategies can be useful for writing a conclusion. I offer explanations, advice, and recommendations in each discussion, but I've reproduced no exemplary models of conclusions. Lacking the body of information from which any model would have grown, examples would have no context for your fully understanding their strategies, and you would be deprived of appreciating how each conclusion successfully illustrates and integrates many of those strategies; however, my explanations, advice, and recommendations do provide specific guidelines and standards.

1. **Broader View of the Subject's Significance**

Because you have imposed a restricted focus on your document or essay, in the conclusion you may want to expand your investigation's, proposal's, or position's significance by applying it more broadly and thus showing its breadth of possibility. For example, assume that your essay proposes an alternative peace-keeping plan for two countries or for a territorial dispute. In your conclusion, you could argue that your proposal has applicability elsewhere in the world as well, or possibly you could show how your proposed methods for international peace-keeping can be applied to a family, or to various departments within a corporation. Or assume that your essay offers a marketing plan for real estate or e-commerce or whatever else you might be marketing; in your conclusion, you could explore briefly how and why that plan has enough business versatility and universality to be applied elsewhere.

2. **Development of an Auxiliary Idea**

Developing one particular aspect of your subject, whose importance you did not need to investigate fully in the essay's body, is another common concluding strategy. Sometimes an essay requires us to include explanations or evidence whose use is limited to one particular context of a topic and whose full meanings you therefore do not expound on in that paragraph of the body. However, if you have more to say about that explanation, or evidence, and believe that it has value as a concluding set of thoughts, then you should feel free to develop whatever you deem valuable.

Also remember that if you have an idea that you're unable to develop fully in the body—especially if it's tangential to a topic's circle of interest—and that you do not want to use as the basis for your conclusion, then you should consider using a footnote or endnote to discuss it as completely as you wish.

3. **What Lesson(s) Your Investigation Adds Up to**

As a possible focus for your conclusion, ask yourself what lessons or meanings your investigation suggests, what logical ideas it advocates, or what warnings it sends. What does one learn conclusively from the body that you have not summed up anywhere in it? Because the body is divided into topics and accomplishes its purpose by investigating, explaining, and supporting the claims of each topic apart from the others, it's not until the conclusion that you have the opportunity to add up the significance of all the topics as a whole; when you do, what concluding lessons, meanings, ideas, or warnings become apparent? Feel free to elaborate.

4. **Ethical and/or Emotional Values to Consider**

If it's relevant to your document or essay, ask yourself what ethical values (see Essay #13) are learned from the body's presentation. Because whatever you are writing likely will have direct or indirect public significance and therefore in some way will affect people's lives, there may be a noteworthy ethical and even emotional impact resulting from what your document or essay has tried to advocate, explain, and prove. Consider that impact, and use it as the basis for your concluding remarks. For example, technical writing sometimes overlooks the impact that new technological mechanisms devices, and software, and equipment and hardware have on people. Is the new intranet software that you suggest for your company not just an intellectually efficient and time-saving system but also user-friendly, promoting feel-good manageability? Conclude with a discussion of that. Many systems of bureaucratic operation in business and industry affect people, so you may want your conclusion to explain how and why a particular system is ethically and emotionally beneficial in the workplace.

5. **The Future Importance of Your Investigation**

What do you foresee as the future development and importance of what you have presented? Although your writing's body usually will be about the "here and now," its relevance needn't be limited to the present. If you think that your investigation's ideas and benefits have the power to persist (and probably you do), speculate why they might endure and what applicability and value they might have in the future. To illustrate your conclusions about the future, you may want to create a realistically based hypothetical scenario.

6. **Consider How Other Business or Academic Fields Apply to Your Subject**

What other business strategies or applications and other academic studies or theories are relevant to and reinforce the validity of the investigation you just presented? Let knowledge from another perspective further inform your document's or essay's investigation. For example, theories that very often apply to business and technology come from but are not limited to psychology (clinical and behavioral, forensic, counseling and rehabilitation, cognitive and perceptual, educational, child and developmental) and sociology (medical, organizational and occupational, racial and ethnic, family-relaed). Take a theory and show how its real-world personal or social implications pertain conceptually to whatever your subject's investigation is about. If child psychology says that children generally behave in particular ways at particular ages, then how might that information apply to marketing? How might established sociological trends pertain to real estate or to tourism and hotels?

7. **Ask a Question and Answer It**

You always can begin your conclusion by asking a question worth pondering about the body's investigation, and then answering it. Often it is useful to frame the question within the context of your summary: "Given the significance of X, Y, and Z [the body's topics], can we assume that / would you agree that / could it be possible that . . . ?" After you present the question, use your answer(s) as the conclusion's content.

8. **Use a Quotation and Proceed from It**

You also can introduce your conclusion with a useful quotation, preferably from a known, reputable source, that summarizes your own point of view or that elaborates on what you've presented. A quick, easy, and often useful source for quotations is Familiar Quotations by John Bartlett. A Google or Yahoo search for subject-specific quotations—business, science, literature, etc.—will list plenty of websites to explore. Depending on the intellectual direction(s) pointed out in the quotation, your conclusion then can proceed with a discussion resting securely on the quotation's solidity.

Think of the conclusion as your document's or essay's most creative opportunity, a chance to go beyond the body's boxed containments. While the body of course is matter-of-fact and purposefully packaged within the limits imposed by your thesis statement, you can design your conclusion according to your preferred purpose. There are no rights and wrongs in a conclusion; just be certain your chosen purpose develops organically, interrelatedly, from the body, giving it stability and a resolute function adding to the wholeness of your document or essay. And hold the interest of your readers, providing a new but related perspective or point of view—a new way of thinking—about what the body has persuasively educated them to appreciate.

REFERENCES

[1] Contrast a) with b). Notice that nothing is lost from the content except the writer's self-conscious narrative—and fourteen words.

    a)   In this term paper, I will explore the parallels that can be drawn between the cultural conditions confronting the late-1960s' "Woodstock Generation" and today's young adults, This essay will question if Woodstock-era beliefs are well suited to 2010. I will propose and test the theory that the contemporary impact of global situations is radically different from what affected American youth over forty years ago; I will further postulate that the substantial influence of the Vietnam War promoted a unifying ethos that today's youth do not have as a rallying point.

    b)   Although parallels can be drawn between cultural conditions confronting the late-1960s' "Woodstock Generation" and today's young adults, Woodstock-era beliefs are not well suited to 2010. Proposed and tested here is the theory that the contemporary impact of global situations is radically different from what affected American youth over forty years ago; further postulated is that the substantial influence of the Vietnam War promoted a unifying ethos that today's youth do not have as a rallying point.

Benbow, Camilla P. and Julian Stanley. "Sex Differences in Mathematical Reasoning Ability: More Facts." Science, 222 (1983): 1029-1031.

Davis, Robert S. and Jack Selzer. Instructor's Manual. Conversations: Readings for Writing, 3rd ed. (1997): 280-81.

http://h-net.msu.edu/cgi-bin/logbrowse.pl?trx=vx&list=H-Urban&month=0509&msg=QbGJsf%2ba/3ywgDyuKHUZdA&user=&pw=

ESSAY 15

Diction

Diction, whose Latin root, "dict,"[1] means speak, refers to the word or the phrasing of words that we choose when speaking and writing. English's spoken and written diction is found in dictionaries. Most of us will go through life thinking about and deciding on precise diction or wording to express accurately what we think and feel about the world outside us and the worlds inside us; most of us also will continue to learn new vocabulary or diction, not just because learning is beneficial, but because additional vocabulary—each new word—is the key to unlocking and opening a new door into the world we inhabit and the worlds inhabiting us. Diction frames and defines our experiences, perceptions, feelings, reactions, speculations, and imaginings, details and explains them, and gives them reality because it actualizes them both to ourselves and to anyone hearing or reading what we have to say. As noted throughout these essays, the English language has approximately one million words, a plethora of diction individualizing all experienced and hypothetical existence, all wholes and all parts in time and in space, animate and inanimate, tangibly concrete and theoretically abstract.

English is the official language of fifty-three countries in the world and twenty-six non-sovereign entities (e.g., Hong Kong, the Virgin Islands, and the South American Falkland Islands). Contemporary inhabitants of those countries and entities originally either were imperialist settlers whose English acquired linguistic influence from native languages, or were indigenous natives who had the English language imposed on them and, in turn, influenced and shaped with unique linguistic content their newly inherited English. It follows, naturally, that we must expect differences in how English diction is used within those seventy-nine locations throughout the world. Let's consider just America.

Within America's geographically diverse fifty states, different immigrant and native populations have shaped and influenced English in significantly different ways as they either adapted their tongues or added vocabulary to it. During its Colonial period, the English of America's Northeast borrowed from Dutch, French, and native or indigenous Indian dialects[2]; numerous African dialects[3] inspired change in English throughout the South and, after 1863, in urban areas of the North; German modified English throughout the Midwest during the nineteenth century; transformations to English were generated by millions of Italian, Irish, and Yiddish-speaking immigrants throughout the Northeast in the early twentieth century, as well as by Scandinavian populations in the Northern Midwest Plains (especially both Dakotas and Minnesota); and Spanish, from the seventeenth-century to the present, both from its own and from native American vocabulary, has influenced English in America's southern border-states, notably Florida, Texas, and California , and now increasingly in the Eastern megalopolis. The point here is simple but has complex ramifications: English contains a mix of style-based usage and diction from one region to another within English-speaking countries, and from one English-speaking country to another. Just a few examples of diction differing between England and the U.S. for the same noun—person, place, or thing—are, respectively, the boot/trunk with exterior space for the number plate/license plate of every car, including estate cars/station wagons. Requiring petrol/gasoline, automobiles sometimes drive on a motorway/freeway, as do lorries/trucks, or drive on city streets, alongside which are pavements/sidewalks. On those city streets, drivers turn anticlockwise/counterclockwise when they reach the roundabout/rotary. Some of those streets have tall buildings with lifts/elevators, boutique stores where people spend paper notes/bills for their purchases or write a check with a biro/ballpoint pen. Along those streets are signs posting adverts/advertisements, vendors selling candy floss/cotton candy, parents pushing prams/baby carriages, and, for everyone's security, bobbies/police officers standing vigilantly at the corners. At home, after someone uses the hoover/vacuum on the floors, cleans the loo/toilet, empties all of the dustbins/wastebaskets, mends a shirt after finding the proper reel of cotton/spool of thread, then washes the baby's nappies/diapers, kitchen flannels/washcloths, and smalls/ underwear, she or he earns the benefits of a biscuit/cookie, maybe an ice lolly/popsicle, and a kip/nap; but, if bone-idle/lazy, that person earns no reward.

  Modern and contemporary diction in the U.S. is regionally different not just because of linguistic origins but also because of local slang and diction. When I grew up in Cincinnati, Ohio, I drank "pop," not "soda"; people still do. I sat on my friends' "davenports," not on "couches." When native Cincinnatians didn't understand something, they said, "please?" A substitute for "Pardon me?" or "Excuse me?" or "Come again," the usage of "please?" became a humorous story in my family: a new neighbor had asked my mother, "Would you like some coffee?" My mother replied, "Please," and the neighbor responded, "Would you like some coffee?" Not just words but also pronunciations can be regional: Cincinnatians washed their hands not in the "sink" but in the "zink." Behind our house was was a narrow "creek," which my friends pronounced "crik." Residents of New Orleans refer to their city as "N'awlins." Many Bostonians were born in "Baaaah-shtin." Hearing that, we smile. But even with seemingly quirky words and pronunciations, regionally variable diction never is "wrong," always innocent, and is accepted and understood by most American native speakers because everyone in America is regional and stays attuned to spoken differences. However, one of American English's more troubling aspects to non-native speakers is the variable regional usage of prepositions. If you are uncertain whether or not to use a particular preposition in your phrasing, consult an English dictionary, but what follows illustrates acceptable multiple American usage of English-language prepositions (italicized):

For three hours we stood *on/in* line [remember: both italicized prepositions are acceptable]. My wife got *along/on* with many people. Impatient, I asked, "What time is it?" "It's twenty *to/of/before/until* five," someone responded. So I told my wife to take a break. "That's fine *by/with* me," she said. Walking *up/down/along* the corridor, she bought us coffee and some food. Later, she spent money *on/for* a magazine, one of whose cartoons she laughed *at/over/about*. Before boarding, my wife told me to have my ticket *with/on* me. *In/Inside/On* the plane I sat *by/beside/next to* her. When we arrived at our destination, the guard asked me to fill *in/out* some forms. I had no idea *of/about* what to do.

I'm very pleased *with/by/about* your art. Many people have heard *about/of* you and your visual innovations. I congratulate you *for/on* accomplishing so much. If possible, please come see me! Stop *at/by/in* my gallery whenever you like. I've been waiting *for/on* you to make an appearance. I'm involved *in/with* you fractal art. Contemporary art has experienced the influences *of/from/by* computer mathematics.

In/with regard to yesterday's dispute, the committee finally settled down and reached a solution. They didn't bother *with/about* superfluous matters. Still, at first there had been confusion *over/about* the major issue at hand, but now they have agreed *on/upon/about/to* a solution. In fact, it's an excellent solution *to/for/of* the problem.

Whereas writers easily can find advice about (or for) the most standard and context-sensitive forms of English usage, as with prepositions, usually they have had by themselves to search for and decide on words that express the highest degree of specificity or precision, accuracy or exactness. However, writers needn't be totally on their own when thinking about specific diction: this essay suggests practical strategies that will help you to think about eliminating vagueness from your writing and, instead, to write well by transforming words' general meanings to those more particular and expressive of your intention. Granted, vagueness exists naturally in some English-language words and phrases because not everything in existence is specific, or logically requires specific expression, or stylistically wants to be specific. But vagueness always will be considered a limitation to your writing well if your language usage lacks distinctness or determinacy and requires additional, clarifying information.

The two broadest classifications of vague words exist when those words indicate, first, a category or kind ("professional," "go-getter") and, second, degree ("much," "a while"). A good way to recognize vagueness is when a broad generalization is unclear or blurred because a thought itself isn't yet precisely focused or determined; we see this in our reliance on "nice," an adjective that we might use to describe, vaguely, a friend or vacation or piece of pie or lamp. Slightly more specific but still undefined kinds of "nice" might be "likeable," "friendly," "pleasant," "stylish," and "attractive." In addition to the diction related to "nice," the words and phrases in the following list are potentially vague and are classifiable either as kind ("good refrigerator") or degree ("big refrigerator"). As a writer using them, you must determine if contextually they need to be elevated to greater specificity or precision.

Potentially Vague Words and Phrases

a bit, deal with, resourceful, a lot, enough, scary, a majority, etc., seem, a minority, experienced, significant, ability, fairly, silly, acceptable, for a while, slight/ slightly, advantageous, goal-oriented, small /large number of, after all has been said, good /good enough, so forth, all that, great deal of, some / some people, anyway, hard working, somehow, appears important, somewhat like, appropriate, interesting, soon, area / areas of, it is believed, sort of thing, aspects, it's, like, special, at the end of the day, kind of, stuff, attractive, knowledgeable, successful, bad, lengthy /long, sufficient, basic / basically, little, team player, beauty /beautiful, loud /loudly, things, benefits, many, to the extent practicable, big, minority, views, broad, motivated, very bizarre, much / to say, whatever, cold, normal /normally, with ability, competent, practical /practically, considerable, professional, creative, quality

But how can these listed words, and others, be elevated to greater precision or specificity? First, we must recognize on our own that a word is vague; then, apply the first level of classification, that of kind and degree, to the three parts of speech most commonly requiring specificity: nouns, adjectives, and verbs (see Essay #5). For each of those parts of speech, include objective description and, when needed, subjective impressions if the diction is potentially vague. For example, seldom does a noun, alone, provide enough visual specificity for your reader to see it as completely as you'd like. Think about the complete image of the "roses" you want readers to see (vague: "She raises roses"), or the psychology informing the "attitude" you mention (vague: "The grocery cashier had attitude"), or the characteristics of "thrift" (vague: "He was known for his thrift"). Then, combine objective description and subjective impressions into your imagery: "With 2½-inch upright petals clinging tightly together on 8"-12" stems, the yellow and white English roses she raises appear negligible individually but triumphantly bountiful in groups." "Dismissively cocking her head while sneering with a belligerent attitude, the grocery cashier looked as if she were smelling and avoiding something foul." "Although neither miserly nor even always frugal, he still is prudent about cost when he spends money, his known thrift based on comparative pricing and a careful selection of high-quality items." To eliminate vagueness in nouns, always ask yourself if you're certain your readers can see and experience the person, place, or thing you mention.

Adjectives add specific characteristics and details to the nouns you choose, but adjectives also can be vague and therefore may require greater specificity of their own. It may seem true adjectivally, for example, that a female gymnast is "small," but what precisely does smallness mean in degree of height and weight? Using objective measurements always helps: 4'10" and 87 pounds. Keep in mind, however, that many adjectives are conceptually relative terms in degree and also in kind. Compared to most of us, that gymnast's height and weight indeed make her small, but that may not be true in relative degree to her 4'9" and 82-pound teammate. And neither of those gymnasts is likely to be a "petite" kind of small: her measurements may be small, but not her power resulting from her compact musculature. Similarly, someone may be "excellent" at the card-game bridge if compared to you but not when compared to her or his partner, across the table. Your module-partner at work may be a "dedicated" employee, but not nearly as dedicated as you. What kinds and degrees of dedication make you relatively more dedicated, your partner less so? The relative intentions of meaning—the subjective perceptions and evaluations inherent in our choices of words—can make our diction vague, true of any of these commonly used adjectives: "bad," "beautiful," "cute," "dumb," "fun," "good," "important," "inferior," "interesting," "intelligent," "large," "major," "minor," "nice," "smart," "significant," and "superior." And there are hundreds more which you should think about before using them as a self-evident characteristic. Each writer knows what she or he means by "a fun time" or "important criticism," but it's not likely that readers will; therefore, expounding on each adjective helps you to express meaning, as with "We had a fun weekend, a good-natured, laughter-filled, enjoyable but only momentary escape from scholastic work," or "The article has important conceptual and factual criticism, providing detailed responses to current theories about capitalism's trends in Asia."

As is true of categorical adjectives—"fun," "important"—which on their own inevitably are general (categories are general) and therefore tend to be vague in kind or degree, or both, verbs also can be categorical and also may require greater specificity. All of the following verbs—and, again, many more—are labels for categories of action and therefore are general and potentially vague:

amuse, grow, put, break, hurt, sin, build, know, sit, cut, lead, speak, do, like, spread, drink, live, take, eat, look, talk, feel, love, think, fight, make, tie, fit, play, walk, give

Sometimes, one or two well-chosen synonyms will provide all the specificity you need, for example with "grow": "breed," "cultivate," "develop," "enlarge," "escalate," "expand," "extend," "increase," "intensify," "mature," "multiply," "nurture," "produce," "raise," "swell." Other times, however, to specify your thought or your image, you may want to add an adverb to your chosen specific synonym, for example with "walk." From any thesaurus listing, you will find synonyms for "walk" that are specific kinds of walking: "amble," "limp," "march," "meander," "pace," "parade," "proceed," "promenade," "sashay," "saunter," "shuffle," "slink," "stagger," "stroll," "strut," "swagger," "tiptoe," "trudge," and "waddle." When you choose the appropriate kind of walking that expresses your intention and captures the image you want a reader to see, and then modify it with an adverb, you treat your reader to a two-word image containing additional physical and often psychological precision: "amble effortlessly," "limp lethargically," "march purposefully," "meander mindlessly," "pace pensively," "parade proudly," "proceed hurriedly," "sashay happily," "saunter dreamily," "slink surreptitiously," "stagger aimlessly," "strut confidently," "tiptoe quietly," "trudge tediously," and "waddle wearily."

Questioning if your nouns, adjectives, and verbs are specific in kind and degree is a reliable but still potentially broad, introductory classification-set for guarding against vagueness. Diction even more refined may come from your clarifying abstract emotions, feelings, and natural abilities. Thus we can take nouns and their adjectival forms—"heartbreak" and "heartbroken"; "courage" and "courageous"—to a deeper level of specificity, not with description but with better chosen words. Nouns labeling broad categories of emotion and kinds of feeling, whose meaning we all recognize, usually lack the contextual significance of each writer's personal, subjective experience, and therefore may be vague. According to W. G. Parrott's "nature of emotion," we may classify emotions and feelings into primary, secondary, and tertiary levels, each level being more specific and thus requiring a more precise label; this is no different from classifying, say, "breakfast fruit" into a secondary level or kind including "citrus," whose tertiary level includes "oranges," and whose quaternary kinds are navel, blood (Moro), and Valencia. As for emotions, the six primary and thus most generalized categories, according to Parrott (375-390), are "love," "joy," "surprise," "anger," "sadness," and "fear." Looking at those words, you immediately recognize the broad, potentially different meanings each suggests. Is the "love" amorous, only sexual or driven by lust, familial, fraternal in the broad sense of loving a friend, or personally satisfying in different ways, maybe love for a dog or love of potato skins? Is the "surprise" jubilantly exciting or startlingly frightful? For "joy," a primary emotion, Parrott classifies seven secondary emotional types or kinds: "cheerfulness," "zest," "contentment," "pride," "optimism," "enthrallment," and "relief." Joy is imbued in all seven kinds, but each secondary kind—for example, "cheerfulness"—can be and usually is different; each difference of course requires a different label, different diction. For joyful cheerfulness, for example, Parrott's tertiary emotions include fifteen more words, each different from the others by kind, by degree, or by both: "amusement," "bliss," "delight," "elation," "ecstasy," "enjoyment," "euphoria," "gaiety," "gladness," "glee," "happiness," "jolliness," "joviality," "jubilation," and "satisfaction." As with the secondary emotions, these tertiary emotions also are all imbued with joy, in this case a cheerful joy, but all eleven express a higher degree of specificity. And remember that each noun has its adjectival counterpart: "amused," "blissful," "delighted," "elated," "ecstatic," "enjoyable," "euphoric," "gay," "glad," "gleeful," "happy," "jolly," "jovial," jubilant," and "satisfied."

Conversely, for the primary emotion "sadness," Parrot classifies six secondary kinds of   emotion: "disappointment," "neglect," "sadness"   itself, "shame,"

"suffering," and "sympathy." "Neglect" has eleven tertiary emotions, any one of which gives greater insight into the sad neglect that someone may be feeling: "alienation," "defeat," "embarrassment," "dejection," "homesickness," "humiliation," "insecurity," "insult," "isolation," "loneliness," and "rejection."

As is true of people's emotions and feelings, people's kinds and degrees of natural ability also can be expressed with generalities and therefore may require labels more specific and refined: "aptitude," "determination," "endurance," "intelligence," "smartness," "talent," and "weakness," all nouns which, again, have adjectival forms ("apt," "determined," "enduring," "intelligent," "smart," "talented," and "weak"), are abstractions requiring specific descriptive information. Assume you tell your reader that a female friend has "so   much aptitude" for succeeding professionally. What kind(s) of aptitude are you speaking of? What will naturally guarantee her professional excellence? What djectives will further help to define her kind(s) of aptitude? The Scholastic Aptitude Test or SAT defines "aptitude" according to verbal and mathematical ability; certainly there are other scholastic aptitudes beyond those two, but at least they provide two additional labels refining the still- vague concept of "aptitude." Further, prospective employers may test people's "spatial or mechanical" aptitude, or "clerical" aptitude, and even "sensory" aptitude. To those labels we should add Howard Gardner's forms of "multiple intelligence," which include "interpersonal" or social aptitude, "intrapersonal" or self-knowledge aptitude, "musical" aptitude, and "bodily-kinesthetic" aptitude, which includes both how and how well a person's mind coordinates with his or her body to accomplish physical skills. Now, we have nine different adjectival labels for kinds of "aptitude," each of which can be further refined to clarify specifically what the female friend's aptitude is.

The degree of anything usually can be objectified, so be careful when you use diction such as "very," "most," "almost," "nearly," "approximately," "a lot," and other vague measurements. If you state that someone is "very tall," then specify the height: 6'9". If you believe that someone won "a lot of money on Jeopardy," then specify how much is "a lot": $84,700. If you tell your readers that "Most people in the world are happy," then let them know what "most" means: "According to statistics from NationMaster.com, 53% of people interviewed in every country in the world claimed to be happy"; the word "happy" also is vague, so as a writer you also would want to clarify what the determinants for happiness were for people responding to the interview.

Am I making too much of the importance of providing greater specificity for potentially vague words? Do writers want their readers to understand precisely what they, the writers, are expressing about persons, places, things, qualities, characteristics, and actions in the world? Your and my responses to those two questions are "no," because "yes."

Yet another way that writers can further clarify or explain their meanings is by using imagery, by which is meant any kind of sensory impression but principally visual impressions. The most typically used, most naturally experienced imagery is visual, which vitalizes writing because it speaks to a reader's sensibilities and remains in a reader's mind's eye; a reader will remember what you say if you clearly and fully paint with words whatever you are talking about. Business, technical, and academic writing sometimes can be lifeless and therefore should be enlivened by striking, literally impressive visual imagery. The second most frequently used imagery is aural; in the next paragraph I'll discuss how music or sound and rhythm can echo and reinforce a visual idea or image being expressed. To a lesser extent, the sensory impact of smell can be intoned to simulate physically an olfactory experience, for example with the high-pitched "reek" that spreads the nose outward and up, or the "odors" that pinch the nose and then pull it down with the lips. Sometimes images can be tactile, when for example readers feel "the soothingly smooth silk, cool and sensuously sliding across his fingertips." Visualization, however, is the most common and reliable kind of sensory imagery; whenever we describe, we use visual imagery to outline and color what we're talking about. Everything we've considered about eliminating vagueness fosters visual imagery, but it's important to remember that visual imagery can be complemented foremost by the music of language.

Like music, all writing is comprised of sound and rhythm. Every word we write has vibrations whose sound frequency can intone feeling and sometimes suggest thought (especially if the word is onomatopoetic, or sounds what it means, such as Rice Krispies' "snap, crackle, and pop"). English's five main vowels range from the high-pitched "e," which can shriek, scream, and pierce your ears until bleeding appears, to the low-pitched "u" or "oo" sounds, whose smooth sonorities surely are soothing and pure. Not just poets but any writer who works with words' sounds can combine words evocatively and integrate them for greater tonal effect—and affect— in phrases and sentences.

Every sentence or syntactic arrangement of words also has its own rhythms; rhythms are patterns of duration. Some sentences stream out easily with simple poise and modest grace while stretching uninterruptedly across the page as if conveyed by a calm spring breeze whose gentle touch caresses one's sensibilities; some bounce, bumpily, banging deeply down upon the page; and some shift, jump, maneuver awkward angles, halt, turn left, and then move on naturally and uninterruptedly about their business.

Arrangement of any sentence's sounds and rhythms can make a small musical composition whose feelings and motion reinforce that sentence's intellectual and visual meaning. Therefore, as writers, we can provide through vowel and consonant tones the sensuous effect of words evoking the mood of a thought's literal meaning, and providing through rhythms a music that reinforces the physical impressions of an idea or image. Poetry frequently does that. And there is no reason why prose can't do the same. In effect, "The sound must be an echo of the sense," as the eighteenth-century Neoclassical English poet Alexander Pope suggested. Additionally, we can be sensitive to the fact that there is "Rhythm in all thought," as the nineteenth-century Romantic poet Samuel

Taylor Coleridge said seventy-five years after Pope, and "also in the sound a thought," which the Victorian poet Matthew Arnold observed one generation after Coleridge.

At the very least, you may want to choose words and simple word arrangements which give momentary affect to an idea. If in a letter you're describing a teacher's boring lectures, then you want not only to make the vague label "boring" more precise, but also to evoke in your writing itself the intellectual nature and emotional feeling of boredom. I won't speak for you, but for me a boring lecture is uninspired, monotonous and thus uninteresting, and probably repetitious, requiring a greater infusion of dynamic intellectual and possibly physical and tonal energy; those, then, are the qualities that you, if you're like me, want to express musically so that your reader feels—while simultaneously learning of—the boredom you're talking about. To express monotony, you might use a repetitive monotone (= monotonous), a drumming sound, maybe with the forcefully alliterative "d" in words suggesting boredom: "droning," "dull," "deadening," "dreary," "dismal." Then, try incorporating into your letter's narrative your music-phrasing for "boring lectures": "True, I like Quantum Mechanics, but I'm ditching it, done with it, 'cuz the teacher's droning lectures are downright dull, damn dry, deadeningly dreary and dismal."

Because English is rich with onomatopoetic diction (re: "snap, crackle, pop," or "droning"), using onomatopoeia is a good start when looking for musical words. Here are just a few I've compiled and classified:

Animals, Insects: baa, bark, bleat, bob-white, buzz, cackle, caw, chirp, cluck, coo, drone, flutter, growl, hiss, hoot, klopp-klopp, low, meow, moo, neigh, oink, purr, quack, rattlesnake, roar, snap, squawk, tweet, yap, yelp

Eating / Drinking: crunch, fizz, gag, gnash, gnaw, gobble, lap, munch, sizzle, slobber, slurp, smack, succulent

Nose, Mouth, Throat: belch, choke, cough, gargle, hiccup, huff, hum, sneeze, sniff, snore, snort, wheeze, whistle

Liquid-Related: drip, drizzle, gargle, gush, pour, ripple, splash, spurt

Forceful Action: bam, bang, bash, clap, crack, clank, clang, plunge, pop, plop, rattle, snap, splat, shock

Rapid Action: click, flick(er), flutter, gush, itch, jitter, knock, prick, shuffle, slap, snip, spin, splash, spurt, squelch, sting, twitter, whirl, whip, whiz, wiggle, zip

Slow Action: beat. drip, flap, loll, plop, plunk, squash, squish, thud

Abrasive Action: brush, buzz, rustle, scratch, slap, slash, smack, squish, whack
Falling Action: fall, tumble

Loud: bang, beep, boom, clang, crackle, explode, pop, roar, slap, smack
Percussive: bang, gong, knock, tap

High-pitched: beep, click clink, ring, scream, screech, sneeze, squeak, squeal, tick, tweet, wheeze

Mid-range pitch: bash, bawl, blurt, chatter, chirp, clatter, clink, crackle, giggle, growl, rattle, sizzle, squish, thud, twinkle

Low-pitched: dumb, groan, grunt, honk hum, low, moan, mumble, murmur, mute, plunk, rumble, smooch, zoom

Sibilance: hiss, hush, sensuous, silence, slash, whisper

Texture, Surface: crisp, flat, fuzzy, mushy, plush, sharp, sheen, slush(y), smooth
Shape: bloated, bubble, enormous, plump, round

When the tonality of these and other onomatopoetic words is infused into a visual image or controlling descriptive idea, readers receive a more thorough sensory and thus emotional experience. Here are a few examples from poetry and prose fiction: "As I gain the cove with pushing prow,/And quench its speed i[n] the slushy sand./. . ./A tap at the pane, the quick sharp scratch/And blue spurt of a lighted match" (Robert Browning, "Meeting at Night"); "The moan of doves in immemorial elms,/And murmuring of innumerable bees" (Alfred, Lord Tennyson, "Come Down, O Maid"); "I heard the ripple washing in the reeds/And the wild water lapping on the crag" (Tennyson, "Morte d'Arthur"); "The market carts rolled along long Picadilly" (George Moore, Mike Fletcher); "A poem should palpable and mute/As a globed fruit./ Dumb,/Like old medallions to the thumb" (Archibald Macleish, "Ars Poetica"); "Bulbs broke out of boxes, hunting for chinks in the dark./Shoots dangled and drooped,/Lolling obscenely from mildewed crates,/Hung down long evil necks, like tropical snakes" (Theodore Roethke, "Root Cellar"); "I must have stood for a few moments listening to the whip and snap of the curtains and the groan of a picture on the wall. Then there was a boom as Tom Buchanan shut the rear window …" (F. Scott Fitzgerald, The Great Gatsby).

Thus far my discussion may seem to have accentuated poetic uses of language with which you're unaccustomed and possibly uncomfortable. If that's true, remember that you never should feel as if your writing must be musical for you to write well; smart prose by itself is good enough, since readers read first for clear, concisely expressed information, not for musical compositions. However, because musical language is partly about tone, and because tone inevitably creates mood, you want to keep in mind that accommodating your audience requires you to write with a voice whose tone creates a mood appropriate to your writing's and your readers' situation. To help you decide the tone and mood you wish to create, go through the following adjectives, and circle those that best describe how you want and need to portray yourself and your information for each new document or essay:

Academic? Ethical? Pleasant? Agitated? Friendly? Professional? Agreeable?Honorable? Questioning? Amusing? Humorous? Reasonable? Angry?Impartial? Reliable? Authoritative? Imploring? Resolute? Bewildered? Inquiring? Sarcastic? Calming? Insistent? Sensible? Challenging? Intellectual? Serious? Charming? Ironic? Soliciting? Curious? Moral? Surprised? Cynical? Objective? Suspicious? Demanding? Optimistic? Trustworthy? Determined? Perplexed? Wise? Enthusiastic? Pessimistic?

Combine your choices from the preceding list, and consider the group of them as the substance of the personal tone, thus mood you want and need to voice in your writing. Find where and justify how in your writing you have communicated that tonal mood. Explain to yourself why it feels appropriate. If you haven't satisfactorily communicated it in particular sections, then you need to revise it by reworking the diction—words, phrases, and possibly entire sentences—that will help to express the kind and degree of tone required in your writing. Creating a tonal mood isn't an exact science, so just do your best to evaluate the prevailing purposes of your document or essay, then rule out diction that contradicts the mood you desire, and let your feelings help to determine how you want your mood to sound and where diction replacements might be valuable. All of this essay's suggestions for achieving greater specificity of diction are applicable to establishing your mood more precisely. If, for example, you want your mood to be "resolute," among other factors, then choose diction that is emphatic and assertive, assured and confident. A report to customers might originally have stated, "We believe that investors will benefit from..." But everybody believes, so find a verb or verb phrase expressing greater resolution: "confirm," "assure you," "are certain," "are confident," "are convinced."

Musical tone and rhythm, and sometimes a general mood, can be important to writing well, but they are auxiliary or supplemental to intellectual ideas and visual imagery from objective and subjective description, all of which helps readers to see what you are talking about; I discussed this earlier, when speaking about the inherent vagueness of most nouns ("roses," "attitude," "thrift") and their need to be brought to life with visual description. Towards further accomplishing that, you might think also about using a metaphor—"my soul/Is a stringed lute on which all winds can play"—or a simile—"Death lies upon her like an untimely frost" to liken your idea to a common but suggestive visual image which, in turn, also may include tonal and rhythmic imagery. Notice how in the first quotation Oscar Wilde says that his "soul," an abstract, potentially difficult concept to define, "is a stringed lute," a well-recognized instrument during his lifetime; adding to the easily understood metaphor is the image of "all winds," which can play on that lute. Thus we realize that Wilde's soul is, first, a receptive power; second, a power receptive to universal influence or "all winds"; third, a multifaceted receptive power, since it is "stringed" (six to thirteen strings) and variably pitched; and fourth, a responsive power reproducing the myriad tones that cross its stringed paths. Shakespeare likens death's impact on Juliet's corpse to "an untimely frost": first, because she is dead, she is cold, like "frost"; second, because no blood flows in a dead corpse, her coloration is like that of frost, pallid; third, she is young, only thirteen, the death of her newly fertile body therefore premature, and so the frost is "untimely" and, as Romeo would prefer to believe, "lies upon her" (as indeed the Friar's inducement of her false death does). The simile's simple, identifiable image immediately establishes an equation that not only makes sense literally or explicitly but also provides implied commentary. The same is true with songwriter Joni Mitchell's simile for a 1968 New York City scene: "A helicopter lands on the PanAm roof/Like a dragonfly on a tomb." Now called the MetLife building, near Grand Central Station, Mitchell's PanAm establishes a deft architectural analogy to a tombstone, while the equation between a helicopter and a dragonfly has eerie visual appropriateness. In 1968, the urban paradigm, urban smog, industrial complexes, and American military imperialism (i.e. PanAmerican) in Vietnam stood in marked contrast to the "Woodstock" imperative, written also by Mitchell, that "We've got to get ourselves back/To the garden" of Eden and of naturalism, spiritual nurturance, and organic development. Her simile ("like") therefore provides commentary about the death-like empire of New York or urban civilization and the devolution of human nature to that of insects.

    Again I have quoted poets and a musical artist with poetic genius to illustrate my ideas, but obviously I do not expect you—any more than I expect myself—to be able to come up with their kinds of similes and metaphors. Still, we can try to vitalize our prose with visual imagery from description and from similes and metaphors as best we can, to help readers see more clearly what we intend to express. So, if you work in business and technology, or are a student, or are a parent at home—if you are anyone who must write—then exercise and stretch your imagination to see what effects result. First, focus on the particular person, place, thing (noun), quality (adjective), or action (verb) that needs to be likened to something else for greater comparative imaging. Maybe in your writing you want to mention your brother's "wisdom," a noun. Ask yourself what is distinctive and extraordinary about his wisdom. How does it differentiate him from other people? Rapidly you realize that you must define his wisdom as a shared, illuminating prudence that benefits seemingly dim and unenlightened people, and that you can use the commonplace "wise" owl as a simple visual starting point; then, you might write that "his wisdom is perched high, like a solitary owl, singularly hooting prudence into dark and gloomy woods." If you want someone to experience fog entering a city, as Carl Sandburg did in Chicago, then let readers see that it "comes on little cat feet./It sits looking/over harbor and city/on silent haunches/and then moves on." It's the cat's "silent haunches" that capture and hold the fog's visual image and that momentarily pause the cat's soundless, puffy motion.

One easy strategy for creating similes and metaphors is to use imagery that is the opposite of what you're describing, to let readers know what something isn't or, if denied existence, won't be or will become. The Harlem Renaissance poet Langston Hughes does this when he tells us that "if dreams die/Life is a broken-winged bird/that cannot fly," a simple metaphorical visual image telling us that dreams inspire flight and enable its accompanying freedom, that they lift us higher, and that their absence literally debilitates and "breaks" us, thwarting our possibility for raised hopes.

My final consideration with diction is to note the definitions of and differences among slang, jargon, and colloquial usage. All three of these verbal categories contain diction infused into our daily conversation, but we need to understand why they may not be appropriate for writing well.

Newly coined and usually short-lived, slang is highly informal and colorfully expressive language used among friends or groups and not intended either for formal business and technical writing or for academic writing. If you don't recognize the adjectives "groovy" and "smokin'," or the nouns "a gas" or "a blast," that's because they're slang used popularly almost a half-century ago, back when "bad" with an elongated "a" was slang for "good." In fact, you won't recognize most words and phrases in a dictionary of slang, because usage and the groups adopting that usage have dispersed, dissolved, or died. My 94-year-old father still calls a five- dollar bill a "fin," but I don't know anyone else who does. He also refers to "jail" as "the hoosegow," a slang English term derived from the Spanish for jail, jusgado. I haven't heard "five-finger discount" used for thirty years as a slang phrase for stealing or shoplifting. Ten years ago someone told me that in my sports jacket I looked "smooth," his comment about the jacket's trendy, suave look, but I've not heard that slang description used recently. A regional slang term used mostly in New England is "wicked," meaning "exceptionally"; Tom's Toothpaste uses the logo "Wicked Fresh" on its cartons and tubes. Since the advent of e-mail, the U.S. Postal Service's mail delivery has become "snail mail." Jokingly, McDonald's has become "the American Embassy" abroad.

Jargon—which often includes acronyms—is acceptable usage within special groups, often professional groups such as marketers, IT workers, or lawyers, to whose members its meaning will be recognizable; however, it's very possible that jargon won't be understood when used for another audience. A musician might refer to "my gig," where he plays his "axe." A businessperson might ask for a "SWOT analysis" (Strengths, Weaknesses, Opportunities, Threats), and, like a lawyer, insist on "due diligence." Because not all money earned by a business is from buyers' direct purchasing of products, some money results from "sweat equity," a slang term used also in home renovation. A new computer program may be "sweet" to my nephew, but, if he were reviewing that software for a magazine, his writing would require greater precision. Other computer-tech jargon that has entered English but remains specialist diction are "cache," "chip," "cookie," "dot pitch," "firewall," "fragmentation," "hyperlink," "interface," and "URL."

Colloquial language begins as slang or jargon but broadens in usage until its understandability is commonplace. Although colloquial language includes words and phrases that make no literal sense, they nonetheless have crept into common speech: "nerd" (origin from Dr. Seuss, 1950-1) and "bull—" (1914) are conventional usage for all of us. However, as with slang, colloquialisms also are inappropriate for formal writing. The following sentences' italicized words have other examples of colloquial usage, all of which are acceptable for conversation but not for writing: "I'll go *crazy* if I hear that song again"; "*At the end of the day* I feel good about my decision"; "That's a *no-brainer*"; "I can't *wrap my head around* that idea"; "I had my *fix*"; "Don't *bug* me"; "It's a *crapshoot*, but I'll give it a try"; "It was a *wash*, so I'm not upset"; "You're paying $2200 a month for that *rathole*?"; "It's my *security blanket*"; "Sitting through that concert was a *drag*"; "There's a *changing of the guard* every six or seven years in professional tennis."

It's important to be aware of slang, jargon, and colloquial usage because our inclinations are to speak and write instinctively, to reproduce what we've heard all our lives in our region of the country, in our community, at home and in school, or at work, and to assume that its comprehensibility is universal. Very possibly, however, it's not, so be sure you remember who your audience is, whom you're writing to, and then be your own best judge about using each of these three categories of diction.

But no matter what diction you choose (and you even can choose "But" to begin a sentence) for greater specificity, sharper visual imagery, and well-pitched tone and mood, keep in mind this final suggestion about diction: if you can say exactly what you mean and what you intend with a simple, straightforward monosyllabic ordinary word, then use that word to write well. Abstruse diction and polysyllables don't signify intelligence; intelligibly intelligent ideas do. Verbose overstuffing and flowery ostentation with words ultimately may signify only one thing: verbose overstuffing and flowery ostentation. Keep your prose clean, clear, and to the point.

REFERENCES

[1] If we foretell something, we "predict" it. If we speak counter to or disagree with someone else, we "contradict." If we speak a letter, memo, memoir, etc. to a stenographer, we "dictate." Possibly an unfamiliar use of the root "dict" is a political "dictator," someone who speaks and writes the rules of his or her totalitarian leadership. An "edict" is an officially explained command or law. An "indictment" is the spoken or written words of a jury charging someone with a crime. And a "verdict" is the spoken decision a jury delivers at a trial.

[2] From Algonquin languages, Colonial English inherited the animal names caribou, chipmonk, moose, muskrat, opossum, raccoon, skunk, and woodchuck; the hickory tree; the food-related hominy, pecan, persimmon, squash, and succotash; Eskimo, (denoting snowshoe-netter), and squaw; and, domestically, the moccasin, papoose, toboggan, tomahawk, totem, and wigwam; and powwow.

[3] There are many African languages, and it isn't purposeful here to individualize their influences on English. Instead, here is a compilation of African diction that English acquired, sometimes modified, and disseminated during the seventeenth through nineteenth centuries: banana, banjo, bogus, bongo, booboo, boogie, bozo, chimpanzee, dig (understand), funk, goober, gumbo, hip (aware of), impala, jazz, jive, mojo, mumbo jumbo, okra, safari, sock (v.), tote, voodoo, yam, zebra, zombie.

Southwest American native language filtered through Spanish into English includes the words armadillo, cabana, canyon, chicle, chili, chocolate, coyote, guacamole, hammock, maize, mesa, mesquite, stampede, and tamale.

Howard Gardner's books and articles on multiple intelligence have influenced educational and psychological theory and practice for the past twenty years. His theoretical primer is Frames of Mind: the Theory of Multiple Intelligences, Basic Books, 1993. A more recent continuation of that theory is Multiple Intelligences: New Horizons in Theory and Practice, Basic Books, 2003.

Parrott, W. G. "The nature of emotion." Blackwell Handbook of Social Psychology: Vol. 1. Intraindividual processes. Ed. A. Tesser & N. Schwarz. Oxford: Basil Blackwell, 2001.